Glass House Books

From Cradle to Global Citizen

Lorraine Rose is a clinical psychologist, psychoanalytic psychotherapist and organisational consultant who worked in private practice for over 40 years. She has lectured at a number of universities and taught in teaching programs for trainees in psychoanalytic psychotherapy. Lorraine established and taught Infant Observation for the Institute of Psychiatry Infant Mental Health Course, NSW.

Her private practice work included work with children, adolescents, adults and families. A particular focus has been adults who have never bonded as babies, needing longer-term intensive treatment.

Lorraine studied group phenomena at the post graduate level and was a member and board member of the Australian Institute of Socio-Analysis (AISA), now known as Group Relations Australia (GRA).

Her previous book, *Learning to Love: The developing relationships between mother, father and baby during the first year*, was published by ACER Press in 2000.

I0023557

GHB

Dedicated to my patients, my greatest teachers.
– Lorraine Rose

FROM CRADLE TO GLOBAL CITIZEN

Finding our way in turbulent times

Lorraine Rose

GHB

Brisbane

From Cradle to Global Citizen

Glass House Books
an imprint of IP (Interactive Publications Pty Ltd)
Treetop Studio • 9 Kuhler Court
Carindale, Queensland, Australia 4152
sales@ipoz.biz
http://ipoz.biz
First published by IP in 2018
© IP, and Lorraine Rose, 2018

Printed in 14 pt Avenir Book on Book Antiqua 12 pt.

From cradle to global citizen: finding our way in turbulent times
ISBN: 9781925231816 (PB) 9781925231823 (eBook)

Contents

Acknowledgements

If it takes a village to raise a child, it is also true that it takes a village to create a book.

I would like to thank Ofra Shabtay who helped me to persevere with this project. Ofra and her partner David offered weekends away from distractions at their beachside home. My writing group, consisting of Dr Michael Dudley, Dr Catherine Hickie, Elaine Kelly, Winton and Lena Higgins, and Maurice Whelan gave me permission to present the material for this book, rather than the more creative intent of the group, which was working on poetry, memoir, novels, and a play. I am grateful for their tolerance and valuable input. My weekly peer group of psychoanalytic psychotherapists, when we discuss our current cases, allowed me to test various ideas over a long period of time. The encouragement and support of Mary Cameron, Sylvia Enfield, Helen Kvelde, Terese Sheridan, Beulah Warren and Helen Hardy, created a space for me to explore various lines of thought and ways of approaching the work we share. Good friends at my Rumi poetry group nourished my body and spirit as we shared special time together, at the change of season, reflecting on Rumi's poetry, eating nourishing food, having a swim or going on walks together. Renee Koonan generously offered to edit the book out of the goodness of her heart, and Celia Glenn did a massive final edit for me. Lewis Rumiz was kind enough to check the psychoanalytically oriented information, while Dr Sarah Mares checked the chapter on the neuroscience, for which I am very grateful. My friend Linda Joy gave me an industry view of the work and Lewis Kaplan augmented my computer skills.

The skill of Madi Maclean made the text more readable, and the professionalism and inside knowledge of Irina Dunn made publication possible! The support and expertise of Dr David Reiter brought the whole project to completion, for which I am deeply grateful.

In the final stages I had invaluable support from Helen Hardy, Jill Henry, Bruce Daglish and Rolf Ruhl who did a complete final edit. I acknowledge my daughter and friends for their patience and support throughout.

Introduction

This book attempts to provide a frame of reference to assist us in reflecting on who we are as human beings and on the world that we have created.

We live in a world in which we're increasingly reacting, rather than reflecting, where it is difficult to take the time to work things through. The rapid rate of technological change encourages us to respond instantaneously to what comes along, rather than take responsibility for where we are going. In this environment, anchors and pointers can help us find our way.

This book is an attempt to synthesise the literature of neuroscience, infant mental health research and practice, psychoanalysis and political and historical commentators to open up a discussion on: Who are we? What is our nature? What is our developmental path? How do we repair the elements of our development that were unsatisfactory? What societal conditions make it possible to realise our potential? And to open a discussion on: How did we get to where we are? Where do we go from here?

Karen Hitchcock, a medical doctor, writing on the current state of medicine in *The Monthly* (September 2015 p. 24, 'Too Many Pills: On lifestyle disease and quick fixes') addresses some of the themes I will discuss in this book:

> A cause for many of our Western ills, organic and non-organic alike, might be found in a catchphrase that has become a cliché: that our society has degenerated into an economy. Read the papers – our main purpose and duty is to acquire and consume. At the expense of others in need; of our planet. Inequity increases. Education standards decline. We suffer existential ills that manifest in our bodies. We drive,

work and eat, become sedentary, fat, diabetic and depressed. Hospital wards fill with social catastrophes
and the outcome of styles-of-life and social policy.
Mainstream medicine alone cannot fix this. Real integrated treatment of our disease requires vast social
action. It requires personal action: use it or lose it.

... And neoliberal to the core, we regard our
population's health as a problem that lies with
discrete, always self-determining individuals.

What are some useful anchors and guides that can
help us navigate our current world and help us keep our
focus? Understanding our needs as a baby, together with
knowledge of our development to maturity over our lifespan,
provides us with our psychological trajectory from birth to
death. This path will include learning to love and gaining
the capacity for intimacy, alongside the growth to maturity
when we augment our family role and take our place in the
community.

Part 1 is an exploration of our nature as human beings, our
needs, and what we must have to thrive. We are inherently
social beings and our interrelatedness is intrinsic to who we
are. We depend on others to come into being, to be born and
to flourish. Without others being there for us we do not have
a self, an identity or a place in the world. We rely on others
for both our physical and psychological birth. Our physical
birth heralds the beginning of the birth of the personality.

I describe the main developmental tasks we grapple with
over our lifespan to explain how we move from dependency
to maturity. The path to maturity is difficult but rewarding.
Each stage requires relinquishing earlier behaviours
alongside opening up new capacities and understanding.
Knowing about the developmental processes over the
human lifespan can show us what is involved in reaching
maturity and help us ascertain where we are going.

If we miss out on any of the developmental stages,
it is possible to revisit our early years to resolve these

issues. Neuroscience, discussed in *Part 2*, tells us that our earliest years have a profound impact on our psyche and our relationships. Thus we need to integrate our early, pre-verbal years into our consciousness. I present three clinical examples of people who have grappled with the process of repairing early difficulties.[1] They were people who, like all of us, struggled with the weight of their early experience, which bore down on them and obstructed their capacity to relate to those around them. With support they could open up to spontaneity and joy and to a better understanding of the ferocity of the primitive forces that operate within.

Part 3 discusses family and society, which also have a profound impact on our psyche. Further, I offer ways of assessing the health of our society so we can better discern our needs personally and as a society. The current disarray in the world has many antecedents. I propose contributing factors to the difficulties we face with war, migration and climate change. I discuss where our society has come from and reflect on where we are at the moment, as well as possible ways of approaching the complex issues we face.

To fulfil our potential, we need to integrate an understanding of our developmental journey from birth to death and the health of the environment in which we live. This will assist us in gaining a greater understanding of the global society, and place us in the best possible position to be reflective and discerning about where we are, and where we need to be in the future.

We are not just pleasure-seeking individuals. When we are born we start developing through trial-and-error learning. What happens to the baby is a metaphor for life. Babies leave the womb where, in most instances, they have an environment attuned to their needs, with continuous nourishment and a consistent temperature. It all changes when the baby is born. He or she has to learn to suck.

---

[1] Two of the examples were first discussed in the *Australian Journal of Psychotherapy*, 'The Shock of the New', vol. 10, no. 2, pp. 144-153 (1991) (Kate), and 'A Stream of Sensations…', vol. 11, no. 1, pp. 35-46 (1992) (Sophia).

The baby is now an active agent in life with their parental "partner". Similarly, the baby needs to learn to crawl first, then stand. Often the baby will stand and fall many times. Next the child takes tentative steps and experiences more falls, but eventually reaches the goal of walking and can delight in his or her achievement. This enables the toddler to be ready for the next adventure. Learning to deal with the task at hand, staying with the challenge and experiencing the reward is the template for all our lives. A sense of satisfaction results from having achieved the task and provides greater confidence in one's ability to handle the next challenge.

"Know thyself" has been the dictum for a full life since the days of Socrates and Plato and it remains true of life today. We need to be aware of our feelings, to understand where they come from, and to use that knowledge reflectively. By combining the mind and the heart we can decide what we want to do. It can be daunting to be in touch with all the aspects inside us. It can lead to exploring our sad and lonely aspects, our guilty or angry desires. We may expose our long forgotten memories; the good, the bad, the ugly, and the profound. The reality of the human condition, that perfection is not our destiny, confronts us. All we have is the present moment. We all need to increase our understanding of, and empathy for, both oneself and others. Then we can mobilise our full human capacity to create a society and an environment that matches our needs and desires.

Note: In this book, "family" includes any group of individuals who rear children, whether they are a married couple, grandparents or single parents and regardless of the parents' gender or biological relation to the children.

PART 1

Normal developmental processes: birth to death

Chapter 1 Pregnancy and birth: our beginnings

A chick pea leaps almost over the rim of the pot
where it is being boiled…
don't try to jump out,
You think I am torturing you,
I'm giving you flavour,
so you can mix with spices and rice
and be the lovely vitality of a human being

"Chick Pea to Cook," p. 132, Barks, C. 1995, *The Essential Rumi*, 2nd ed., HarperCollins: New York

Pregnancy

What I am hoping to achieve is an imaginative journey into the experience of pregnancy and birth. What is it like to be the mother? What is it like to be the baby? What is it like to be the father? If we explore all of these perspectives we understand more about who we are and the context into which we were born, how the experience was for us, and its impact on those around us. According to the neuroscience literature, at this stage of life we need someone who is intimately connected to us and who understands us. This allows us to comprehend ourselves more fully, beginning with our time in the womb.

The experiences of a baby's early care may be unconscious but they impact powerfully on our development. When there are unconscious conflicts, they need to come to the surface to be aired so that ultimately they lose their power over us. The trauma of wartime experience provides a good analogy. In the past, not talking about what people experienced in wartime was considered the best way to protect oneself and the family. What we have since realised is that these experiences cannot be put aside since they can affect our behaviour negatively. Recognising the trauma, speaking the truth of the experience, and becoming aware of its impact can help it to be neutralised.

From the moment a couple conceives their baby they enter a triangular space. This expanded space adds a creative dimension, which develops their relationship. Simultaneously, there will be a regressive pull to go back into the dyadic or couple space. The arrival of a third person raises the question of whether they will be a friend or foe. As the newcomer, the baby brings great joy but also displaces or interrupts the couple. The baby may be a demanding rival who can damage the mother's body and disrupt the couple's equilibrium. These tensions are not generally problematic as they resolve over time.

The healthy resolution of these tensions comes when a mutual dependency emerges. The mother feeds the child but depends on her partner's support. In turn, the partner needs the mother's support, and together they experience their mutual hope in the growing foetus in the womb. After birth, the baby expresses its dependence on the parents in its smiles and other non-verbal expressions of emotion.

The French philosopher Jean-Paul Sartre explores this reliance in the relationships of the trio that form the basis of his play *No Exit (Huis Clos)*. In this play all humanity is reduced to three people who are trapped in a room in Hell. Eventually, one of them finds an exit but as he decides to leave he realises that life would be meaningless without the other two: all three must find a way to co-exist with each other.

Likewise, all members of the family trio face the joy and fulfilment of being wanted, together with the realisation that they were also unwanted. The child will always be a threat to the ambivalent, more self-centred part of the biological parents. To other aspects of the parents, the baby will be a blessing. Each member of the trio has to bear this reality, even though it is often unconscious.

All members of the trio need to find a space "to be" and

not just "do". Pregnancy is the beginning of learning how to do this. A character in a Woody Allen movie commented, 'I don't have time to be pregnant,' but the reality is it does take time. There is a different quality to "being" during pregnancy and after. It is slower, it comes from inside us, and it is not only reacting to the external world; it includes feeling, and reflection on that feeling. It is not just a process of linear cause and effect but a place where we can experience the fullness of things.

After conception, early hormonal and metabolic changes produce minor symptoms in the mother such as morning sickness. Pregnancy disturbs her body and psyche and she may have many dreams that parallel the physical intrusion of the new body inside her. She may be anxious about whether she wants the pregnancy or not. Is she ready to be a mother and move from her child-free existence? Is she allowed to have this baby? Will she be punished for having dared to take this step? Will she cope? The parents can be in harmony, in conflict, or a mixture of the two. Their own individual fantasies can lead to both joy and panic.

Together with a male colleague, I ran a parent group of four couples during the period of pregnancy. Three of the couples had confirmed pregnancies while one couple was hoping to become pregnant. It was a life-enhancing experience to be in the group meeting weekly for six weeks, then monthly for six months, and a final meeting twelve months after the first.

In the early sessions, the women shared violent dreams with us that were confronting. These dreams would have been very disturbing if they had not been in the context of pregnancy. Previous issues relating to their family of origin surfaced and old hurts and rivalries arose. At this stage the women frequently talked to each other as if what they were going through was "women's business". My colleague was able to challenge the men to stay in the dialogue and remain connected to what the women were saying and feeling. Subsequently, the men found a way to discuss their own fears and anxieties. When we kept both partners engaged in the discussion, they created an "ecosystem," with the sum of the couple being greater than the two individuals. Other colleagues ran mother's groups that were enormously helpful to the women but found that they did not have the lightness and humour of the mixed group. With both parents attending the meetings together, the group developed a greater sense of having enough resources and support during and after the pregnancy.

The men became preoccupied with the loss of income to the household due to their partner not working or working less. Initially, they thought they would have to earn more money to compensate. However, the men gradually thought more about being a supportive presence for their partner and new baby. They realised that rather than working more, they would need to work less. They thought about asking the boss to allow them more flexible time, or to travel less, and they were able to prioritise what was important in the situation.

Pregnant women generally become more preoccupied with their bodies as the first trimester progresses. They focus on the extraordinary idea of a separate and unknown being growing inside them. This often corresponds with feeling the baby kicking. As the symptoms of tiredness and nausea ease, mothers experience great wellbeing and contentment. The mother's hormones leave her in a happy state to "hatch" her baby and her focus is now turned inward to this other being. The mother begins to feel her attention is divided between the demands of the external world and the bid for attention from within. During this period, the couple variously give the baby characteristics or a pet name, or attribute likes and dislikes.

Women who have experienced rape or incest may find the baby's growth alarming. In the primitive world of the psyche, it may be perceived as the outcome of the earlier invasion by a predator and not the outcome of the current relationship. This can unconsciously reactivate past angers around the intrusion into the mother's body, and if these feelings haven't been acknowledged they may limit her capacity to bond with her baby.

In the final trimester, the mother-to-be begins to consider that her baby is viable and could survive outside her, if it were to be born prematurely. As the pregnancy progresses, the expectant mother becomes more aware of the momentous, irreversible change that is about to occur. Faced with the unknown, and as the tension and uncertainty increases, many women attempt to control what is happening to them by predicting possible birth dates. Internal conflicts can arise from old family issues, together with moodiness, heightened emotions and irrational fears of retribution for past sins. These could be an abortion, illicit sexual encounters or past hatreds. All the hopes that have accrued in the mother's life may be placed on the baby. Her child can be the fulfilment of her dreams or the messiah who will cure all her suffering.

The other side of this amazing and creative process is that the mother, father and baby can develop negative feelings about the experience. At the earliest age, hate inevitably comes with intimacy and cannot be avoided. We may try to bypass it, individually and collectively, but it is built into the human condition. I remember facing up to my hatred in relation to some conflicts with my mother while in therapy. My skin broke out in itchy hives all over my legs. I walked a great deal around my neighbourhood and finally realised that if the same circumstances with my mother recurred, I would be angry. I became painfully aware that I was not able to avoid being angry. It was a natural response, given the circumstances, and I had to accept that it was an integral part of my being alive. Having accepted this, I then opened up to the positive things my mother had given me.

It is natural that the mother will have mixed feelings about the baby. The baby will hurt or tear at her body, challenge her old identity and keep her endlessly sleep deprived. The baby starts life ruthlessly loving its mother before developing reciprocal love. Hate develops as she or he becomes a whole person who can be both loved and loving. The baby must push through the body of the mother and take his or her nourishment, even if it is at some expense to the mother, in order to live. The mother needs to understand this and learn to tolerate any negative feelings without acting on them.

Pregnancy and birth remain a magical yet terrifying experience for everyone. Mothers can experience elation, terror, anxiety and joy that they need to process. It is a time when feeling overwhelmed is utterly appropriate and to contain this range of feeling prematurely is to limit the experience. It is a special time for all involved.

Birth

This is the first moment of a cooperative partnership between the mother and baby as they work together to give birth. This critical time will influence how their relationship develops and, for the baby, it will establish a pattern of relating that will affect future relationships. It is important that we all understand our own physical and psychological origins by reflecting on this experience from each of the differing perspectives.

The mother and baby require a certain state of mind to engage in the process. The parents need to be able to stay with their thoughts and feelings and also to understand the baby's experience. Achieving this state of receptiveness is difficult in a culture that values doing over being. We should acknowledge this quality of human experience. Otherwise we can only act or react rather than "be with". This "being with" state includes being aware of our feelings in a situation and also the baby's feelings. This is the path of empathy.

What I discuss is only the tip of the iceberg. This book cannot cover every permutation of this state but I hope it provides an entry into these different perspectives and shows how we can be attuned to the experience of each participant. It is an imaginative exercise since each of us has been a baby and many will have subsequently become parents.

Mother

A first-time mother and father, interviewed for a study involving full-term and premature babies, clearly illustrates the strong and conflicting emotions involved in the birthing process. The couples I discuss had full-term babies. This research is comprehensively discussed in *Premature Babies: Their emotional world* compiled and edited by Norma Tracey (2000):[2]

> We rang the birth centre because the pain was worse. Later when I went to the toilet there was a bit of meconium in it so I went straight in. Because the meconium was thick I couldn't stay at the birth centre and went upstairs. They plugged me into the machine and put straps around me but that made the contractions worse. Everyone was in and out. They took blood but, because I was bloated, it took six times before they could get it. The new registrar said I had to have a caesarean. I started to cry. It was just the situation. So I had an epidural. There was no pain and a lot of pushing and pulling. Finally half of him arrives and I asked if it was a boy or a girl.
>
> It was a boy. I didn't know if that was right because we had been told we were having a girl, but they had to race him straight off because he had swallowed some of the gunk so they suctioned him out. Finally they brought him back to me and it was still not real, it had all been so quick and everything. They brought him back and they just laid him by my head so I couldn't focus on him. I don't know whether it was the drugs or whether he was just too close, but I could see this little thing lying there but I could barely move to do any more.

---

[2] This unique research was conducted by Norma Tracey and designed by Dr Henry Luiker. Norma interviewed twelve couples; six had normal term babies that are discussed here. The other six babies arrived more than nine weeks early. These couples were interviewed 18 times each over the first four months after birth. Mothers and fathers were interviewed separately.

Responding empathetically to this mother would mean acknowledging what she had been through. She anticipated a natural birth at the birth centre but because of the meconium she had to go "upstairs". This is the first change of plan she has to face. Next, not only does she have to relinquish the birth centre for the hospital ward, she faces a caesarean birth. Further, while expecting a girl, she has a boy. By this time she is exhausted and overwhelmed. Finally, just after the birth, the staff took the baby away for a procedure just when she might expect to hold him in her arms. When the baby finally returns it would have been helpful if someone had encouraged her to make her first meeting with her baby more comfortable and positive.

All mothers experience difficulties and even shock at the new experience of giving birth. Most mothers will need to talk through her birth experience, in detail, many times. Mothers leave hospital so quickly these days that they may not have "processed" the birth. The unprocessed birth experience can interfere with how a mother first meets her baby. The mother's partner and family, or staff, can help by listening and taking an interest in her experience.

Both mother and baby will naturally feel overwhelmed and need time to deal with those feelings. Busy hospital wards are not always easy places to create a nurturing environment. A few days after the birth the hormonal functioning of the body can lead to many mothers feeling quite teary for a day. This is a normal part of the biochemical reaction to the mother's milk coming down into her breasts. It is also an expression of the loss of the union that the mother and baby shared and should not be mistaken for a clinical depression.

At the time of the birth, the mother is very open, vulnerable and receptive both physiologically and psychologically. Her body opens in a mysterious and dramatic way to allow the passage of her baby. The openness and sensitivity are adaptive mechanisms attuning her to her baby and entering a state of "maternal preoccupation". This state helps her understand what is happening for her baby and to intuit what he or she needs.

Mother and baby have to allow for a "getting to know you" phase, just as the mother and father will need to get to get to know each other in a different way. The beginning of any relationship is a time of adjustment. Previously unresolved relationships, particularly between the mother and her mother, may re-surface. Unresolved needs and conflicts may need to be acknowledged.

One new mother put it this way:

> It was really quite overwhelming. A lot of the time
> I find myself just crying at the thought that… she's
> here and I love her and… the fear that I might lose
> her (crying). It's funny because it took a few days
> to feel anything much, especially after having had
> a caesarean. I was in pain and so drugged for a few
> days. She just lay there next to me and I'd lie there
> feeling very afraid for her, thinking I can't look after
> her… I can't even look after myself (crying).

> My mother was sick when I was little. She died of
> cancer when I was five. It also hit me how my mother
> must have felt. She had three babies when she died.
> She had to leave us (crying)… it never struck me
> before just how traumatic that must have been for
> her (cries) not just to face death herself but to know
> her babies weren't going to be looked after. And we
> weren't, we weren't well looked after (crying).

This poignant story shows how unresolved past issues surface at the crucial time of birth. Giving birth will inevitably remind mothers of their own early childhood. If there are many unresolved issues the mother may need to talk about her experience with someone who will listen and be open to the feelings evoked.

The use of drugs in childbirth requires a thoughtful approach. Drugs can help with a painful or prolonged labour but they can cloud the experience that the mother and baby are going through together. A successful drug-free birth frequently gives the mother a "high" or joyful experience. Even routine drugs can inhibit this experience and limit the intensity of the mother's first meeting with her baby.

In one case, a family had agreed to join an infant observation program, where a trainee visited the mother and / or father once a week for at least a year to observe normal developmental processes. The mother rang from the hospital to let the trainee know that her baby was born. The trainee promptly attended the hospital. The mother had asked for a caesarean birth and her doctor had told her to bring earphones and some of her favourite music so that she could listen to it while the caesarean section was performed. When the trainee arrived, she saw the new mother lying turned away from her baby with the earphones in her ears. In a wistful, sad tone she said, 'I am listening to the same music I had at the birth'. The mother was melancholy and flat, and seemed oblivious to the live baby lying next to her in her crib. It was as if she was looking for something. We discussed this birth in our seminar and wondered whether the mother was trying to reconnect to the lost experience of the birth. What had happened in the oblivion the music created? Had she given birth? Was this her baby? How could she go back to have the experience?

The mother also needs time to unravel from who she was before the birth and take her time to become someone different, with new and different capacities, after the birth. In this context, the mother "getting going" too soon after the birth may not be good for her.

Father

The birth of a child will also reactivate the father's own past histories. They will often review their own parenting and revisit their relationship with their father. A father said of his experience:

> Basically we had a good upbringing, although I wasn't
> all that close to my dad. One thing we didn't do was
> talk about things very much, and I would like that to
> be different – that we could discuss things more.

For the father, seeing what his partner experiences in childbirth can be an ordeal and even traumatic. The father, like the mother, is facing massive changes to his life. To transition to fatherhood, he will also need to be more open and connect with his own vulnerability. He may experience new feelings. Acknowledging these feelings helps him to bond with his child:

> It's been harrowing, I am enjoying parenthood but
> I am scared. Sometimes you feel great love when
> they snuggle into your neck… but if they continually
> scream, then you understand how parents can
> accidently squash or beat their child. It is confusing.
> It is difficult to describe my relationship to the baby
> at the moment because he likes to be picked up by
> anybody.

> They're the baby, and they know what to do, but we're
> really the babies because we don't know what to do.

The father has a crucial role. Mothers need the father to protect them and their baby and to foster the mother-baby relationship. The mother needs to be protected from the outside world intruding too soon. This allows the mother-baby couple time to find each other. The father can moderate any intrusions of family and friends that are initially too much for the mother-baby couple. It helps if the father can be sensitive to his partner's needs as well as his own.

While happy about their new child and sharing the mother's sense of achievement and elation, fathers can feel outside of the experience. In fact they have to be generous to their partner by allowing the growing intimacy between their partner and their child. This is not always an easy task:

> I was excited when I found out about the pregnancy.
> I was supportive of my wife – just watching it grow.
> You're not living it like they are, in that respect you
> are a bit left out. After the birth you can participate
> more but the baby is so time-consuming for my wife:
> he is a perpetual feeder and she is on edge all the
> time.

The father is often concerned for the whole family unit while the mother focuses on her engagement with the baby. He may be worried about having enough money for the family and what the future will bring.

> I am worried financially, and I worry about the
> future, mainly in terms of my study now and how I
> will relate to our child as he gets older. I worry about
> how I will get my study done, and at the same time
> be more available to the baby than my father was.

In time, he moves the twosome of the mother and baby into the threesome (or more) of the family. While initially fostering the twosome to form a connection, once bonded he helps draw the unit into a family group.

The father's role is a difficult one. The father's relationship to the baby is not as immediate and physical as the mother's. He needs to find his own connection and role rather than replicating that of the mother. The father is critical to the development of the mother's capacity to be a mother, but it is harder for the father to see this role. His task is a protective, mediating one with the outside world, which leaves the mother freer to engage in the relationship with her baby

Baby

For nine months the foetus has grown inside the mother – in a sac of fluid that stays at a steady temperature. The experience of hot and cold is alien to the foetus. It has lived in a warm constant temperature to which it is perfectly adapted. Around that fluid are the firm walls of the uterus that provide a safe container for the foetus, preventing a sense of "lostness" and a feeling of "I don't know where I am". The continuous supply of nutrients through the umbilical cord and into the foetus means that the developing foetus does not experience hunger.

In normal circumstances, the birth process begins through the mutual activity of the baby and mother. Having matured, the foetus is ready to leave its protective environment and fulfil its potential outside. First it has to breathe. After taking the first breath a number of new experiences confronts the baby. The light is stronger and sounds are louder. The baby feels hot and cold air hitting the sense receptors on the surface of its skin for the first time.

Losing the enveloping "arms" of the uterus that provided constant protection exposes the baby to its vulnerability, hence its need for holding, for firm arms from mother and father, firm wrapping, and being held in the mind of the parents. The baby has a natural impulse to look for the parent. The baby seeking the nipple symbolises the readiness to be met in the outside world.

Gradually the task of integrating the birth and the baby's first separation from its mother takes place. The baby now totally depends on the mother. The mother provides a sense of security; there is a warm, firmly held place that provides milk to fill the empty gnawing stomach. However, now the baby has to wait in between feeds. He or she communicates feelings of bewilderment, distress and frustration to the mother. The mother may feel overwhelmed. In time, the mother's and father's reliable responses will reassure the baby, who will develop trust in its parents. The parents need to be wondering about what the baby may be going through. This "reverie" acts as a "mental skin" that holds the parts of the baby's personality together and buffers its experiences. Gradually, the baby can build up an image of its parents and establish a relationship.

Understanding the baby's experience helps us to attend to his or her needs. We can begin to see the baby as a little personality with individual differences. It is important to be emotionally open to the baby. We need to let their cries speak to us so that we understand what they are experiencing.

Premature birth

Before birth, parents have mixed emotions about the baby-to-be. For the mother and father of a premature baby in intensive care, a premature baby can seem to fulfil their worst fantasies. They may fear that their own negative thoughts, about not wanting their baby, have overcome the positive ones. The parents may even fear that they have caused the prematurity and the baby's illness. For a fuller discussion of these issues read Tracey (2000) with particular reference to Chapter 14 by Helen Hardy.

The baby is the mutual gift of the parents to each other; a mutual sign of her fertility and his potency. This holds whether the baby is full-term or premature. However, when negative events occur there is greater potential for difficulties. The baby was to be the mother's gift to her partner and her parents and it can be devastating to see her gift going "wrong" and bringing grief instead of joy. Her body and the baby's body may bear the scars of their experience; there is no glowing mother and perfectly formed baby to show to the world.

In time, much of what the parents and baby experience will fade into the background. I will explore what can arise so these feelings can be better understood at the time and therefore recede into past experiences more quickly.

A mother and a baby in the last trimester are still part of each other. A premature birth interrupts the natural separating process and it occurs before either of them is ready. This destroys the seamless transition from inside to outside, which occurs in a natural birth. The mother has carried her baby inside her body in a state of fusion and when birth parts them she feels empty. The full-term mother has a healthy feeding baby to nurture but if the baby is premature and in intensive care the mother can become anxious and afraid.

She does not have a healthy living baby but a very small, not fully formed one. Often, for medical reasons, the mother cannot touch her baby or can only have limited contact. Both mother and father may be afraid to attach to this little being in case he or she may die. There is no baby in the carefully prepared nursery at home.

Instead of the natural maternal preoccupation enveloping her baby, the baby is now outside and wrenched away from her; her maternal preoccupation is broken. She may feel incapable of protecting her baby and that she is "bad" for her baby. A mother vividly spoke of this experience when her first baby was born three months premature. She carried feelings of failing her baby. She felt he was inaccessible in his humidicrib and attempts to make contact with him were met with 'you must wash your hands, you might give him an infection'. Such comments discouraged her. She lost confidence and felt the nurses would do a better job. In her distressed state she also felt that her baby's father would be better for him and that he should take over and spend time with their baby.

For the mother, the baby was to be her final moment of separating out from her own mother. This was to be the moment when she would become a successful mother. If her baby is in any way damaged or ill she struggles with a sense of being inferior to her mother or even robbed of her opportunity to become a full woman.

The mother has not had the opportunity to work through the normal life and death fantasies that arise in the last trimester. In fact she is catapulted into an actual life and death situation. Mothers of babies in neonatal intensive care units don't always feel the baby is theirs. Rather than her breast providing the milk the baby is in a public ward with a humidicrib sustaining the baby, and a tube may be providing the milk. A team of nurses is the mother.

The vital elements of soft bodily contact and smell, which are a normal part of every intimate relationship, are essential to the new mother's bonding with her real baby. She loses this physical contact when her baby is in a humidicrib. Even when she is able to nurse her baby, it can be difficult to negotiate the equipment attached to the baby's body. The mother has to express soothing intimate words to her baby without any privacy. The premature baby may not always find the touch soothing. It may be painful after all the medical procedures that have intruded into the baby's sensitive body.

The mother has already missed out on those precious moments of having the baby being placed on her chest after birth, allowing it to find her nipple and have skin-to-skin contact while it hears the familiar heartbeat of the mother. Establishing and maintaining the bond with a fragile baby that is hypersensitive and not robust enough for the world outside the womb is difficult.

Circumstances can overwhelm premature mothers and they need to process these events. Without support, they will be left to manage as best they can but the shock and unprocessed events may prevent them bonding well with their baby. Fate has dealt them a blow. This is not what they wished for. Their dreams are dashed; it has all gone wrong. They need to grieve what they have lost, but it is hard to grieve when everything is so uncertain. Some mothers will grieve and be able to move on. Others will overreact and find it hard to find their "alive" baby. They may need to cut off their feelings and become emotionally dead. Without good support it is too painful to deal with what has happened.

When the numbness persists, the mother may become hyper-alert to her baby. In her mind she has failed to protect her baby so she is overprotective. On the other hand, she may be neglectful and indifferent to her baby. Being overprotective or indifferent are ways of coping with the hostile and frequently angry impulses that they feel towards the hand that life has dealt them. Why should this have happened to me? What have I done to deserve this? Why is this baby bringing me stress and difficulty instead of joy? This can develop into self-hatred and feeling unworthy which get in the way of connecting with her new baby.

With an early birth, the mother and baby can feel that events are pushing them when they are not ready and that life has been unfair. She has lost control and does not know what to do. Without being able to touch her baby, the mother cannot even physically feel that she is getting to know her baby. To dare to know her baby emotionally is an enormous risk until she is assured that the baby will live and come home with her.

The father of a preterm baby faces similar difficulties. If the baby is impaired in any way, or there is a threat to the baby's life, this may challenge the father in his role as the protector of his family. It is a time of crisis for him as well. He needs to cope with a changing wife, preoccupied and emotionally unpredictable, who needs his support. If their baby is in a different hospital from the mother, he may be the one with close and direct contact with the baby.

Circumstances may not allow the mother and father to work things out together even when they are consulted by medical staff. By gradually trying to claim their baby, the mother and father struggle to properly work through how they want their baby looked after. Unspeakable thoughts and feelings get in the way of the normal discussions between husband and wife. She may assume all control of the baby and make unilateral decisions leaving her husband out, or she may criticise him because she unconsciously feels criticised. With the bonding disrupted she may not always know what is best for her baby and in her emotional state may not be able to enjoy being a mother. She may be overly dependent on her husband, or alternatively, feel that she is the only one who knows what to do. She may bewilder her partner because she seems so unreasonable.

What is it like to be a baby in this situation? I spent time in a neonatal intensive care unit to understand a patient of mine who had a difficult early experience. The sight of tiny babies connected to tubes, alone in their humidicribs, even with attentive staff and parents, was very distressing. The babies looked vulnerable and unready to be in the world. They relied on impersonal technology and specialist medical and nursing care in order to maintain basic needs like temperature control, breathing and feeding.

The baby has arrived abruptly in this world and not had the continuous sound of his or her mother's voice, smell and taste. Not being able to be breastfed, the baby misses out on being in their mother's arms. The baby is likely to be too fragile to be held and too weak to snuggle. Even if the parents can nurse the baby, he or she may not experience touching as comforting due to painful medical or nursing procedures. Unable to feed orally a baby loses a sense of continuity, of having been safe inside the walls of the uterus, followed by being wrapped and gently held.

Preterm infants do not develop the normal behaviours that enable full-term babies to respond to their parents and engage them by gaining their attention and comfort. These babies cannot initially develop periods of calmness and alertness. Immature movement patterns and an inability to settle affect the baby's responses and communication. The parents may not recognise the baby's cues and facial expressions because they are weaker or less obvious.

With such a disruptive start, what can be done for these infants and parents? Studies have shown that receiving individualised supportive care involving the family can enhance the comfort and brain function of premature infants. The intensive care unit can be made more baby-friendly, with softer lighting and quieter machines, thus lessening the stress on the baby. Staff can adapt medical interventions to fit the baby's sleeping and eating cycles. I have seen videos of nurses taking the time for the baby to recover from each intervention, holding them until they settle, then proceeding when the baby is ready. Thus they allow the baby to have some agency. Nurses can modify handling and routines to be more in keeping with the baby's cues and take the baby's readiness into account. Pillows or towels placed next to the baby's skin can be comforting and supportive as they feel contact against them rather than nothingness. Massage may be beneficial in comforting a preterm baby where skin contact can be tolerated.

Infant mental health work indicates that the self-organisation of the brain is developed in the context of a relationship with another thinking/feeling self. To achieve this, someone needs to understand enough of what is going on for the baby. In its disorganised and unintegrated state, such a vulnerable little baby must be terrified. An "integrated state" of mind can only be achieved within this partnership and is not possible if the baby is left to it alone.

Chapter 2 Psychological birth

Little by little, wean yourself.
This is the gist of what I have to say.
From an embryo, whose nourishment comes in the blood,
move to an infant drinking milk,
to a child on solid foods,
to a searcher after wisdom,
to a hunter of more invisible game

"Wean Yourself," (Barks, p. 70)

This chapter deals with the stages that take place, for all parties, during the period of the baby's "psychological birth". It is a critical period of learning and maturing as parents help their child develop the capacity for intimacy. It creates the template for all their future relationships and responses to change and life events. This occurs with whoever provides the early nurturing for the baby whether they be male, female or grandparents; whoever has an emotional investment in developing a bond with the baby.

Psychological birth begins as the baby, who is born with his or her own characteristics, begins to interact with the environment they inhabit. This environment into which the baby is born includes the atmosphere within the parent's relationship or, if a mother is on her own, with significant others. It also includes attitudes in the family as well as the family's cultural inheritance. Boys may be prized, girls undervalued, or vice versa. Families may pass major trauma down to the next generation to deal with. For example, the grandchildren of Holocaust survivors are over-represented among people with anorexia nervosa. While not consciously doing so, the grandchildren can replay some of the issues that their grandparents faced but were not able to process at the time.

It is important, wherever possible, for the baby to be met by parents who know who he or she is. The baby needs someone who is attuned to them rather than to an idea in the parent's mind of who the baby should be. The analogy here is with a couple. Often when I am conducting therapy with couples, I am amazed at how frequently they are unable to see each other as they are because of the intrusion of the past. The issues each complains about in the partner are frequently related to their own past experiences. Couples very often look to each other to provide what they missed out on in their childhood and so cannot see clearly the person they are relating to.

We also often look to our partner to make us happy, something that neither party can do for the other. We are responsible for our own fulfilment. Only we ourselves can make our lives the way we want them to be. However, we can share the ups and downs of our life with the other. Sharing our own process of development, and expecting sustenance and support, are legitimate demands on our partner, but not giving us happiness. This is also true for the baby. Parents meet the baby's needs and develop a relationship, but the baby is not there to meet the parent's needs. It is a challenging time for a couple as they are forced to develop new capabilities and mature in ways they had not expected.

The baby's context includes the psychological environment each parent brings to the relationship. The baby is highly sensitive to the emotional environment he or she inhabits. There will be greater obstacles to developing a good relationship if one or both partners have a difficult history; unless subsequent experiences have alleviated the earlier difficulties. On the other hand, some past difficulties, if not too great, can be a spur to do better. Easy past relationships do not always provide the ability to handle more complex relationships. Too many gaps in development, however, need attention so people can do things differently and expand their capacity for intimacy.

The couple will also impart their values to the baby. Life is a gift and our deepest desire as human beings is to make the most of the experience of living, to fulfil our potential as human beings. This is also true for the baby. However, much depends on how the parents interpret the notion of potential. It is important for the couple to clarify together their values around their baby. Whether explicitly stated or not, the baby will pick up the underlying message of the parents' unconscious demands of him or her and parents need to be sure the baby receives the message they want him or her to get.

What are the parents hoping for on behalf of the baby? What do they wish for in terms of the baby's development? Is the baby there to fulfil his or her potential or the parents' expectations? Do they want the baby to excel, to know how to compete or achieve what they weren't able to do? Do they want the baby to carry the burden of putting the parents in a good light and showing off the parents' achievements? Do the parents want the baby to be a loving and thoughtful human being who values relationships? Do they want to have a child who is engaged in and able to deal with the world and fully use their capacities? It is difficult for parents to manage all the expectations, desires and resentments they hold towards the baby and yet remain attentive to the baby. No wonder this is a critical time for parents to receive support.

For parents, having a child is a wonderful opportunity to revisit their own childhood and recall their early experiences, with all the associated pleasure and pain. They can also discover the world in a different way through the eyes of the child. Being part of the development of a new human being is an enormous but enriching responsibility. It is a maturing process as well as a source of deep joy.

What are the processes that parents and babies go through together?

To answer this we need to look at the processes that enable psychological birth. Physical birth heralds the beginning of the psychological process of the birth of the personality. Certain things need to happen to make this possible. Developmental studies, psychological theories, infant observation and neuroscience research have given us a comprehensive picture of what a baby needs to be able to form intimate relationships.

These processes, which we learn from our parents when we are babies, recur over our lifetime because they represent a prototype for all later developmental processes.

"Being with": the first two months

Just after birth, the baby and the new parents experience a lot of change that can be overwhelming. Everyone feels a degree of shock with the massive changes once the baby is outside the womb. Every member of this new family struggles with their own aspects of who they are. The mother has just faced her first separation from her baby with the transition from the womb to the outside world. Her identity is now entwined with the new baby. The baby is facing enormous changes coming into the world, while the father has to find his place within the new matrix that has formed.

Everyone is confused and that is to be expected. A new unit has formed. Everyone needs to feel able to "not know" the territory and gradually find their way. Avoiding this experience will prevent a transition from fully taking place. As a community, we need to support the new family unit to find its way. Reducing external demands will allow them the time needed for a successful transition. The parents can be in touch with the baby's helplessness and needs. The baby has nowhere else to go, no one else to look to. The parents are the baby's whole world.

While our society does not value vulnerability, it is a crucial part of opening up to being in touch with the baby. The parents need to respond to the baby's needs sufficiently for the baby to develop a sense of security. If observed carefully, the baby will give cues as to when he or she wants eye contact, or needs to look away when they have had enough engagement, or when they are following a voice. Parents in touch with these cues put their babies in touch with themselves.[3] Friends or family members who are sensitive to these cues are important, too. In our infant observation seminars, we found that mothers, when their partner was away, would lose momentum while waiting for their partner to return. Support is crucial.

Parents are asked to manage the feelings that babies' experiences evoke in them. This requires parents to adjust to their needs, to be quiet with the baby, or respond when they indicate they would like connection. From birth, babies fall into a state of what is called "alert inactivity". They are physically quiet but alert, apparently taking in external events. This may require the parent to slow down to be with the baby and not just be more efficient at "getting the job done". Being with a baby also means dealing with crying. This can be difficult. The parent needs to wonder: does the crying make me feel helpless, angry, over-protective, or a mixture of all of these? Parents can feel angry at the seemingly endless demands a baby places on them. They need to acknowledge these feelings, understand what is going on and move on to dealing with the baby. The baby, like the parents, will be a bundle of sensations, disoriented in the new environment and needing to find his or her way. In this transition the baby will seek the familiar sounds and smells of the mother's heartbeat and skin. Parents can begin by observing what is going on in themselves while wondering what it might be like for the baby, and responding to the baby's needs.

---

[3] *Getting to Know You* is a delightful video on picking up the cues in the first three months of life. It is available from the Northern Beaches Child and Family Health Services or the NSW Institute of Psychiatry, institute@nswiop.nsw.edu.au.

At this time, parents and baby are trying to organise their experience. The mother and father attempt to gradually create some pattern around night and day, negotiating feeds and time for digestion in between. They spend time stabilising sleep patterns. The baby is trying to make sense of his or her experiences in a simple way and actively forming a sense of what the literature calls "an emergent self". Research shows that babies recognise the smell of their mother's milk from birth and at three days can respond to music that became familiar to them in the womb. Newborns prefer the human voice, particularly the voices they heard during their mother's pregnancy. They prefer to look at faces rather than inanimate patterns.

A basic flexible routine develops out of the baby's invitation to engage when crying, smiling or gazing. In response to this invitation, parents attend to feeding and getting the baby to sleep, engage in rocking, touching, soothing, talking, singing and making noises and faces. All of these activities are part of getting to know each other and assist the physiological regulation of the baby's body.

If well responded to, the baby startles less and gradually absorbs the impact of new situations. How the mother picks up the baby, changes the nappy, engages in the feed, all communicate how she feels towards her baby. In turn, the parents are modulating the baby's emotional state. The baby begins to feel wanted in the world in which they now live. The baby responds: three-week-old babies can imitate adults sticking out their tongues, opening their mouths, smiling, frowning or showing a surprised face.

Initially, the mother's lap becomes an extension of the womb. This is the first step in the baby understanding he or she is now outside, not inside, the womb. The mother assists the baby to determine where he or she begins and ends and where the mother's body begins and ends. Hence an early task is to ascertain who is who in the relationship and the separateness between them. This helps "embody" babies within the physical self and helps them to identify the boundaries of the mother's body. This is often done in simple ways, for example, when the baby sneezes and wonders where this comes from, inside or outside, and the mother clarifies its origin. A slamming door, an airplane passing by, if identified, all assist this process of clarification in very natural ways. The mother too grows into her new body that has been profoundly changed by the birth experience. Both mother and father will develop into an expanded version of who they are as they claim their status as parents. Mothers who enjoy the total dependency of the baby can find it difficult to let go of this period while others who struggle with the dependency needs of their baby, because their own have never been met, look forward to the baby becoming less dependent.

A way to make sense of the world and establish rudimentary categories of experiences, is to divide experiences into those that are sensually soothing or those that disturb. It is as if the whole world can be reduced to these two states. The parents and the baby need to develop the psychological muscles to handle both of these states. Babies have to face that they no longer live in a world totally shaped to their needs, as when having to wait for a feed. The baby has to digest the milk before another feed is possible. The mother's milk is not on tap. The parents can soothe themselves by holding their feeding and sleeping baby or having periods of short gazing and connection. Some parents may find it difficult to enjoy these moments of intense love and stillness when they have not experienced much of a loving gaze themselves. On other occasions, the parents will have to bear the baby's fractiousness with equanimity rather than being irritated and resentful. Again, this can be difficult for those parents who have not had their own cries responded to as babies.

What the family members have to face is that not all experiences are soothing. All are realising that there are both "soft" and "hard" experiences. Soft experiences are those that help the baby feel secure and held in the outside world that is so different from the womb. Being firmly wrapped, being held and sucking at the breast, are all unifying experiences that produce a sense of security. Hard experiences, on the other hand, help the baby experience their individuality and to feel their separateness. Having a nappy changed, being bathed and being taken away from the breast at the end of feeding are all experiences in this domain. Speaking soothingly and assisting the baby through these experiences can ease these "hard" experiences. However, both hard and soft experiences are necessary for them to develop. Too many soft experiences and babies are unable to develop their own skills to deal with the world. Too many hard experiences and babies are left feeling alone. Babies then often become anxious as they work hard to cope with the world on their own.

As the baby begins to feel the presence of the parent, a partnership develops and a sense of working together flows from this interaction. Two people are involved in the exchange. The baby gives the cues; the mother or father responds, and a partnership is formed. This interchange constructs a web of safety around the baby.

In one of my infant observation sessions, a young migrant mother returned to work, leaving her baby with her mother. We knew nothing of this grandmother's background, but she fed, changed and put the baby to sleep totally in line with her own regime. She never responded to a cry of hunger or a gesture of need from this little person. Consequently, he became like a stuffed little toy with no sense of his own agency and his integrity lost. On the other hand, parents should not just follow the baby's cues as if the parents are not part of the conversation. Two is the operative ecology, followed by three, as dad enters the picture. Later, the conversation may include siblings and finally the larger world.

Having achieved some sense of night and day, a flexible routine and some idea of who their baby is, the triad moves to the next period of development. In the meantime, if all goes well, the baby, mother and father have forged a connection.

They have come through a peak period of change, faced doubt, experienced disturbance and managed to survive. A similar process will be repeated as changes occur.

Falling in love: two to six months

This phase heralds the baby's growing capacity to relate. The world begins to treat the baby as a little self with a more integrated sense of the baby's identity. At this age they smile infectiously, gaze into the parent's eyes, coo and are irresistibly social.

Babies' growing competence at relationships is evident in how they use their gaze to have some control over relationships. They will engage someone, stare past, look away, take notice of an event or watch others intently. In this way, babies regulate the initiating, maintaining, ending and avoiding of contact with their parents. By using their gaze, they can reject, distance or defend themselves against their parents. Using the gaze is their way of saying "no". They can then reinstate contact through gazing, smiling and vocalizing. There is an increase in "talking" to those who are close. People respond to the baby by using exaggerated "baby talk" with a raised pitch and simplified syntax delivered at a slower than normal speed. Mimicking exchanges take place and exchanges of sounds are like wordless conversations. These exchanges are engagements with another but they also regulate the baby's level of arousal and excitement within a tolerable range.

Babies are not just more social, regulated or attentive, but now seem to have an integrated sense of themselves as distinct bodies with control over their own actions. At this age, research shows that babies know that the various faces of their mother, whether happy, sad or angry, all belong to her, and they have no trouble identifying their mother's face from photographs. They actively explore their parents' faces by stroking or pulling their hair. They have their own feelings, a sense of continuity, and they recognise other people as being separate from them.

Physically, babies master rolling over and begin to explore the world more. Their motor patterns mature and sensori-motor capacity reaches a higher level. Engagement with the world increases, but the baby is not yet willing to share intimate relationships with others. They ignore pets until they are ready to include them in their circle of intimates.

Around four months, babies will move from wanting to curl in and be cuddled to also wanting to turn outward to face the world while being held. This heralds their full arrival into the world and "hatching" out of their parent's arms. When needing reassurance, they will turn inward to receive comfort. At this time, their rhythms of sleep and activity cycles become more predictable. Evidence suggests the baby is capable of acts of cued recall memory around three months.

Emotionally, however, babies are volatile. The calm presence of the parents can regulate the intensity of the baby's feelings. Gradually, during interactions with the parents, babies learn to manage feelings of elation and ecstasy or distress and disturbance. The growing intensity of the babies' feelings can be handled safely within the relationships with their parents. This requires maturity from the parents at a time when they are also dealing with their own fluctuating emotional states.

Underlying all these changes, there is much psychological work happening through the baby's everyday activities. During the early few months, *mutual idealisation* helps all the parties stay the course. This is nature's way of supporting parents through a complex transition. This is analogous to the falling in love stage of a relationship and a precursor to getting to know each other at a deeper level. This idealisation includes an initial belief that the other can fulfil all our needs. The mother and baby form a pair, a complete unit that seemingly needs no one else. If all goes well, they mirror one another, the gaze of the baby seeking the beloved and the mother basking in the glow.

Intense highs and lows in mood accompany this *falling in love phase*. The relationship is volatile on both sides. The mother, who speaks in a heartfelt and loving way of her beautiful baby in the morning, is the same mother who, later in the afternoon, cannot wait to offload the baby onto the father when he returns from work. The baby occupies a similar state: the mother is blessed with intense loving gazes as if she is the only one for him or her, yet this can turn abruptly when the baby is upset. Then it is as if the whole world has fallen apart and the baby is inconsolable. The father has to calm the volatility of his partner and baby. This time can be quite bewildering for him. He needs to provide a secure and safe harbour for the ups and downs of the relationship between the two people closest to him without feeling left out. The father can feel displaced when he sees how lovingly his wife gazes at the baby. Of course, if the father is the main carer then these roles will be reversed.

The gradual let down into the real world follows the idealised view of parent and baby. In time, this idealisation diminishes and the *reality of the relationship* takes over. Babies realise that their mother or father cannot take away all pain but they will assist them in living their life. For the parents, this new baby, who was somehow going to repair all past hurts or heal the gaps in the marriage, can only be an ordinary delightful human being. It is at this point, however, when they begin to understand the reality of who each other is, that real love begins. It is an important learning process for the baby for all future relationships. The early time of togetherness assists the pair to bond. Later, they further explore the relationship and the individuals involved so that what unfolds is the reality of both sides. Of necessity, there is *some mutual disappointment* alongside accepting those realities. However, the true nature of each other gives birth to a more realistic and authentic love. In this way we love in the context of what we are given and of what we are not given; we accept both sides of the coin.

The parent, usually the mother, does this in the context

of the feeding and the separation that occurs when the baby moves to and from the breast. Mothers assist their babies with these *transitions to and from the breast*, giving them time to pass through this experience. The baby is learning to be with the mother in the intimacy of feeding at the breast, then to let go of the breast and the mother. This mirrors their togetherness and their separateness from each other. How to be apart and *rejoin* remains an important and continuing lesson in life. Here are the seeds of learning to be alone, but still with the sense of being accompanied.

Additionally, all three have to learn to *wait*. The mother allows the baby time to settle at the breast and patiently waits for the baby to find a way to the nipple. This also applies to the end of the feed. The mother indicates the end is coming but, rather than abruptly pulling away, negotiates the end of the feed. The father has to stand aside while his partner negotiates this budding love relationship. In time, he will reclaim his primary relationship with the mother, but in the early months he too has to wait.

Closely related to this is the notion of limitations. The experience in the womb is seamless because the temperature is adapted to the needs of the baby's body and hunger is kept at bay by the continuous flow of nourishment from the placenta. The baby learns that breasts do not have a continuous supply of milk, and time is needed for digestion. This creates some *frustration,* but it is in these times, in the absence of the mother, that the baby begins to develop the capacity for thought. The baby's frustration when the mother is absent helps the baby to hold the idea of the relationship in mind. This is an important relational achievement.

If all has gone well they work through the *illusion of the perfect mother/baby.* The mutual demands on mother and baby become more realistic. The mother can now find alternative ways to relate to her baby. Her voice or her eye contact may sometimes be sufficient to soothe the baby. *Father* becomes more important with the development of smiling, which allows him to enter the intimate space of the two-person relationship with the baby. His different relationship and way of interacting with the baby allows the baby to increase the capacity to relate and embrace differences, adding an enormous richness to the baby's experience.

Negotiating: six to nine months

Around six months, once a baby can sit up, their perspective grows. From the sitting position the baby will watch her parents speaking, first noticing one parent, then looking to the other when the partner replies. The baby "follows" the conversation. Babies also follow the mother's line of vision when she turns her head, just like the mother follows the baby's line of vision. Researchers were able to make babies of this age laugh in response to a hand puppet that moved, "spoke" and played peek-a-boo, disappearing and reappearing. A week later the infants smiled when shown the un-activated silent puppet. What appears to be happening is that the baby has now entered the domain of *"intersubjective relatedness"*. Stern (1985) uses this term to refer to the fact that sharing experiences becomes possible and the baby's capacity for interpersonal exchanges expands. For example, without using any words, the baby can now communicate something like, 'Mum, I want you to look over here (shift your attention to match mine), so that you too will see how exciting and delightful this is' (so we can share my experience of excitement and pleasure). This sharing encompasses the notion that states of mind are shareable. What is going on in my mind may be similar enough to what is going on in your mind, and we can somehow communicate this, without words, and experience togetherness or inter-subjectivity. Mothers frequently comment around this time how difficult it is to get things done because the baby enjoys having company. When this happens it is a tribute to both that they have found a companionable world with each other.

It is a major step forward for the baby to sense that an empathic process, the bridging of two minds, has occurred.

The caregiver's empathy becomes a specific element of the baby's experience. Babies at this stage begin to notice the congruence, or non-congruence, between their own emotional state and the expression on someone else's face. They begin to realise that mum and dad have their own emotional states and they do not focus all their attention on him or her. Watching mum get the dinner while sitting in the high chair, the baby recognises the phone ringing as interfering with his or her dinner being served. The baby can tolerate some reasonable intrusions but too many will lead to frustration. Parents have to decide how much time to give their child and what is not reasonable.

Repairing relationships enters the picture. The baby becomes aware that mum or dad can be cross or baby can be cross and yet they all persist in a relationship beyond those moments of conflict. Parents and the baby now require a greater sense of *negotiation* between all of them. The baby's need to be taken into account becomes an imperative. When the parents discount the baby's needs there is frustration, which may lead to aggressiveness. There will naturally be upsets and the baby's now more complex feelings will include aggression. This happens around the time that the baby's teeth emerge. At this time, babies can be aggressive in their play or in biting the nipple. Parents need to respond to these in an ordinary way and allow time for handling frustrating events during the course of the day. Some planning helps them through these events. The parents may be thinking about weaning the baby around this time. *Weaning* provokes mixed feelings in the baby and the mother. Both have a natural sense of moving on to another phase of the relationship, but they have to manage their feelings of loss, disappointment, hurt and anger. Taking time over the weaning, and doing it in small steps, helps.

Babies' greater awareness makes them realise that others can do things they cannot. Often, they are working quite hard dealing with all the new capacities that are evolving within them and they also become more aware of *failing*. They want to make their parents happy and wish to be like them. They want to eat what their parents eat, to be like them or an older sibling. This is a compliment to the parents but can frustrate the baby.

The gesture of pointing and the act of following another's line of vision are among the first overt acts that permit inferences about the sharing of attention or establishing joint attention. Nine-month olds detach their gaze from the pointing hand and follow the imaginary line to the target. At this age babies can follow someone else's line of regard, using a coordinate system of the world, rather than one in which they are the centre. Then they add a further step. By nine months they visually follow the direction of the pointing hand and after reaching the target, look back at the mother to confirm if she is looking at the target. This is more than a discovery procedure. It is a deliberate attempt to ascertain whether they have shared the focus of attention. Babies themselves begin to point at this time and join the enterprise.

Both parents and the baby contribute to this interplay. Parents of nine-months olds add a new dimension to their behaviour that reflects the baby's new status as an interactive partner. Parents and babies begin to expand their behaviour to a new level called *affect attunement*; the parent acknowledges the emotional state of the baby so the baby feels understood. Both parties are able to add and play with this emotional conversation. Attunement includes, but is not just about, empathy. Parents slip inside the baby's feeling enough to capture it but then add something of their own. They add enough to alter the baby's behaviour but not enough to break the attunement. This addition continues the play and expands its potential so that something new is created together.

As intimate relationships intensify, the baby becomes *possessive*. The baby will prefer parents above others and one parent above another at times. Having found intimacy the baby wants to prolong the two-ness. Possessiveness and jealousy naturally occur as the baby transitions from the world of two into the world of three and then beyond. Parents need to recognise and understand such feelings. Moving towards the world of three goes together with a return to the world of two. In the parents' relationship, the father also seeks to realign relationships and strengthen his pairing with his partner. He draws his partner back into their twosome as the baby gradually develops a capacity to live happily in the world of three. All three are finding a way to move fluidly between these configurations.

Moving away and coming back: nine to twelve months

This is a time of physical and psychological movement. The baby crawls, stands up and their first steps are taken. The growing mobility brings with it the capacity to move away from the mother. Parents support this process, but stay around and wait for their baby's need to return. Adults need to be mature enough to enjoy babies' movements away from them yet allow for their continuing dependence. Moving about gives babies a different perspective on the world that fosters the realisation that others share, or don't share, the same perspective. They can also check whether their parents are sharing their excitement or are worried, curious or upset. They become very interested in what the parent is thinking and a notion of "we" is possible. Further, after nine months babies communicate more rather than just influence. Soon after nine months, the beginning of the baby teasing, or making jokes, emerges. You can't tease someone unless you can correctly guess what is "in their mind" and make them suffer or laugh because of your knowing.

When the baby returns to the mother, it is not only to be *refuelled* or reassured about their relationship. It is also a reaffirmation that the baby and mother, as separate beings, are sharing in what the baby experiences. The baby is understood and shares a common knowledge base with the parent. The creation of sharing permits the exploration and pursuit of curiosity.

Managing new situations comes to the forefront as the baby's exploration leads to all sorts of new circumstances. The world is opening up and it can be a dangerous place. Parents need to allow their baby to try out new skills and engage in the rough and tumble of life without too much worry about their safety. However, parents need to take precautions such as ensuring the baby cannot touch hazards like heaters, wall sockets, and so on. They must strike a balance between letting the baby explore and being protected.

All three members of the trio have more freedom at this time. While the baby is exploring, mum and dad can have more time for each other. An important learning at this time is how to be *together but each in their own space*. There is a greater range of possibilities now and they can connect with each other by just glancing in each other's direction or by sharing in the baby's adventures. The baby's sense of self benefits from "holding onto" something when others are engaged with each other nearby. Babies can understand that their own activities are important and that the parents' acknowledge the world in which they live. It confirms that the baby is important on 'their' terms and not only when engaged in the adult world. The baby may be intensely occupied with the world and seemingly forget all else, but still needs to touch base with the parents.

Reciprocity comes into play at this time. The baby may wish to feed the parents, to show the parents something they have found or offer them something the baby owns. Both sides can gain from this sense of reciprocity, and mother can say, 'I'll cut up your apple after I pour my tea.' This articulates the two-way relationship. The baby begins to realise the possibility of identifying with someone else's needs. Everyone can be taken into account. Differing needs do not mean someone has to miss out. There is room for all.

As the baby learns first to crawl and then to *walk*, we encounter learning to learn. Watching a baby begin to stand up while holding on to firm support, fall down again, and try again is a wonderful example of the baby engaging in the learning process. Finally, when the baby takes the first tentative steps to walk, there will be many falls accompanied by getting up again and having another go. This *trial-and-error learning* is a normal process for a baby. The principles of learning that are encountered at this time set the baby up for all future learning situations throughout life.

There are a number of principles involved in learning that apply to us all. First of all, learning involves facing the fact that we don't know how to do something. Facing our limitations is a natural part of getting to know what to do. Babies need to be left to feel their vulnerability and given some space to work out how to manage something. Being able to feel vulnerable but press ahead and find a way through is a great confidence builder for the baby. Second, learning entails a few steps forward and then some backwards. This is how we build our skills. We learn in small steps and knowing this can reduce the baby's anxiety. At this stage, we can learn to be patient and wait through the steps involved. Parents need to model this patience and not have unrealistic expectations of their baby. Third, new learning requires practising new skills. Parents can praise the baby's efforts. Fourth, parents need to recognise the trial and error nature of learning. Making errors is intrinsic to learning. In the beginning, mistakes are inevitable. The process of learning will entail returning to old patterns and trying the new skill again until it becomes established. Finally, learning proceeds more easily when parents expect the baby to improve incrementally. A certain amount of challenge is necessary for development, but too much change too quickly can be overwhelming.

Toddlerhood: the second year

In the baby's second year the parents will have to revisit all the issues that surfaced during the first year. Importantly, the second year consolidates and expands the child's development. Moving on from a preoccupation with their parents, the emerging toddler begins a love affair with the world. On a physical level, the toddler is beginning to walk. This is an important achievement of which the emerging toddler feels justly proud. At this time, all things seem possible. The child concentrates on *practising* and mastering skills and is exhilarated by many *discoveries*. This new relationship to the world does not mean mum and dad are not important. There is still a strong desire to return to the parents and share their adventures. Parents need to be available to receive things, to look at objects and share discoveries.

Mothers being able to take up to twelve months' maternity leave has been a positive development for meeting the needs of babies and their relationships with their parents. However, parents may have assumed that by the end of the first year the baby no longer has intense *dependency* needs and can be left in the care of others quite easily. In fact, leaving the baby in the second year still requires considerable thought and care. A parent needs to be around sufficiently to meet the dependency needs of the growing and more mobile baby in a different way. They need to be present enough so that the baby feels sufficiently secure to move away and to return. This means that babies can go and explore their world – the next room, or the garden – and return to them when ready. Once mobile, children run off to validate their idea that their parents will want to catch them and swoop them up into their arms. Their elation at running away and their parents catching them shows them that they can *escape* mum or dad yet return to that *security*. They are preoccupied with the dual task of how to be with their mother or carer and how to be without them. When their mother is not present, they will recall her.

At fifteen to eighteen months infants develop a further skill in their relationships with mum and dad. They can now draw on a lot of accumulated information about themselves and the world. They can think, 'I remember what happened the last time I wanted to play that game. Maybe if I do that again mum/dad might play with me'. They can draw on their memory to help them do what they want in the world.

By eighteen months, the baby is a toddler, more aware and making greater use of his or her physical separateness. Alongside this development comes a return to earlier behaviours as they increasingly realise that they are their own little selves and different from their parents. Like all major steps in life, this is both exciting and scary. Toddlers begin to express greater frustration and have a greater need for others to be present. They want to *share all their experiences* with the parents and they depend more on their approval. The emotional availability of the parents is crucial at this time. The parents' love and acceptance of the toddler helps them reconcile their feelings of love and hate, of wanting to grow up and wanting to stay attached.

Toddlers begin to function at a much higher level, learning to speak and using *play* to work things out. Learning to speak is another major step in their development. They can now symbolise and act out issues that trouble them. They also become aware that the mother's wishes are not always identical with their own, so they feel less "on top of the world". Perhaps they sense their parents' inevitable ambivalence about them. All is not always well for the toddler.

Two characteristic patterns of toddlers are *shadowing* and *darting*. Toddlers shadow their mother by watching and following her every move. Getting upset and clinging can re-emerge if the mother leaves them. They want to be reunited with their loved ones but, at the same time, they do not want their parents to *engulf* them or take their separateness away. This is why they *dart* away and force the parents to chase them; they re-enact running away and being pursued. The toddler's demand for their mother's constant involvement can seem *contradictory*. They are more independent than they were at the end of the first year and want to be so, yet they are also more insistent about sharing every aspect of their lives. Although they may realise that their relationship with their mother continues when she is absent, this is not always sufficient to reassure the toddler when they are missing their parents.

For the mother and father, the demands of the toddler can be very trying. What is difficult for the child is the growing acceptance of their separateness. Everyone can find this time difficult. Gradually and painfully, toddlers let go of the delusion of their *central position,* often through dramatic fights or tantrums. Nearly all children express their growing sense of self and their recognition of their littleness through rapid mood swings and tantrums. If the parents can be quietly available to share the toddler's adventurous exploits by playfully responding to their games and understanding their ambivalences, children begin to *internalise* their relationship with them and verbal communication takes over. Toddlers can see the world as it is, rather than how they might want it to be. Predictable emotional involvement from the parents facilitates the unfolding of the toddler's thought processes. The unique way in which they approach the world becomes apparent. Their constant questioning is one way of testing reality and finding out how the world works.

By the time toddlers are two or three years old, they often face the *birth of a sibling.* Three years is a helpful gap because by then they have the language to express their feelings about this. This is a major event as they lose their position to the baby. On the other hand, a new baby arouses the toddler's curiosity. 'How does this happen?' Frank but simple responses to questions, and involving the toddlers in the pregnancy, can help them feel part of the new experience. The new pregnancy, however, may wound their sense of self: 'How come they wanted another one when they had me?' There is a temporary sense of misplacement as the toddler rethinks the world to see how they fit in. In time, the benefits of confronting such questions and thoughts becomes clearer as they enjoy the benefits of the new family.

Being a parent is a continuing story. As parents we need to draw on different capacities in ourselves at different times as we move from empathy to firmness in response to the needs of each situation. To do the task well, we need support from grandparents, friends and the community. Although parents have the major role in bringing up their children, it is also a shared task. Perhaps long day-care centres could become family support centres that help parents deal with babies and older children, as well as minding them.

Parents can view their involvement with the baby as an engagement in their creation, both physical and psychological. They have to partner the baby and this means meeting, welcoming and helping him or her if they are to truly come alive. Without this, and left to their own devices, or to impersonal care, this process cannot take place.

Chapter 3 Ongoing development to maturity

So the sea journey goes on and who knows where!
Just to be held by the ocean is the best luck
we could have. It's a total waking up!

"Buoyancy," (Barks, p. 105)

To understand further development over our life span, we can perhaps divide life into natural divisions or stages. I have focused on the first two years of life since they are the years that neuroscience, infant mental health, developmental psychologists and psychoanalytic literature highlight as being crucial. In the earliest years we are developing our sense of self through an initial period of dependency. This next stage is our growth towards individuation and differentiation from our parents and caretakers, while still maintaining these connections.

The following outline of our further growth in sociability focuses on psychological developmental processes. This is not meant to be prescriptive, or to discount cultural and social factors.

Excitement and worries: from two to five

At this time, parents and children are mutually engaged in a range of tasks. These include:

Consolidating a secure emotional base between the parents and child

- This involves the mother and father being with their child sufficiently so that they can make sense of and understand what is happening with their child. This enables children to feel that someone is essentially "there for them" and helps them deal

with their emotional experiences and their experience of the world. Both parents and children feel
they are accompanying each other on the child's
journey of becoming a person.

Establishing and maintaining this sense of security

- Both parties must, by trial and error, learn how
  to persevere and work together. In this way they
  begin to see who is who in the relationship and
  the role that each needs to play in the process of
  development.

Separating then being reunited

- These transitions need to be negotiated in a
  thoughtful way. By making transitions gradual,
  and building on small steps, both parties are able
  to say goodbye to each other and to hold on to the
  relationship when they are apart. Taking time to
  reunite is also important.

Working together to allow for parents' and children's separate needs

- The child can progress from not being the centre
  of things and can take up her part in the family
  and the world around them. This gives children
  maximum opportunity to express and fulfil their
  unique contribution to the world.

Entering the linguistic world is a major milestone. The
development of language creates complex capacities with
which to understand the experience of others. Children can
now take "roles" and join the social culture in which they
operate. They understand past, present and future and they
can picture things that are not present. They also develop
the capacity to suffer since the child can now worry, and feel
guilt and regret. With the development of language comes
the flowering of the mind. The two- to three-year-old is a
questioning being who needs to figure out how the world
works. They ask "why" about the external and internal

world. Conscience emerges and they explore "naughty" alongside the world of "no".

Children want to engage in a mutually respectful dialogue with their parents about what is going on around them in a way that acknowledges their growing little self. By three to four years of age this mutuality is a shared source of pleasure for both parties. Children enjoy socialising with others as well as having quiet times alone. Both are important. Time on their own with their thoughts, desires and feelings is crucial to their sense of being at ease with themselves. Enjoying being by themselves and engaged in their own activities is also important to feeling that what they are doing is valuable.

As the child's socialising grows they develop a fear of failing and a concern that they are not good enough. These fears naturally accompany all our attempts to grow. At this time the child's growing sense of reality means an ability to explore the world of "pretend", and know the difference between the two. Children may share dreams they have experienced and may wake from a nightmare. Parents and children can talk together about these normal developmental processes.

Childen's capacity to work with a group and cooperate with others gradually grows as their sense of self is strengthened. Shared play can be a very satisfying activity. By four- to five-years-old children possess an even greater sense of their self in the world as their mental processes allow them to reflect on who they are and their place in the world. The child wants to be not just an individual, but also part of things. This desire to do the same as the others, together with sorting out the internal relationships between siblings and parents, ultimately leads to joining groups like cubs or entering team sports. These activities provide a safe environment of routines and guidelines by which to explore the child's internal and external relationships.

The world expands: five to twelve years

The primary school years bring an exciting period of greater exploration of the world, as well as an increase in anxiety as children attempt to meet new demands. Stories and make-believe can be imaginative ways of trying to clarify the complexities the child faces. This stage is often referred to as the "latency period". I will draw on the discussion of latency in Waddell's (2002) book *Inside Lives*. During "latency," the child develops a sufficiently strong sense of inner identity to enable undertaking the psychosocial tasks of going to school and ultimately contemplating high school. The family relationships, even though they are still central to the child's world, begin to loosen slightly to include wider friendships formed at school and brief stays away from home.

How the child traverses this phase depends on how well the previous developmental stages have gone. If all has gone well the child can engage with this new world playfully and with curiosity. Acquiring skills and new information is a form of thriving. However, opening up to the world, as mentioned earlier, can cause anxieties often expressed as bodily complaints, or developing phobias, like a fear of spiders or eating only certain foods. The challenges of the outside world are worrying as well as stimulating. The child is faced with recognising limitations when embarking on acquiring skills, and learning reading and writing. As the world opens up in its richness and diversity, it becomes both more tantalising and more frustrating.

Children need relative stability and routine to assist them to manage the new demands. They often want order and discipline as a way of supporting the fragile balance between the disruptive internal impulses and acceptable social behaviour. These diverse feelings are not easy to manage. On a psychological level, children can reduce their dependence on the external figures to whom intense feelings are directed, and become more securely related to the internalised idea of a parent inside. They can strengthen their internal "holding" of their parents in their absence to create some stability inside themselves, yet they will still need their parents' reassurance. With the acquisition of knowledge and skills, children can repair their unconscious fear of their internal "badness". Helping mum or dad can be another form of repair.

Being read to, and in time learning to read for oneself, expands a child's ideas of what is "good" and "bad," "them" and "us". Good literature can challenge the child's limited categorisation of the world and help increase reflective capacity. On the other hand, comics or television programs can give children time out from their efforts of self-awareness and reduce the confusion and anxiety that is under the surface at this time, by simplifying concepts like "good" and "bad". Children need a world of their own that is separate but not cut-off from that of adults where they have space and time to think. Parents need to support the child to find enjoyment in their own company and in their own thoughts. Allowing children to become bored and to find their way into their internal world, and not rely on constant stimulation, is important.

During this time children can play with gender roles; girls can be tomboys, and boys can play with dolls. It can be exhilarating to explore these roles before more rigid social mores begin to exert themselves. Children also like to collect and exchange objects. This can be a combination of an anxious greediness to acquire, as well as a desire to enter the wider world in which they live, and to feel they have an impact on it.

Children are constantly exploring the question of whether their destructive impulses will prevail over other more positive, loving aspects of their nature. This question arises from various interactions between the inside and outside world. Do their destructive feelings make them bad, or do they just need to control them? Children need to feel there is a containing and sustaining presence that supports them in these states of mind. With support, primary school children can hope to find their way to a loving productive life despite what might be painful, bleak and negative experiences. They are learning how to keep alive the process of self-discovery against external and internal demands.

Persona: between thirteen and twenty-eight years

The next phase, from thirteen to twenty-eight years, is related to the development of our own persona. The emerging issue is the various roles prescribed by the society in which we live. What we gradually identify with is beyond the family and their rules. We initially break away from the family to find the "tribe" that best fits how we think and feel. Again I will draw considerably on Waddell (2002) who is worth reading for a fuller discussion of the issues arising at puberty and adolescence.

In puberty, bodily changes occur more rapidly than in any other period of life, except in the womb. Enormous psychological upheaval accompanies these changes. The physiological changes of puberty tend to occur earlier than the emotional ones and a range of behaviours appear. The teenager can conform or rebel. It may take several years for the disturbance to settle. A more recent way of understanding this troubled and exciting time is to regard adolescence as a necessary restructuring of the personality

Whether the adolescent and the family can tolerate this disturbance depends on the quality of the original containment provided as a baby, how stable the latency years were and the pressures that the adolescent has to deal with. Very often, issues have accumulated over time. Any unresolved developmental issues can be re-visited and worked through. Adolescent upheaval has the creative potential to resolve past and present issues. However, the adolescent can feel that these conflicts or difficulties are overwhelming and delinquent behaviour can be a way to let off steam. The quality of the early containment and conflicts around the family, and who is in, and who is out, re-emerge quite acutely. Adolescents can act out many of their fantasies and desires. This can create anxiety in early adolescence and lead to strong relationships with same sex peers. Sometimes these relationships are a way to explore and reassure, and do not indicate a specific sexual inclination. Such friendships can be a natural precursor to a heterosexual relationship, or clarify that they prefer a same-sex partnership.

Adolescents prefer getting rid of painful emotions rather than being aware of them and containing them. Adolescents will "act out" internal conflict rather than resolve it, and replace thought with action in order to reduce internal conflict. They blame others rather than reflecting on their own actions and feelings. The constant tension between self-awareness and projection is typical of the adolescent approach. Their behaviour can cause anxiety in others and their attempts to avoid suffering by refusing to engage with it can lead to extreme behaviour. When does drug and alcohol abuse, as self-medicating behaviour, become addictive and unhelpful? When does being withdrawn become a way of avoiding experience? When does the self-doubt and hatred become self-mutilation? How does the body's need for sleep sit alongside the desire to party and push boundaries? Do you become a know-all to avoid reality or do you withdraw from intimacy altogether when overwhelmed by your feelings?

Identifying with their peer group, and making peers their primary attachment to each other, can lead the adolescent to be more distant or negative towards adults and other groups. This negativity is often difficult for parents to understand or to tolerate. Yet adolescent group life can offer something of a holding space for the confused young person, providing both a challenge and "time out" until the ability grows to hold separate feelings together within a single self. At this time, endless hours can be spent talking with each other about their feelings, their reactions and what they are doing. The group and other members can offer ways to try out different versions of themselves and discover how others react to them. On the other hand, it is not helpful for adolescents to fall in with others in a gang-like structure, or to reproduce an atmosphere of fear and oppression, because they have felt intimidated and oppressed. What adolescents need is to think rather than just act, and to take responsibility for their actions while in the group. Where the projection is not too extreme, other ways to explore curiosity and uncertainty about the self include changing appearances or music style to see which one fits.

But a deeper inner exploration is also being asked of the adolescent. They have to build a safe environment to explore the more painful, unacceptable or repressed side. They need to get in touch with a deeper sense of who they are, their angers and heartaches, and their unlikeable side: their meanness, pettiness, jealousy and envy. All the sides of their nature are there to be gradually owned. Facing up to the truthfulness of the self heals those aspects of the false self that have grown inside to cover the "whole'" of who they are. Feeling turmoil and confusion is an important and necessary aspect of this time.

The desire to establish a more authentic self and become the best we are capable of is in all of us. In adolescence, this impulse is particularly strong if the environment supports it and internal struggles do not get in the way. This requires getting rid of the impediments that limit our potential. Removing impediments involves being in touch with and locating the feelings in the body. It is important to feel the flow and sense the growing excitation of the body. This requires giving up any rigid control, so that deep body sensations can reach the surface. Knowing oneself includes knowing one's body. An intimate and subtle knowledge of the body and the way it functions, and how it experiences emotional states, is essential. How we breathe and where we hold our stresses in our body are an important key to opening up to a real knowledge of ourselves. Since the body does not lie, this knowledge helps us bypass the internal forces inside that resist inner exploration.

We need to uncover not only the tendencies that we may have disowned like anger and jealousy, but also assertiveness, joy, and courage. If we are to get to know ourselves then we must allow for all aspects of the human condition, conscious and unconscious. Our unconscious is not just the place for our negative traits as it also contains the roots of our creativeness and joy, and has its own ethics and values. To know who we are is, therefore, not just a process of fearing ourselves, but of getting to know our strengths and weaknesses. Alongside the joy of gaining a greater sense of autonomy comes the greater potential for the suffering that marks the birth of creative insight. When we suffer we do so because intelligent insight is emerging, but we need to know what that suffering means, and why it is occurring, to make that suffering worthwhile.

If we properly negotiate this stage, we learn the roles and skills we need to live in society. Our developmental process shifts us to living in an inter-subjective culture where people care about others. This awareness of others expands the self, so that we can look at the world through someone else's eyes as well as our own. The world can continue to expand and become an even more amazing place. If we do not negotiate this stage properly then we are left out of touch with our social group and develop self-defeating ideas about our place in society.

Our capacity to relinquish parental and authority figures on whom we have been dependent and to replace them with an internal version is intrinsic to the maturation process at this time. We can use these figures to inspire and encourage the independent development of the personality. The capacity to be alone is essential to the capacity to be in a relationship with another. Adolescents are striving to achieve a capacity for intimacy. To be with someone also means being able to be without someone, as we have encountered in our earlier chapters. We need to have a relationship with ourselves that is nourished and developed so there is a self to share with others, such as friends, children or colleagues. To be alone is to be in touch with all the parts of the self inside: our wishes, hurts and angers. Being in touch with all these aspects allows us to reconcile these threads of the self. This requires, time, attention and commitment to the self. Enjoying solitude is one of life's great pleasures and accepting who we are is an important precursor to the acceptance of someone else. Developing intimacy may take many years and possibly several different attempts to achieve.

In late adolescence, the young person will emerge from the safety and complexities of group life and face a deeper separation than previously. This involves letting go of the unacceptable and idealised versions of the self, of other people, and of relationships, in preference for the real. This includes grieving the loss associated with facing these realities. We have to negotiate dreams, hopes, choices and lost opportunities. At the heart of the process is the central challenge of a more mature engagement. This is the realistic estimation of the actual qualities of the self and the other, and accepting what is found there. It is being able to bear the loss of the external presence, yet still retain the presence internally, as well as managing doubt and uncertainty, loss of trust and even fear of betrayal. In the end it means to make something of experience whether it be "good" or "bad".

In this phase we can acquire the capacity to reflect on our thoughts and to imagine a range of possibilities. We open up all sorts of possible lives and possible selves. We can dream of things that belong to the future and work towards attaining those ideals, or create a world in which those possibilities may occur. Introspection is now possible and creates a psychological space where one begins to have one's own thoughts, not just those of the rest of the group. While there is the opening up to society and a lessening of the sense of the world being an extension of the self, it is still a time when a kind of tribal loyalty operates. This means that while there is a greater inclusiveness of some others, there remains a "them" and "us" grouping. Some are in, others are out, and the capacity to care belongs to the group in which

one belongs and not always to the group that is the "other".
To take the idea of inclusiveness further is the domain of the
next stage of moving into the society.

The middle years: twenty-eight to fifty years

The psychoanalyst Wilfred Bion (1970) saw maturity as
continually developing. His concern was the individual
continuing to move from knowing about reality to becoming
real. The difference between maturity and immaturity hinges
not on chronological years but on a person's capacity to bear
intense emotional states, think about them and reflect on
psychic pain. In this sense wisdom is more to do with living
and feeling than with acquiring knowledge. It is not born
out of infantile impulses and longings, but understanding
the undeveloped aspects of the self and being alert to their
potential effects, particularly their destructiveness.

In the middle years, adolescents emerge into the adult
who is eager and willing to share their identity with others.
They are ready for intimacy, and can commit to partnerships
and friendships. These connections can be committed to
even though they may call for significant sacrifices and
compromises. On the other hand, avoiding such experiences
because of a fear of losing one's sense of self may lead to a
deep sense of isolation and subsequently self-absorption.

We may constantly repeat or deny our early difficulties.
More fortunate people may have understood those earlier
difficulties, integrated them into their personality and
moved on. It is not a matter of imitating a grown-up, or just
living out the role. It is the task of being one. Part of learning
to be an adult, is to realise that life is about internalising
adult ways of being, together with the knowledge that those
functions may require struggle, that life is both difficult and
pleasurable.

Our need to survive and protect ourselves from internal
and external pressures dominates our early states of mind.
By contrast, the mature person can experience other people

as genuinely other, that is, as persons who have independent needs and priorities. They can also suffer grief and have concern for damage inflicted on others by anxiety-driven greed and unreasonable demands. It involves carrying the burdens of being grown-up as well as claiming the rights and privileges. Ultimately, it leads to appreciating the care received and being able to repair and identify with parental concern as the growing adult contemplates having children. It involves a shift from a more self-centred frame of mind to internalising figures that function as helpful inner resources. Further, through having relationships and sexual activity in caring relationships, there is a wonderful experience of the mutual regulation of two beings. Both can support and soothe each other. Such experiences take the edge off the hostilities that arise because of differences between male and female. The nourishment of a happy sexual life softens the sharper edges of our desire to control and helps us feel warmer towards other human beings, and therefore less likely to assert control over others.

During this time, we need to hold a duality of positions in the private and public domain. Here we have to juggle the loyalty to our growing family (if we have one) and negotiate the more public space where we earn a living. The roles we play in the home and in society are now more complex. We are the son and daughter who now becomes a father or mother learning to take the place of the adult, while maintaining some inner contact with the child we were. We have to work through both the positive inheritance we have received, as well as the debris from our families of origin, which resurface in the next generation when we establish our own family. We need to be careful not to see these family influences as the determining influence by which we are formed but rather the raw material from which to build a life. Over-identifying with one's childhood and family can be very limiting and crippling and reduce our potential for developing a creative life for ourselves, since the demands of family life carry the seeds of a generative experience. Reworking one's own childhood through being a parent can free us and satisfy us, alongside the burden of responsibility and steadfastness that the task requires.

The demands of the growing family at this time are enormous and limit how much we can do in meeting the needs of the society. On the other hand, we have to maintain a sense of the group to which we belong, and the society in which we function in the outside world. Ralston Saul (1995) has been critical of the idea of individualism that is so prevalent today and which is a narrow view of self-interest with a denial of a public good. In reality, the notion of a public good is one that has been held within society for a very long time. It was Socrates who said, 'I cannot (just) mind my own business'. So while there is self-reflection, there is also a need to reflect on the society, and the social milieu in which we live. The capacity to see the broader perspective is part of the maturation process. Having a family is therefore not just about the good of "my" family, and having our own children can put us in touch with the needs of all children.

During middle age the primary developmental task is one of contributing to society and helping to guide future generations. When a person makes a contribution during this period, perhaps by raising a family or working towards the betterment of society, there is a sense of accomplishment. In contrast, a person who is self-centred and unable or unwilling to help society move forward potentially feels dissatisfaction from the lack of productivity and contribution.

The development of the study of group processes helps us to understand how we function and optimise our participation in groups. Much is now known about the stages of group development, as well as the strategies that groups use to make it difficult to do the work of the group. Social Systems Theory, in conjunction with psychoanalytic concepts and the work of Bion, and Lewin's field theory and General Systems Theory are helpful. It was Agazarian (1983) who brought these various theories together. She postulated that while there are many levels of possible intervention in a group, having the capacity to wonder about and observe the group as a whole, has the greatest potential for resolving conflict, while deepening the insight for each individual. It is Agazarian's view that if we can hold a perspective at the level of group-as-a-whole there can be a potential influence on the level of reality in all the subsystems of the group. Within the family, this may mean holding the overall functioning of the family in mind while holding the individual needs of family members. Knowledge of roles, boundaries and functions serve to prevent distortions occurring, such as the eldest son being the alternative parent, or strong dyads distorting the family constellation. In the workplace, understanding the purpose, roles and functions of the various members of the workplace, and where the individual fits, is important to maintaining an overall perspective and equilibrium. Knowledge of how groups develop and function can lead to a greater understanding of how we function in the collective.

Developing a broader perspective involves integrating a personal awareness and sensitivity to unconscious processes with the conditions under which such awareness can be used. Both of these perspectives are necessary for real change to occur. The social perspective on its own brings only a two-dimensional view, unless it includes the psychological aspects of a group or organisation. Similarly unconscious needs alone cannot be expressed unless there is structure that allows for the expression of those needs. Holding both provides the ecology for better functioning in the family and in the workplace.

Research into how people operate in a large group has revealed the opportunity to experience a sense of "fellowship" as opposed to operating on a more personal level. It is possible to explore the notion of citizenship or, as Patrick De Mare (1991, p. 3) puts it, "Koinonia", meaning impersonal fellowship. This is possible if the initial differences and tensions can be worked through.

De Mare's goal in a group is a dialogue that is:

> ... a different way of thinking and communication.
> It is tangential and quite different from the distinct
> binary logic of the one-to-one dyad. It is articulate,
> circular, giving rise to lateral, more creative thinking,
> as distinct from linear. This form of dialogue
> has enormous thought potential. It is a dialogue
> from which ideas spring that can transform the
> mindlessness and group-think that accompanies
> social oppression. This groupthink can be replaced
> with higher levels of cultural sensitivity, intelligence
> and humanity. These experiences can help us
> understand some of the ways in which we can
> connect with the larger societal group around us,
> without denying who we are, and how relationships
> work and function on that broader level.

Bion (1962) suggests that becoming a member of our tribe requires us to develop what he called "binocular vision". This is the movement towards being socio-centric as well as egocentric, moving from narcissism to a social-ism. As humans with both personal and social needs, we will oscillate between these two states but we will need both if we are to attain any kind of happiness. Grotstein (1997), following Bion, discusses his notion of "transcendence". While remaining true to Bion's notion that we continually oscillate between periods of uncertainty and not knowing, followed by some gradual resolution, he adds a further notion. This is being able to know that these phases are part of life. Grotstein suggests we are able to gradually traverse these states with less distress as we accept that they are part of the process of ongoing development to a new phase. At this point, we are able to be in touch with our need for connection to society at a broader level. This is a sense of at-one-ness with all others with whom we share this developmental process.

In this position we create a thoughtful stance that is less emotionally engaged. While based on knowing the emotional content of an experience, a step further is taken; we also connect to both our needs and the needs of the group. Then we can comprehend our own feelings, the feelings of others and the point at which the group is operating. Diversity of views are included, but transcended, in order to look at the world from the perspective of "community".

Maturity of being: the later years

Our capacity to continue engaging with the meaning of our experience in an imaginative way, with courage and integrity, is the foundation of development at any age. While fifty years or more may seem "mature," our physical decline tests a mature state of mind. Death is more possible. There may be many external losses such as elderly parents, or friends may be ill or dying. Children will be leaving home. Retirement will become an issue. The ultimate test of all is to face dying rather than activating defensive measures to evade it.

Early experiences return. The good mother or father could make bearable the baby's fear of the precariousness of life. If babies feel sufficiently understood in the relationship with their parents, they can retain a tolerable and growth-stimulating part of the personality. This can instil in the baby the sense of a self that can endure setbacks and loss. Those who are ageing have similar needs and their internal and external attachment figures will be needed to help navigate this phase.

If we have had a supportive childhood, we may be less afraid of aging. We can let go of the redundant parts of the self, be separate as well as dependent, and have the courage to face an honest self-assessment. This modifies excessive love and hate and helps hold ambivalent feelings. Where we have had strong ambivalent feelings about a loved one, there is no longer just good and bad. Both are the same person; one who sometimes fulfils and sometimes frustrates. We can see that person as a bit more "ordinary," which includes the self. Both remain in proportion, to fit with how it really is. This stage of life is about embracing the complexity of experience and integrating the painful with the pleasurable, rather than seeking to avoid the hard bits and clutching onto the "right to be happy". Loss will shadow this period of time with decline of sexual potency, professional ideals, appearance and health. With maturity we can resist the pull of earlier modes of functioning and bear the emotional burdens and progress into some new adult states of mind.

In later life, we can continue to mature but we remain interdependent. To tolerate psychic pain we need to project feelings into someone else, whether to communicate those emotions or to get rid of them. Much depends on whether the person acting as the "container" can tolerate these projections and whether we go on thinking about the meaning of the experience. By that time, we will demonstrate where we have come in our developmental process. Have we avoided or denied the aging process? Unresolved experiences of loss may cast a dark cloud or the sense of failure may have dogged us over the years. However, there is still time to examine the underlying anxieties and inhibitions and find the courage to address them. The fear of suffering may be worse than the suffering itself. Each person carries within the potential to develop a personality of richness and depth and the potential to draw from his or her own experience the essential elements for further growth.

Care of the elderly in the last stages of life, as discussed by Waddell (2002), requires a painful reversal of the original pattern of the adult holding the baby in mind. Now the young need to offer reverie to the old. Turbulent feelings, whether joy, frustration, helplessness, rage, fear, pleasure, persecution, is quite as intense in the old as in the young and tests the partner or carer in similar ways. However, the carer is also enriched. The basis of self-knowledge comes from the capacity to contain and observe emotionally powerful psychic phenomena. When there is that level of contact with psychic reality, this enriches the carer's authentic core. In this way exchanges between the carer and cared for can be mutually life enhancing.

The process of finding one's own place in the world from one generation to the next needs constant mental and emotional work, from the earliest struggles of the unborn child to those of the final years of life. It involves learning from others without merely becoming like them and imparting to others without seeking to restrict them. It involves conflict but also opens limitless possibilities. Life need not be a place of distress or hard work, but also a process founded on the growth of the mind, the development of the personality and an opening of the heart.

What are some of the elements of maturity?

What are the elements of maturity that hold a lateral sense of development rather than only a linear one; that is, a fleshing out of the self-identity rather than a sense of continuous progression? Some of the concepts involved here are providence, destiny, presence, values and compassion in the context of commitment and struggle on our part.

The concept of *providence* connects to the psychoanalytic notion of internal objects. Our original internal objects are our parents and other helpful people, but as we mature we need to develop a more broadly based notion of what sustains us in living our life. This "providence" can include what we look to for inspiration in our lives, be it teachers, colleagues, art, theatre, nature or sport. If we have been provided for in a good enough way from a variety of sources, then it would seem natural to gain a sense of having been cared for. The experience of enjoying the wonders of nature can also nourish us.

Coupled with this is the sense of being able to handle what life brings us, as we gradually gain confidence by moving through stages of development and many difficulties, and gaining helpful skills and capacities. In our later stages it is perhaps important to acknowledge providence as meaning our partnership with life: life working with us, and us working with life. In feeling provided for we can feel confident and able to meet the challenges that will come along.

We can also revisit the notion of *destiny*. James Hillman (1996), in his book *The Soul's Code,* discusses his "acorn theory". This is the view that we can perceive our lives in terms of "a calling", or our fate, or as something innate. His belief is that you are born with a character, that is, a gift 'from the guardians upon your birth.' Thus it is our responsibility to find out what that "calling" is, fulfil this in our life span and experience fulfilment in living it out. Whether this is so or not, we can look at the patterns in our lives, and thoughtfully consider what those patterns tell us. A "calling" may be clearer for an obviously gifted person, but it is useful for each of us to consider what qualities we wish to express in the world.

Maslow (1980), who identified a hierarchy of human needs in the 1950s, also discusses the term "vocation". He noted that self-actualised people have a very clear idea of their purpose in life. They were all involved in a cause outside themselves. They were working at something precious to them; a calling or vocation whereby individuals can discover where they best fit in the world and where their capacities and qualities can be used for the greater good.

Presence is a capacity to enter the present moment in such a complete way that it is experienced as timeless. The paradox of temporality and timelessness can therefore be combined, so that we can momentarily be beyond time through being completely absorbed in what we are doing. Going deeply into the present is like entering into eternity. At this point we can be fully human and fully ourselves.

Such experiences of timelessness last a very short time. They are the result of sustained effort to discover who we are, in the moment, in many varied situations. It involves making the choice, over and over again, in diverse circumstances, to be authentic to oneself. The momentary times of complete absorption grow out of learning who we are and clearing out past misconceptions; learning what is. and what is not, good for us; knowing what we can and can't do; and clearing the long-held illusions in order to live increasingly in the reality of our experience. Maslow notes that in all peak experiences, whether giving birth or listening to music, for example, it becomes difficult to differentiate between self and non-self. Presence also relates to a notion of depth and the fullness of the self that allows us to experience a completeness of being.

Closely related to presence is the development of a set of *values* that we have gradually established out of hard-won experience. We have, over time, been able to acknowledge the reality of things, as opposed to a perception of how we want things to be. The "truth" of things can then emerge. Experience has also, hopefully, taught us some answers to moral and ethical dilemmas that have confronted us over many decades.

We develop our values gradually over the course of a lifetime. They are something we discover from the lessons of living rather than something we invent. Life is our teacher, so it gives us a sense of unfolding if we can allow it. As a result, large concepts like "morality" and "ethics" will coincide with ones closer to home like a sense of "rightness" and "wellbeing". If we take responsibility for understanding our own value system we will naturally behave in a way that facilitates change in the society in which we live. Our movement toward psychological health, if authentic, is also a movement toward social harmony.

Compassion is our capacity to understand and empathise with another human being. This requires an active agency on our part to act in ways that facilitate the greater good of that person and others with whom we come in contact. At later stages of development, compassion broadens to include the behavioural, social and cultural components of the community. Our concern is not just for individual sections of the community but includes the best interests of the whole community, or mankind.

At this stage, we express more than a benign attitude to the world as it passes; we are deepening our concern about the ramifications of our collective actions. Our thoughtful interest is needed to act as a "container" around the very real issues the human race and the planet face. This mirrors the holding and concern of the parents for the baby. The compassionate reflection we hold at this stage is an active, as opposed to a passive, activity and is an appropriate role in the latter stages of life.

Resacrilising is also a term used by Maslow to indicate creating a meaningful daily life. We can re-enchant our life by taking time to give fully to our relationships and the minutiae of our daily lives since it will be the everyday experiences that occupy our life at this stage. It can mean a re-discovery of meaning in ordinary mundane activities. This requires valuing our everyday experience by respecting it and giving it the reflection it deserves. A delight in living is there to be experienced alongside a sense of world-weariness.

Another way of maintaining a broader perspective is to use *dis-identification*. This involves holding on to a sense of the wholeness of our life even when another aspect of our self is in the forefront. This process creates a space or perspective from which we remain in touch with the totality of our experience, or the full reality of what is happening, and not just the aspect that is pressing at a particular moment. It means watching ourselves as we operate in the world, personally and with others, experiencing both our involvement in the circumstances and maintaining a distance from it. The emphasis here is also on the benefits of mobilising our willpower to assist with development. This involves the ability to observe or witness our own functioning without over-identifying with one aspect of it. Meditation employs this technique, but I am thinking of it in terms of holding on to the notion of our wholeness, while observing the parts of ourselves in action.

Dis-identification means we can create a thoughtful stance that is less emotionally engaged. This stance helps us to know the emotional content of an experience and the needs of the group so that a diversity of views can be included, but transcended, to look at the world from the perspective of "community".

Acquiring these concepts requires a great deal of effort and struggle. As with all human endeavour, we have to repeat and refine many times before new concepts and ways of being establish themselves. Each stage of development has its own pain as we leave one state and move to another. How we progress is not necessarily hierarchical or linear, as it may seem to be portrayed here. We develop one stage, but at another time it may be necessary to double back to attend to an earlier issue again. It is natural to resist moving from one state to another, but being discomforted is part of a continuing unfolding. It may become progressively harder to allow discomfort. It may seem easier to cut corners if we have reached a reasonable, workable way of living our lives, yet without the discomfort we do not make the gains.

Each emerging stage brings with it a new demand, a new responsibility. But as Ken Wilbur (1995, p. 85) views it in *No Boundary*:

> The movement of descent and discovery begins at
> the moment you consciously become dissatisfied
> with life. Contrary to most professional opinion,
> this gnawing dissatisfaction with life is not a sign
> of "mental illness", nor an indication of poor social
> adjustment, nor a character disorder. For concealed
> within this basic unhappiness with life and
> existence is the embryo of a growing intelligence,
> a special intelligence usually buried under the
> immense weight of social shams. A person who
> is beginning to sense the suffering of life is, at the
> same time, beginning to awaken to deeper realities,
> truer realities. For suffering smashes to pieces the
> complacency of our normal fictions about reality, and
> forces us to become alive in a special sense – to see
> carefully, to feel deeply, to touch ourselves and our
> worlds in ways we have hitherto avoided. It has been
> said that suffering is the first grace.

Conclusion

As we move away from developing our social self in our early years, what state of being are we striving for? The term that Wilbur uses is *a global perspective*. To have such a perspective means that we incorporate the paradox of life so that there is a unity of opposites. Having explored differentiation and learning about the self and other, the task is to re-unite with life. This is not to regain the state of fusion we had in the womb but to encompass the differences among ourselves.

We have a template for this in modern physics. In relativity theory, the old opposites of rest versus motion have become indistinguishable, that is, "each" is now "both". Likewise, the split between wave and particle has vanished to "wavicles". Mass and energy are no longer divisions, and so-called opposites are now viewed as two aspects of one reality. Irreconcilable opposites are in fact complementary aspects of the same reality. This gives us the key to what seems the paradoxical notion of looking inside yourself for who you are. The answer is inside, because if you look carefully inside you sooner or later find outside, so the inside and the outside form a unity. Hence we can experience a deeper connection to other human beings. Being in touch with ourselves is inclusive of being in touch with others.

The relinquishing of the boundary between the self and others is, of course, not always something we wish to do, or do easily. We may have spent years establishing a sense of who we are in relation to others. To add a sense of a deep unity with others, without this boundary, may appear threatening. Again we face the illusion that to have a self is in opposition to a sense of union or communion with others. Yet it is possible, as modern physics indicates, to traverse this seeming opposition. In fact, the sense of identity is not threatened but expanded.

Having a global perspective also requires a particular kind of love. This can be a state of being in touch with the nature of things and how they are, allowing for their intrinsic nature, and letting go of all other prescriptions about how they ought to be. This includes knowing our own nature and the nature of others. At the same time there remains a basic sense of acceptance and love despite this knowledge. At this point we do not love others because they love us, affirm us, reflect or secure us in our illusions, but because they are who they are. It is also the point at which love becomes so great and so without ambivalence that the good of the other is what we want, not what others can do for us. In this state, love passes beyond being a means and becomes an end. Real love can therefore delight in the other and in the notion of love itself.

We can see that our early growth from finding a self through others, to establishing separateness, leads to the sense of oneness with others. By coming to understand who we are and the roles we play, we take our place in the family and the community.

Finally, a sense of belonging to the global family of humankind may express the stage we can achieve during our life span. To do this requires developing a mature sense of trust in the world, establishing our own value system, understanding our place in the scheme of things, and being able to see and respect the place of others. We are progressively capable throughout our life, if we so choose, to begin to shift to a more universal consciousness. If we shift through the various stages of development, then finally we are not just looking at the world through our own eyes but also through the eyes of the collective human spirit.

PART 2

When it goes wrong: how do we repair?

Chapter 4 Attachment and neuroscience

This being human is a guest house,
every morning a new arrival.
A joy, a depression, a meanness,
as an unexpected visitor
welcome and entertain them all!
… treat each guest honourably
he may be cleaning you out
for some new delight

"The Guest House," (Barks, p. 109)

Neuroscience research, together with infant mental health research and observational studies, are converging to produce an understanding of our emotional life. As this occurs, these disciplines begin to influence each other, offering a deeper understanding of how we become fully human and learn to relate emotionally to others. We now know that our earliest experiences as babies, have much more relevance to our adult selves than we formerly realised. It is as babies that we first feel and learn what to do with our feelings and organise our experiences in a way that will affect our later behaviour and thinking capacities. These concerns form the basis of what is called "affective" neuroscience.

This chapter covers the development of Attachment Theory, which has worked closely with neuroscience to better understand how we form bonds with each other, both physically and psychologically. On the other hand, we also have a better picture of what happens when things go wrong, when we may need intervention and exposure to different experiences in order to change the template that has been established. Cross-sections of the brains of neglected and abused children show disruption to the neuronal pathways in the relational areas of the brain. This has led to much valuable research on the brain and its role in developing our relationships. More recent research points to a more holistic view of ourselves and the importance of the heart as a central organ in our bodies, and further, the importance of the flora of our gut for our general well-being. As highly interactive beings, we possess highly interactive bodies.

We all begin life getting to know those around us and learning to feel safe in their presence. Babies have an array of reflexes that are designed to help them bond and communicate their needs. They are born able to bond, sustain attachment and encourage mutual care. At the same time, parents have a variety of nurturing instincts that influence their behaviours, emotions, and neurochemistry. These everyday human experiences, activated and processed within the networks of the social brain, connect the bodies, hearts and minds of both sides of this partnership. When parents nurture their babies and children, a process of neurogenesis takes place in both parties. Being together builds the baby's brain, and the brain of the parent changes as well.

The neural circuits of the social brain are referred to as experience-dependent, because they are shaped by the baby's interactions with their caregivers. The nurture we receive from the first moments of our life can set us on a course of physical and psychological health. Later in life, broader interactions become a primary source of brain regulation, growth and healing. Friendships, marriage, any meaningful relationship, at any time of life, can activate neuroplastic processes that change the structure and functioning of the brain, the foundations of which are laid down early. As we grow, our brains convert these experiences into the way we relate to others, the feelings we have about ourselves, and our implicit expectations for the future. How we bond and stay attached to others is at the core of the health and longevity of the brain.

The beginnings of convergent research

John Bowlby, an anthropologist and psychoanalyst who developed Attachment Theory, believed that psychopathology originated in real experiences of interpersonal life. He emphasised our dependence on others, especially during infancy, and the importance of psychological experiences that are occurring in an interpersonal context. In the 1950s Bowlby engaged a husband and wife team, James and Joyce Roberson, to make a film depicting the impact of separation on children in hospital. It was not usual for hospitals at this time to allow parents to visit their children. This film, *A Two-Year-Old Goes to Hospital*, made in 1953, recorded the plight of a young girl, Laura, who was in hospital for eight days to have a minor operation, with no parental visits allowed. Without her mother and with nurses that were changing frequently, she had no familiar person to soothe and support her during this difficult period. On the first day, after the routine bath, Laura ran naked to the door and tried to escape. She was frightened, hurt and reacted badly to a rectal anaesthetic. Normally bright, her expression became dull and sad as she clung to her teddy. She became quiet and eventually showed a mixture of submissiveness and resentment. By the end of her stay, Laura was withdrawn from her mother, shaken in her trust, sleeping poorly, soiling herself and having temper tantrums. She showed clear emotional deterioration from being in hospital and separated from her family.

Between 1967 and 1971, James and Joyce Robertson made five more films. They observed children, aged between eighteen and thirty months, whose mothers were in hospital for the birth of their second child. In each case, the children were securely attached to their parents with no previous experience of separation. The children went through an initial period of angry protest, searching and crying for their mother and father. Next they went through a phase of deep sadness, despairing of being able to be reunited with their parents. After these intensely distressing states came a phase of detachment. The children had given up. Emotionally they became withdrawn and indifferent. Angry responses upon reunion with their mother and conflicted feelings towards her, now with a newborn, were well documented. The sequence of protest, despair and detachment of a child separated from his or her mother was clear.

Further study of attachment relationships led to the initial classification of attachment relationships into two broad categories; "secure" and "insecure". Young children, who had experienced consistent, reliable and empathic parental care, were observed to behave in ways that suggested they felt securely attached. Children who experienced various forms and degrees of abandonment, rejection, abuse or inconsistent care were classified as being insecurely attached. The study of defensive reactions against separation anxiety showed that these were responses to real-life interpersonal events rather than to internal conflicts, as would have been explained by psychoanalytic theories dominant at that time.

In the USA, Mary Ainsworth inferred, through her research, that what determined the child's security, and therefore potentially their development pathway, was the caregiver's sensitive responsiveness. Sensitive responsiveness in infancy includes noticing signals from the baby, interpreting them accurately and responding appropriately. Out of these experiences the baby builds internal working models of relationships.

Ainsworth and her colleagues described infants as using the mother as a secure base from which to explore, identifying a reciprocal relationship between security and exploration. Confident infants, who experience attachment figures who are reliable and consistently available, are more likely to venture into the world to explore, knowing that the attachment figures will be there when needed. Her team developed the "Strange Situation Procedure". This experimental procedure was designed to mildly, but progressively, stress the infant's attachment system. It consisted of several episodes involving the child, his or her mother, and a "stranger" (a member of the research team), and took place in a room with two chairs and some toys. This exposed the young child to an unfamiliar situation.

The child enters the room with his or her mother. A large array of toys is there to explore. An adult who is friendly, but unfamiliar enters the room. The mother leaves the room and leaves the child with the stranger. Within three minutes, the mother returns and there is a reunion between mother and child. Next the mother leaves the room again and so does the stranger. Therefore the child is left alone in the room. The stranger returns before the mother does. After the second reunion between mother and child, the procedure comes to an end. Afterwards, the researchers spend some time with the mother and child in pleasant interactions, offering the opportunity to discuss what happened.

A *securely* attached child would be expected to stay close to the parent initially then move on to play with the toys, showing signs of being upset when the mother left the room. When the mother returns, the secure child will interrupt his or her playing or exploratory behaviour and show distress and desire for reunion clearly. He or she is easily comforted, settles and resumes playing. The chief characteristics of their reaction include: greater ability to play and explore the environment with enjoyment, confidence and curiosity; greater ability to clearly communicate distress as an appropriate reaction to separation; and finally, greater ability to be soothed. The researchers hypothesised that secure children, who have built an internal working model of their relationship with their mother are more likely to respond with these behaviours. Over 60% of children in Ainsworth's initial study behaved in this way.

Some children behaved differently. A quarter of the infants actively explored, but sought less proximity with the mother and failed to cry or to be overtly upset when she left the room. When the mother returned, these children actively avoided contact with her and busied themselves with the toys. Throughout the procedure, the children appeared independent and more attentive to inanimate objects than to interpersonal events. The researchers interpreted this to show that the child had learnt that expressing distress did not lead to closeness and might lead to anger in the parents. Later physiological studies have shown that these children have learnt to hide or minimise their distress. They avoid seeking proximity in order to keep under control feelings of neediness that would not be dealt with adequately. These children were classified as "insecure-avoidant".

A third group, roughly 10%, stayed closer to the parent throughout, explored less and reacted very strongly to separation. When the mother returned they did seek reunion and comfort, but they also showed anger, did not settle easily, tended to cry in an inconsolable way and failed to return to exploration. These children were classified as "insecure-ambivalent". These three groups are classified as "organised" attachment strategies.

There was another small group of children initially called "cannot classify" because their behaviours didn't fit easily into the other three patterns. A Berkeley research team, led by Mary Main, later called this fourth pattern "disorganised-disoriented". The infants in this category reacted to reunion with their mother in a confused and disorganised way. They showed contradictory behaviours such as approaching the parent backwards, or asking to be picked up, but then collapsing onto the floor. The researchers found that the parents of these children were unpredictable and frightening for the child. This pattern is seen in higher rates in children who have experienced maltreatment, or where the parent is preoccupied with past and/or current trauma from their own childhoods.

Bowlby and Ainsworth's initial work emphasised the role of the mother. However, in the mid-1970s, there was an increased interest in children's relationship with their father. Michael Lamb found that children gave prompts to the father in order to elicit care in the same way as they did to mothers. While the quality of the child's relationship with the father differed, a child could be securely attached to both, or have a different attachment style with each parent. There has been a great deal of research interest in this area, looking at patterns of relating as well as the psychobiology underpinning these experiences. In addition, interest in trans-generational attachment processes led to the development of the adult attachment interview, a semi-structured method for identifying attachment patterns in adulthood. A striking 75% correlation was found between attachment patterns identified using this interview with parents before birth and infant's attachment patterns at 12 months of age.

Further developments

In recent years, Bowlby's conception of attachment has expanded to include the influence of interpersonal experience on the shaping of neurological structures and biological processes involved in emotional regulation, learning and bodily health. Particular attachment behaviours parallel internal changes that can be measured in the body via physiological arousal, levels of stress hormones, patterns of brain activation and actual neural structure. His work and subsequent research demonstrated some of the links between early attachment and wellbeing in adulthood.

Bowlby came to the view that attachment schemas are unconscious memories of our experiences in early relationships that stay with us for the rest of our lives. They are stored in networks of unconscious memory and affect our development, the quality of our relationships and our ability to regulate our emotions. According to Stern (1995), securely attached children have internalised their parents as sources of comfort, leading them to feel safe as they explore their world. The resulting states of mind, brain and body are a secure emotional base from which to establish subsequent relationships. Secure attachments build the brain in ways that optimise neuronal activity, autonomic arousal and positive coping responses. Insecure attachments build brains more vulnerable to stress, suboptimal performance, and less adaptive abilities. Fortunately, the neural plasticity of the brain means that engaging in positive relationships can alter these networks later in life.

Attachment literature informed the work of Stern, Trevarthen, Schore and Fonagy. New scanning techniques have enabled neuroscientists like Damasio, Le Doux, Watt and Panksepp to make a visual map of the brain's activity when emotions are being experienced. Developmental psychology has also refined its tools for understanding relational patterns, so that Stern and others use video footage of mothers and babies, studying them frame by frame to better understand what is happening in the relationship. Allan Schore has synthesised a huge quantity of multidisciplinary information. He has many on-line articles on the neurobiology of secure attachment, attachment trauma and the effects of neglect and abuse on brain development. This includes the central role of affect regulation in development and treatment. Understanding emotional life biologically and socially can now show relationship patterns that are integrated into our body and brain in babyhood. Mercer (2011) has a more recent paper that offers a critique and discusses the complexities of the Attachment Model.

Neuroscientist Doug Watt, whose affective neuroscience articles are also available online, refers to the earliest years as "unrememberable" and "unforgettable". This means that while we cannot normally consciously recall any of it, it is not forgotten except under specific conditions, because it is built into our organism and informs the behaviour and expectations we bring to relationships. The psychiatrist Dr Bruce Perry, senior fellow of the Child Trauma Academy in the USA, along with Mary Maine, were among the first to notice that patterns of sensory input result in a concomitant pattern of activity of neurons and neuronal systems. Dr Bruce Perry's slides of the brains of normal children shown alongside those who had suffered violence are distressing to observe. He also notes that early experiences act as a template for all other processing of experiences.

What neuroscience tells us

We are all affected by, and affect, the biology and behaviour of those around us. Human beings are social animals and the human brain is a social organ, which serves to connect us to one another. Stanislas Grof (2000) suggests that the birth and the postnatal period have a profound influence on the emotional and social life of the individual and have important implications for the future of our society. These lay the foundations for the baby's loving and altruistic attitude toward society. They may also be a critical factor in determining whether the individual will be able to cope with the vicissitudes of life in a constructive way, or will escape the challenges of life by opting for alcohol or narcotics.

French obstetrician Michel Odent (1995) has shown how the hormones involved in the birth process, and in maternal behaviour, participate in this imprinting. The catecholamines (adrenaline and noradrenaline) play an important role in evolution as mediators of the aggressive/protective instinct of the mother at the time when birth occurs in unprotected natural environments. Oxytocin, prolactin, and endorphins induce maternal behaviour and foster dependence and attachment. The busy, noisy and chaotic milieu of many hospitals induces anxiety, unnecessarily engages the adrenaline system and imprints the picture of a world that is potentially dangerous and requires aggressive responses. This interferes with the hormones that mediate positive interpersonal imprinting. Providing a quiet, safe and private environment for birthing is therefore essential.

We can look more generally at the brain and its division into three levels; the brain stem, the limbic system and the cortex, to provide background information about interactions within our bodies and brains.

The brain stem sits at the base of the brain and is connected to the spinal cord and controls the flow of messages between the brain and the rest of the body. It also controls basic body functions such as breathing, swallowing, heart rate, blood pressure and consciousness. All our sensory experiences feed into the brain stem, waiting for processing and understanding. Next, the limbic system, including the neocortex, regulates emotions and memory. Finally, the cortex controls higher-level thinking, and is where our experiences are understood and "filed away". We can retrieve and add to our experience later.

The thalamus communicates with the rest of the brain and the neocortex. The thalamus functions as a command centre that controls what information goes between different parts of the neocortex and the rest of the brain. Nearly all of the signals from the senses go to the thalamus, as do the signals from other subcortical areas. The hypothalamus controls body functions like temperature and circadian rhythms. Below the neocortex and the thalamus are several important subcortical brain areas. One of the most important is a network of distinct old nuclei called the limbic system. There are several important structures within the limbic system:

- The hippocampus has a crucial function in the creation of memory.

- The amygdala is primarily involved with emotional processing and, together with the prefrontal cortex, processes the major emotions of anger, happiness, disgust, surprise, sadness and fear.

- The orbitofrontal cortex connects the amygdala and other structures of the limbic system to with the pre-fontal cortex. If you have experienced a difficult situation the orbitofrontal cortex will store the circumstances and the amygdala will store the fear.

- The anterior cingulate cortex monitors the progress toward whatever goal you are pursuing and generates a signal when things are not working to indicate a change in strategy is necessary.

- The basal ganglia have five major nuclei comprising a highly interconnected system that interacts with the thalamus and neocortex to regulate behaviour.

Another central process during brain development is the emergence of networks of connective fibres, or white matter, linking distant regions of the brain and establishing network communication, co-ordination and integration among the brain areas. As these networks grow and interconnect with one another there is a gradual synchronisation of brain wave patterns.

Cozolino (2008), Professor of Psychology, Pepperdine University, California, has identified four major systems in the brain that are shaped by early nurturing:

1. *The Attachment System:* The orbital and medial portions of the prefrontal cortex (OMPFC) are the first regions of the prefrontal lobe to develop during childhood. These are connected with subcortical networks of learning, memory and emotions, while the OMPFC guides arousal, relatedness, and our ability to cope with stress. These connections reflect the role of the OMPFC as the executive centre of attachment, emotional regulation and higher-level input into bodily homeostasis. We build these systems during childhood through physical contact and emotional attunement between parent and child and maintain them through emotional connection with those around us.

Although we usually think of the cortex as associated with learning, it also has an important inhibitory role in regulating lower brain functions. For example, at birth newborns have a grasping reflex that allows them to hold onto their parents. Over the first few months of life, descending cortical circuits inhibit this brain stem reflex so that we can learn to use our hands and individual fingers for more complex cortically controlled tasks. The OMPFC plays a similar sort of inhibitory role with the amygdala, which is in charge of activating our fear response. The OMPFC allows for the important function of learning to be soothed by others early in life. This important gain allows for the later capacity to self-soothe, using our own thoughts, memories and behaviours, to modulate our fearful responses and levels of arousal.

2. *The Social Engagement System:* While the basic flight-fight reaction to fear is an adequate defensive strategy for non-social animals, caretaking, cooperation, and sustaining relationships all require more subtle and continuous emotional self-regulation. In other words, an all-or-nothing trigger of the autonomic nervous system is inadequate. We need to stay in proximity to and nurture, not harm, those we love, even when we are upset or angry. To assist us in this process, in addition to the attachment system, natural selection has shaped what is described as the social engagement system or the smart vagus. The complex nerves of the vagus system connect the brain with the heart, lungs, and facial muscles (among other structures), allowing us to modulate bodily and emotional reactions in a social way. It is believed that just like our attachment system, early relationships shape the social engagement system.

Children with poor vagal tone have difficulty suppressing emotions in situations that demand their attention, making it difficult for them to engage with and sustain a shared focus of attention with others. As adults, "good" vagal tone allows us to become upset, anxious or angry with loved ones without withdrawing or becoming physically aggressive. In conjunction with the other systems, the vagal "brake" allows us to regulate our emotions and be able to sustain pair bonding and caretaking.

3. *The Social Motivation System:* The social motivation system involves the social brain drawing us to one

another. The most primitive neurochemicals involved in social motivation, as well as attachment, are oxytocin and vaspressin, which are associated with mating, reproduction and mothering. As humans developed a complex variety of social relationships, emotional and cognitive reward systems involving the neurotransmitters dopamine and norepinephrine, link social interactions with exciting and rewarding states of body and mind. Over time, the repetition of positive experiences stored in attachment circuitry shapes secure attachment schemas linked to the activity of dopamine and norepinephrine.

4. *The Stress Regulated System:* The hypothalamic-pituitary-adrenal (HPA) axis is the central communication system involved in the body's stress response. It also converts the perception of danger into hormonal messengers activating the body's fight-flight response. This system evolved to respond to brief stress and then is designed to quickly return to homeostasis. In conditions of chronic stress, the HPA system stays activated and can damage the body and the brain through sustained high levels of cortisol, ultimately shortening the life span. Chronically high levels of cortisol inhibit the protein synthesis necessary for neuronal maintenance, brain building and proper immunological functioning. Because relationships regulate HPA activation, the calmer, safer and more supportive our social world, the better regulated our stress-response system.

Positive attention to young children generates in them more benzodiazepine and endorphin receptors throughout the brain, creating a resilience that assists them to face future challenges. It also enhances brain growth and develops the brain system that supports affect regulation and problem solving. Early touch is crucial. For example, the handling of rat pups by human researchers increases density of the cortical receptors, which lower the levels of cortisol in the bloodstream. We can see then that the brain is a social organ built on the interaction between experience and genetics, where nature and nurture join together. Genes begin as a template to organise the general structure of the brain and trigger sensitive periods of development. Later, the brain adapts to its environment through a process called transcription, whereby genes orchestrate the ongoing translation of experience into neural material.

The delicate early period

The story of the baby's journey from the womb includes the pioneering work of two remarkable men, Michel Odent and Frederick Leboyer. They emphasised the importance of the heart and the positive or negative impact on children's psyche and emotion of the way they are brought into the world. Leboyer described the acute pain, terror and distress that the newborn baby experiences if they are insensitively handled. He advocated welcoming the baby gently into a dark, quiet atmosphere without loud voices, bright lights or cold surfaces. Odent's more recent work (2004) discusses the importance of the baby triggering the birth process, as this triggers other hormonal responses that help the mother bond with the baby. The increase in caesarean sections means more women are missing this important input. Where a caesarean birth is necessary, it still may be possible to wait until the birth process starts before carrying out the caesarean section.

We need to treat the first nine months with enormous respect. Following conception, the human brain will develop 100 billion neurons and 10 trillion glial cells, the greatest activity in our lifespan. From the ages of three to ten months, a culling takes place with the loss of 50,000 connections between brain cells every second; cells that are not used during this time die. Every nerve cell or dendrite has multiple branching dendrons, allowing communication and connection between nerve cells. The more the cells are used, the more these connecting dendrons and pathways between neurons and brain regions develop. The parent's empathic response to their infant in the early months and years is vital to the development of these dendritic connections. If care and love are absent or deficient, there is less neuronal growth. The highly plastic nature of the brain means that these patterns are open to later change, but such change requires a great deal of consistent and specialised effort.

The first three years of life are the most important for the emotional and mental development of the child. Until the age of three to five years, the neural connections between the older limbic brain and the heart and the frontal lobes of the neocortical brain are not fully established. Until then, we live through the reflexes of the limbic brain and through instinctual (unconscious) behaviour, assimilating sounds, sights and encounters with people and our environment at a phenomenal rate. If there is insufficient verbal and sensory stimulus in these years, we will not be able to develop to the optimum level of what we are capable of at birth. Our natural instinct is to reach out to people and respond to them, to explore through the senses everything that surrounds us.

Between three and five years the neocortical level of the brain and the frontal lobes become activated and we begin to develop a sense of self, which differentiates us from our environment. The memories associated with the older brain during the earliest years gradually become "unconscious". Yet these earliest memories, imprinted on the older brain and held in the limbic brain and the heart's memory field, have immense power to influence our lives and our behaviour. A wound in this early time can affect our lives in negative ways to the end of our days unless and until we become aware of them and other more helpful experiences intervene.

Compared to other animals, humans are born with extremely immature brains and an immense number of uncommitted neurons in the postnatal period, making us highly adaptable creatures. At a microscopic level, we find that individual neurons are separated by small gaps called synapses. A variety of chemical substances engaged in communications between neurons inhabit these synapses. This synaptic transmission stimulates each neuron, forming functional neural systems. As a result of our relationships, millions of changes within and between neurons combine, organise our brains and influence our emotions. Through interacting with others, we activate our senses, regulate our brains and bodies and change the shape of our neuronal structures.

When all goes well

In the early months of life after birth, the parents and their baby establish the normal range of arousal and develop an equilibrium that the baby will attempt to maintain. When there is a drop below or rise above the normal range of arousal, the systems go into action to recover the set point or normal state. The norm has to be established first. Babies don't do this by themselves, but coordinate with surrounding people. Within their brain, there are many loosely connected pathways that communicate with each other through their chemical and electrical signals. These systems keep things going within a comfortable range of arousal, by adapting to the changing internal and external circumstances.

The baby is still physiologically and psychologically an extension of the mother in the early months. Babies depend on milk for feeding, to regulate heart rate and blood pressure, and to provide immune protections. The mother's touch regulates muscular activity and the baby's growth hormone level. Her body provides warmth and she disperses stress hormones by touching and feeding. This basic physiological regulation keeps the baby alive.

Early regulation is also about responding to the baby's feelings in a non-verbal way. The mother does this mainly with her face, her tone of voice and her touch. She soothes her baby's loud crying and over-arousal by using her voice to calm the baby, while soothing the tense baby by holding and rocking. Conversely, she stimulates a floppy baby back into a happier state with her smiling face and dilated alert eyes. By a range of non-verbal means, she gets the baby back to set points where comfort is restored. Well-managed babies come to expect a world that is responsive to feelings and helps to bring intense states back to a comfortable level. Through the experience of having it done for them, they learn how to do it for themselves.

Looking at faces is hard-wired into human beings from the beginning and smiles help the brain to grow. Positive looks are the most vital stimulus to the growth of the emotionally intelligent brain. As the world comes into focus, vision plays an increasingly important part in relationships. Eye contact now becomes the main source of information about other people's feelings and intentions; feelings are seen on the face. By toddlerhood, the human child has started to use the parent's face as an immediate guide to behaviour. 'Is it safe to crawl out of this door?' 'Does Dad like this visitor?' This is known as "social referencing" with the infant using visual communication at a distance to check out what to do and what not to do.

Schore (1994), quoted in Gerhardt (2004, pp. 41-2), has put together an amazingly integrated picture of what is going on biologically and psychologically:

> When the baby looks at his mother (or father), he reads her dilated pupils as information that her sympathetic nervous system is aroused, and she is experiencing pleasurable arousal. In response, his own nervous system becomes pleasurably aroused and his own heart rate goes up. These processes trigger off a biochemical response. First a pleasure neuropeptide called beta-endorphin is released into the circulation and specifically into the orbitofrontal regions of the brain. "Endogenous" or homemade opioids like betaendorphin are known to help neurons to "grow", by regulating glucose and insulin. As natural opioids they also make you feel good. At the same time another neurotransmitter called dopamine is released from the brainstem, and again makes its way to the prefrontal cortex. This too

enhances the uptake of glucose there, helping new tissue to grow in the prefrontal brain. Dopamine probably also feels good, insofar as it produces an energising stimulating effect; it is involved in the anticipation of reward. By this technical and circuitous route we discover that the family's doting looks are triggering the pleasurable biochemical that helps the social brain to grow.

We can see that there is now a biological as well as psychological understanding of why those who grow up in a safe and loving environment, tend to be happier and healthier adults. The psychological explanation is that early relationships teach us that we are valued and loved and that the world is a safe place to live in. The biological explanation lies in the construction and regulation of multiple systems and processes within our social brains.

Babies need mothers who are highly sensitised to them through their maternal preoccupation. In this state, the baby's needs feel like the mother's needs, because the baby is physiologically and psychologically an extension of her. When the baby is unhappy, this is upsetting to the mother, so she will wish to do what she can to relieve the baby's cries or distress. This is what regulation means. While it is possible for others to do this, parents are usually the most physiologically honed by their hormones and therefore naturally attuned to fulfil this task.

When things go wrong

In *Why Love Matters* (2004), Sarah Gerhardt elucidates the processes that take place in early childhood, as well as what can go wrong in early relationships. Early experience has a great impact on the baby's physiological systems because they are so malleable and open to being influenced. This impact can be positive or negative and biochemical systems can be set up in a negative way if early experiences are difficult. Both the stress response, as well as other neuropeptides of the emotional system, can be adversely affected. Even the development of the brain itself, which grows at its most rapid rate in the first year and a half, may not progress adequately if the baby doesn't have the right conditions for development. Over time, the baby begins to store images of patterns of relating, whether they are soothing or hostile.

Early regulation is about responding to the baby's feelings in a non-verbal way. As noted before, the mother does this mainly with her face, her tone of voice and her touch. The baby also depends on her being able to tolerate uncomfortable feelings. All parents will struggle at this point. If we as parents have not had a good response as a baby or a child ourselves, then we will find it harder to feel in tune with the baby. It will be more difficult to notice and regulate our own feelings and it will be harder for us to help the baby learn to monitor their own states and adjust to them effectively. It is usually angry, conflicting feelings that are the most difficult for parents and baby to bear. Under these circumstances, we cannot regulate the baby's system because our own system is full; our brain stem is overloaded with unprocessed experiences. If our own issues consume us, or if we have closed off any connection to our own state of mind, it will be harder to notice what the baby is feeling. We will struggle more to bear our children's feelings if we have been unable to learn from our parents, how to manage negative feelings comfortably. Further, we will reject these feelings when the baby attempts to communicate them for understanding and processing. The baby then has to manage their feelings alone and protect the parents from the feelings they are experiencing if we are unable to respond.

When the child is repeatedly rejected and the parents' gaze withheld, researchers found that children learn to appear calm and unconcerned, but when measured, they have a high heart rate and high autonomic arousal. Such children are unable to get help to return to their comfort zone. The child is learning there is no one to help settle them and cope with such feelings. The child avoids seeking help and closes down the feelings they cannot manage.

Resistant or ambivalently attached children are more likely to express strong feelings explosively, with no sense of their impact on others. These children are living with parents who respond inconsistently to the child's feeling world. They are sometimes in touch, sometimes disassociated. As a result, babies or children focus closely on the parent's state of mind to optimise a chance of getting a response. This preoccupation can make children overly aware of fears and needs, undermining a sense of independence. These children learn to exaggerate their feelings in order to receive parental attention. The parent's unpredictable behaviour ensures that the child's attention is always focused on them.

Children caught up in any one of these patterns of attachment, will have a less secure sense of self than a securely attached child. The parent may not have provided enough information about the child's own feelings, to equip the child to enter the domain of psychological interpretation of self and others with confidence. Instead, children may try to protect a less formed sense of self by withdrawing from others when feeling uncertain (the avoidant pattern) or clinging to others to try to elicit more feedback (the resistant pattern).

Disorganised attachment occurs when much has gone wrong for the family so they cannot coherently model how to handle interactions. Very often, intense traumatic feelings that have not been processed effectively, such as a loss, or abuse, have overwhelmed the parents themselves. If that is the case, support will be needed to provide the basic parental functions to protect children and create a safe base from which the world can be explored.

Depressed mothers generally offer few positive interactions. Research has shown that about 40% of the time they are unresponsive or disengaged, while much of the rest of the time they can be angry, intrusive and rough with their babies. The most painful experience for a baby is not being able to get the parent's attention. This experience is seemingly worse than maltreatment. Cohn *et al.* (1990) found that babies of depressed mothers experience more negative than positive feelings. There is a hopelessness attached to depression, which is not just the lack of self-esteem, but also not being able to make things right. Schore calls this the "disruption and repair" cycle. When conflict occurs in relationships, it is crucial to feel there is a way to repair the rupture. The baby of a depressed mother is unable to "repair" the mother, so does not believe repair is possible. Babies of depressed mothers adjust to low stimulation and can get used to a lack of positive feelings. This can adversely affect their stress response, as well as other neuropeptides of the emotional system.

At the *neglectful* end of the scale, depressed mothers will find it very hard to respond to their babies and tend to be apathetic and withdrawn. As a result of their own experience of neglect, they may not make eye contact with their babies or pick them up, except to clean them or feed them. The babies will respond by developing a depressed way of interacting with people themselves. They may show fewer positive feelings and the left-brain becomes less active. In toddlerhood, they may perform less well on cognitive tasks and be "insecurely" attached to their parents. Later in childhood, their emotional problems tend to persist. In my own experience of depressed mothers, I have seen their baby become very interactive and watchful of their mothers. The baby works to lift the mood of the mother by frequently engaging and encouraging the mother to make a connection. These babies do this at the cost of being in touch with their own responses. The mother is centre stage and not the baby's needs. This is a painful position for both parties.

At the *intrusive* end of the scale, there is another type of mother who may also be depressed, but is much more angry, even if only covertly. For the mother whose own needs have not been met there is a natural resentment of the baby's demands and feelings of hostility are aroused toward the baby. She may convey this to the baby by picking up abruptly or holding stiffly. Active involvement with her baby may be insensitive; she may fail to read signals and this interferes with the baby's initiatives. If we are agitated as mothers, we can leave our children aroused and struggling to self-regulate. Babies remember negative looks and interactions. A negative look can also trigger a biochemical response, just as a positive face does. The mother's disapproving face can trigger off stress hormones like cortisol that stop the endorphins and dopamine neurons and the pleasurable feelings they generate, which is a great loss for both parties.

All of these children will be prone to a stress response in their bodies. The hypothalamus triggers a particular flow of chemical reactions when experiences are negative. One of its end products is the stress hormone cortisol. A key part of the subcortical response to stress is the hypothalamus, situated in the centre of the brain. In response, the hypothalamus triggers what is known as "the stress response". This means that the hypothalamus activates the pituitary gland, which in turn triggers the adrenal glands. The adrenal glands generate extra cortisol, to provide extra energy to deal with the stress and put other bodily systems on hold, while this is being dealt with. What seems to be most crucial for the baby is the extent to which the parent is emotionally available, to notice signals and to regulate their states, something the baby cannot yet do. As a result of being poorly handled, the baby develops a more reactive stress response and different biochemical patterns from a well-handled baby. He or she is unable to learn how to soothe states of intense feeling.

Babies of agitated mothers may stay over-aroused and have a sense that feelings just explode out of you and there is not much you or anyone can do about it, or they may try to switch off their feelings altogether to cope. Sarah Gerhardt points out that all these kinds of dysfunctional parental responses disturb the body's natural rhythm. Being aroused physiologically by some intense emotional state will normally lead to action of some kind, and once the feeling has been expressed, the baby's body will wind down and come back to a resting state. This is the normal cycle of the sympathetic and parasympathetic nervous systems. When arousal is not dealt with or soothed, this rhythm is lost. The baby or child can move either into a hyperactive mode, or withdraw and turn away. In response, there are bodily reactions like muscle tension, shallow breathing, immune or hormonal disturbances. The cardiovascular system, in particular, will remain activated, even if the baby suppresses the feelings.

Securely attached children use others to successfully modulate their stress and unlike insecurely attached children, do not produce a cortisol response when attachment figures are available. Thus secure attachment is an indication of positive coping, while the behaviours of insecurely attached individuals are more like states of arousal than forms of coping.

Conclusion

Neglect or abuse of babies and small children can alter the balance of their neural chemistry and program them for later depression, or violent behaviour. When constant anxiety and distress are present, the adrenal glands produce a high level of the stress hormone cortisol and this upsets the optimal formation and equilibrium of the autonomic nervous system, the endocrine and immune systems. This also interferes with the neural connections between the heart, the two hemispheres of the brain and the frontal lobes. The stress of constant anxiety may prevent the higher brain centres from developing.

The orbitofrontal cortex, together with other parts of the prefrontal cortex and anterior cingulate, is probably the area of the brain most responsible for what Daniel Goleman called "emotional intelligence". The capacity to empathise and wonder about the state of mind of someone else requires a developed orbitofrontal cortex. It is linked to the right side of the brain, which is specialised for understanding the general feel of things – the whole picture – and is linked to visual, spatial and emotional responses. In fact, according to Allan Schore (2000), the orbitofrontal cortex is the controller for the entire right brain, which is dominant throughout infancy. It is only later that the left side of the brain integrates.

Much current research is focussed on the brain, but we need to keep a holistic perspective. I would like to put in a plea for the heart as an important centre of focus. The neuroscience work has focused on the right brain, because the right brain is the most active and utilised in the first few years. However, the emphasis on brain activity need not detract from the importance of the heart, both physiologically and psychologically. The use of the breath highlights this fact; the restful moments are not those where there is mental activity, but a sense of peace and wellbeing flowing from the heart to the body. This will be the next stage of neuroscience research: studying the body, the brain, the heart and the gut flora, and how they work as a whole.

I watched an interview with a Palestinian family after the bombing of Gaza. The parents spoke of their concern for their son. He had been playing in front of their house with his best friend, when a bomb hit the house. Debris killed his best friend in front of him.

The boy spoke of his best friend in very loving terms, but said, 'I don't want my heart any more; it hurts too much. I wish I could take it out and get rid of it'.

Very clearly, this boy experienced his sense of loss through his heart in a very physical way. The heart is the primal organ of the whole body-mind organism. When the heart is deeply distressed and cannot function in an optimal way, this affects the hormonal, immune and autonomic nervous systems and all the other organs of the body.

Most recent research shows that the all-important flora of the gut establishes itself in the first thousand days of life and after that we are constantly seeking to manage that flora. We need to continue to grow in our understanding of the brain in tandem with the heart and the gut so that we get a fuller picture of what is happening. We also need to add this to our knowledge of the impact of psychological states on our functioning as babies and adults. Children who have been subjected to a chronically abusive environment, for example, grow up to be hyper-vigilant of other people's moods and body language as a protective measure. They sense changes in mood or a subtle inflexion in the voice or body language long before others do. This hyper-vigilance affects every system in the body, programming it to live in a state of constant arousal and anxiety.

The Institute of HeartMath in Boulder Creek, California, has been at the forefront of research into the importance of the heart and suggests that the heart communicates with the brain in four ways: neurologically (through the transmission of nerve impulses), biochemically (via hormones and neurotransmitters), biophysically (through pulse waves) and energetically (through the interactions of their electromagnetic fields). Baring (2013, p. 400) provides the best summary of the emerging material regarding the heart:

> The heart is not just a pump circulating blood around the body. Speaking in purely physiological terms, the heart is now known to be another "brain": an organ that is a centre of intelligence and consciousness as important, if not more important, than the brain we associate with our mind. It is now thought that the heart is the main organ in the body that coordinates the functioning of the autonomic nervous system, the immune system and the endocrine system and that the heart communicates continuously with the brain.
>
> … Cardiologists call this whole system the "heart brain". These four different transmitters of information function below the awareness of the conscious mind, yet continually interact with the brain, exchanging information with it and

profoundly affecting the way we think, feel and behave from moment to moment. It is now known that there is a continuous highway of neural communication between the older limbic emotional brain, the heart and the two hemispheres of the neocortical brain but that the neural connections from the emotional to the cognitive centres is greater than those going the other way.

We need to continue exploring the connection between the heart, the older instinctive emotional (limbic) brain, and the newer neocortical one, which we usually refer to as our mind. This can help us to understand, in terms of brain chemistry and neuronal connections, why the heart is so important, why the instincts and emotions are so powerful and why they can have a positive or negative effect on us.

The biologist Candace Pert (1998), whose AIDS drug Peptide T was featured in the 2013 Oscar-winning movie *Dallas Buyers Club,* discovered that our emotions are the crucial link between mind and body (discussed in Baring 2013, p. 405). Specific chemicals called neuropeptides relate to specific emotional states, and further, these neuropeptides are found to be active all over the body, including in the older limbic brain, the neocortex, the stomach and the intestines. This was a ground-breaking discovery, because she realised that neuropeptides are the connecting factor between the emotions and physiological processes. Each specific peptide (chemical) mediates a specific emotional state. We can no longer speak of objective rational thought, because thought is inextricably involved with emotion. She found that neuropeptides connect the brain, the hormonal system and the immune system, acting as messengers between them and able to alter mood and behaviour. This means we can no longer view the body as a machine, but as an incredibly efficient information network with inbuilt intelligence. That intelligence is not only to be found in the brain, but in the cells of every part of the body.

In early childhood, we store memories of our emotional

states in the heart and limbic brain. These feelings remain imprinted on them throughout our lives. The development of the frontal lobes of the brain can be affected in a positive and negative way by these feelings. With the development of the frontal lobes comes the ability to reflect, to reason and to apply knowledge gained to specific goals.

Additionally, the frontal lobes develop the ideas conveyed by the imagination to make intuitive connections between apparently unrelated things and ideas. Trauma can affect the heart, and the whole instinctual system connected with it can be traumatised. This causes a deviation from a normal path of growth, with intense anxiety and fear aroused by neglect, abandonment or abuse. Trauma impairs the capacity for harmonious and balanced interaction between the heart, the nervous system and the brain. Hence, for the wellbeing and creativity of a whole society, nothing is more important than the care of the mother, father and child at this time.

Chapter 5 The body and the breath

The body itself is a screen
to shield and partially reveal the light that's blazing
inside your presence

"Story Water," (Barks, p. 172)

The body

Plato's rationalistic epistemology, and the dualism of Descartes, served to separate us from our bodies. Many of the religions of the world saw the body as an impediment to the spiritual life, and viewed the body as something to be treated with revulsion and contempt. These beliefs have deeply misrepresented the nature of our bodies. However, we are beginning to open up to the Eastern view of the importance of the breath and the association of breath and breathing with psyche, spirit or soul. Traditional Tibetan medicine and current energy therapies employ tapping points on the meridians or energy fields of the body. Researchers are examining the Western separation of body/mind. The fundamental mind-body dichotomy has coincided with research into neuroscience, embodiment and consciousness, and how the unconscious mind may "speak" through the language of the body.

Affective neuroscience is moving us more into the body and researchers are now confident that the mind-body gap can be bridged. When you focus on feelings, as opposed to cognition or thoughts, you need to turn to the body. It is no longer possible to talk about feelings purely in terms of a mental state. You also have to include changes in heart rate, respiration and muscle tension. The psychobiological models of infancy and adulthood will lead to more powerful models that will assist in the treatment of psychosomatic disorders. This important unity between body, emotions and mind, is now evident in both neuroscience and the growth in body therapies.

Neuroscience findings challenge us all to rethink what we do. This re-think covers reflection on child-rearing practices, support for parents during the early years, and the organisation of our work places to better accommodate work-life choices for families. It also includes the need for helping professions to reflect on how best to treat people. This information needs to inform how best to frame and understand individual and collective treatment programs. With psychological services already under enormous pressure, it is hard to imagine how this re-think can take place, yet it remains important to do so. Neuroscience has focused our attention on the body. This information should be integrated into our treatment approaches, because our primitive feelings that have no words are found in our bodies.

Finding the body

At birth we are "a stream of sensations" seeking someone to "contain us", and to think about what is going on for us. If we have someone's mind and feelings available to us we are able to live in our bodies, fulfil our potential and progress toward psychological birth. In a mother's or father's arms, where it is safe and warm, the baby's muscles can relax and breathing can deepen as tensions are dispersed by gentle stroking or calm rocking. Research has shown that the baby's heart rate synchronises with the parent's heart rate if the parent is relaxed. The parents' autonomic nervous system communicates with their baby's nervous system, soothing it through touch. When babies are held, they know they are supported. So often this is not the case. Because of circumstance and temperament, development does not automatically occur. To access these early difficulties when we are older requires tuning in to what is "held" in our bodies. It is not difficult to imagine that babies left to cry for long periods will eventually learn to hold their breath when very anxious. This may lead to symptoms of bronchial asthma, and the asthmatic reaction may then arise in any situation that arouses anxiety. As Henry Maudsley, London's famous nineteenth century anatomist, said, 'The sorrow that has no vent in tears makes other organs weep.'

Sensorimotor Psychotherapy integrates sensorimotor processing with cognitive and emotional processes in the treatment of trauma. Traditional therapies have relied largely on cognitive and emotional engagement, but Ken Wilbur (1996) postulated the idea of a hierarchy of information-processing systems so that there are three levels of arranging our experiences; the cognitive, emotional and sensorimotor. Cognitive processing occurs in the frontal cortical upper parts of the brain, emotional processing takes place in the limbic parts of the brain, and the sensorimotor level is located in the lower rear portions of the brain. These three systems interact and influence each other and all need to be attended to if healthy functioning is to occur. Babies and children explore the world through the sensorimotor and emotional systems and, if supported, progress to using the cortical areas in more adult activity. This is called top-down processing where, for example, as we mature, we may override tiredness or hunger in order to complete a task.

If we are traumatised, however, we experience intense sensations and are unable to regulate our physical reactions and strong feelings. In response we will behave either hyperactively or passively, or alternate between the two. If we are hyperactive, we are subject to uncontrollable bouts of rage and are hyper-vigilant. When we feel helpless, we are unable to set boundaries and we feel inadequate, or remain in a victim role. Trauma has physical symptoms. They are the subtle physiological experiences that occurred in the body at the time of the event or events. What we experienced in the body needs to be re-experienced in the safety of a sensitive relationship. Just as we notice the emotional states of each other, we also need to notice the physical expression of the skin, the breath, heart rate, muscle tension and body posture of those we are interacting with.

In their online article "One Method for Processing Traumatic Memory", Pat Ogden and Kekuni Minton (2000, p. 11) from the Sensorimotor Psychotherapy Institute state:

> … when clients are asked to describe sensations,
> they frequently do so with words such as "panic"
> or "terror" which refer to emotional states rather
> than to sensation itself. When this occurs, clients are
> asked to describe how they experience the emotion
> physically: for example, panic may be felt in the body
> as rapid heartbeat, trembling and shallow breathing.
> Anger might be experienced as tension in the jaw,
> an impulse to strike out accompanied by a sense
> of heaviness and immobility in the arms. Similarly,
> a belief about oneself, such as "I'm bad" might be
> experienced as collapse through the spine, a ducking
> of the head, and tension in the buttocks.

This will help us to observe our experience and be able, with support, to experience what was formerly unbearable. Once we achieve this it is possible to work on the emotional and cognitive levels of functioning.

Working with our own, or a client's, implicit knowledge of early experiences, somatic psychology studies the non-verbal qualities in most human communication, especially in the first years of life. We can learn to incorporate them into other models of therapy. The writer Alice Miller (2005) bluntly speaks of the body in her book *The Body Never Lies*, referring to the body as the ultimate rebel. This rebel body will be the one who will speak the truth for us. Whatever we do to our body with substances or medicine will not work because it will ultimately have its say, whether it is in the form of a temporary or more serious illness. She sees the body as both the host to the brutalities we have experienced, and at the same time our most authentic voice.

Tim Winton (2014, p. 42), in his insightful piece "Havoc: A life in accidents," an article in *The Monthly*'s Tenth Anniversary edition, resonates with this view when he writes of a severe accident his father was involved in. In the aftermath:

> The grown-ups who visited spoke in riddles and whispers. I had to imbibe the gravity of our situation the way a dog will, reading the smells and the postures and hierarchies. You forget how much a child absorbs physically and then has to process unaided.

Focusing on the body

We all tend to make physical those moments when inner and outer circumstances combine to overwhelm our ordinary psychological ways of coping. In the aptly named *Theatres of the Body; a psychoanalytic approach to psychosomatic illness* (1989), Joyce McDougall speaks of psychosomatic phenomena that disappear as a side effect of psychoanalytic treatment, even though there has been no specific exploration of the underlying significance of such illnesses in the psychic economy. As a psychoanalyst, she was struck by how little the body had been focused on, and often wondered why this was so. To her, the silence became understandable when she realised that the roots of such physical manifestations were linked to early experiences; her adult patients were functioning psychically like infants in part of their personality. It is hard to incorporate these experiences in ourselves as alive and well, and in the main, we prefer not to acknowledge them. McDougall herself recounts having recurrent attacks of hives as a child, which always occurred during her biannual visits to her paternal grandmother, called "Mater", whom she didn't like. The hives were routinely blamed on the jersey cow milk, which she loved, but was forbidden to drink. Subsequently, her grandmother shifted from the farm, with the farm remaining within the family. Visits from then on were "Mater free", as well as hive free, and she was able, on future visits, to resume drinking jersey cow milk.

Not all experiences are psychosomatic, but at times we all use action instead of reflection, when our usual defences against mental pain are disturbed. Instead of becoming aware that we are guilty, anxious or angry, we might overeat, drink too much, have a car accident or get the flu. These are simple examples of expressing ourselves in action so that the emotion is dispersed, rather than thinking about what has been unconsciously reactivated and its associated feelings.

While the psychotic person may use language in a "thought-disordered" way to fill the empty space of terrifying nothingness inside, the thought process of the psychosomatic sufferer, is more likely to drain words and language of emotional significance. The body either expresses itself without restraint, or is highly inhibited in a dysfunctional way. McDougall speaks of the unconscious need of the patient to preserve these illnesses as proof of psychic survival. Patients preserve their psyche by asking their body to carry the unprocessed thoughts and experiences. They do this in the hope that at some later time someone might understand their needs. They "freeze" the elements that lead to gaining a psyche, waiting to be thawed if different conditions are provided.

The body and trauma

In the last chapter we spoke of the baby/child who does not appear to react to mistreatment, yet their body registers what is taking place. When the psyche treats potentially traumatic events with unusual calm and insensitivity, it is not recognising the overwhelming emotions that have been activated. This increases the likelihood that there will be a bodily reaction. These are defensive measures against inexpressible pain and fears of a psychotic nature. These fears include the danger of losing one's sense of identity, of becoming mentally fragmented or perhaps of going mad. The background stories taken from adult psychosomatic sufferers frequently contain references to their infancy. Just as frequently, there are reports of precocious development, of walking and talking early, which add to the clinical picture. These patients had to maintain a camouflage of "pseudo-normality" in order not to think or feel too deeply about inner pain and conflict that they might otherwise experience as highly disturbing. They do not deny or repress their experience and so unconsciously register it, but rather they destroy memories of the troubling perceptions. A part of the personality is constantly avoiding any recognition of primitive anxieties with psychotic overtones.

Under the veneer of their pseudo-normality, psychosomatic patients feel that love leads to death, because it was their relationship with their parents that led to their psychic death. This death can result from being taken over, being forced to adapt to the point where boundaries do not exist, or where their mind has been colonised. Their parents' behaviour forces them to conclude they can only survive by being totally indifferent to any loving attachments. In their experience, relationships destroy. An area of inner deadness occupies the psychic reality of such patients and often leads to a lack of physical self-care. Like all manifestations of mental illness, these responses are in fact directed towards survival and restoring health. These constructions are the psychic work of small children faced with mental pain, arising from external factors beyond their control. They attribute their ills to outside circumstances and cannot achieve any understanding that has meaning. Growing children understand that it is forbidden to think – they are only permitted thoughts that belong to the mother, father or their environment. Some create their own imaginary world; others feel entrapped in their parent's mind. Highly charged emotional thought, which the mother or father cannot bear, becomes forbidden territory for the child. The child's image of the parent is a confusing mixture of an omnipotent figure, who is also frail and easily broken. The child then becomes a narcissistic extension of the mother or father and attends to the parent's needs. Such people question their right to exist as a lively and independent being.

Pre-verbal injuries to our psyche, will remain locked in the body if there has not been a process of repair between the parent and child. Later circumstances can unlock these fears and anxieties, so that an adult may revisit, for example, a fear of spiders, and come to understand why it came about. More severe cases, like those discussed above, will turn against their feeling/body/self to such an extent that they need help from someone else to understand what happened. Their experience is that no one has been there for them. To release these feelings would overwhelm them again. They would be open to the threat of falling into a black hole that would annihilate them. Many people who appear to be coping carry around these anxieties in their everyday living. It is important that the community works toward finding effective ways of alleviating their horrors. Collectively, if we can integrate the understandings being discussed here, all of us could be aware of these terrors and make access to these states easier.

Engaging with the breath

The breath is an important way of connecting with the unconscious primitive material that resides in the body. Like our heartbeat and the contractions of our intestines, the breath functions independently. It is an unconscious function that establishes a basic body rhythm, a pulse of energy like a wave. There is a taking in and a letting go. If all has gone well, we are born with a rib cage that is vibrant and flexible. The ribs, where they join the spine at our back, move easily and rhythmically with each breath. With a full and natural breath our bodies maintain a high degree of energy. Emotions like anger or excitement flow through our bodies easily and we are open to love and pain alike.

In most instances, over time, our full breath is reduced as we face the challenges of living within our culture and society. As a result, our ribs may have grown inflexible in response to difficult experiences and our breathing may have quickened. These difficulties lead to a tightened diaphragm, our breath no longer connecting the upper and lower body. Holding our breath and contracting our diaphragm are early mechanisms used to suppress sensations of both anxiety and pleasure. When we experience anxiety, or intense pleasure, we frequently feel it in our chest, diaphragm, and the abdomen.

The body experiences life through the five senses. Taking the time to become acutely aware of sensory experiences, is a form of meditation that slows the bodily systems. It puts us in touch with our body and the rhythm of our breathing and our heart. As we slow down, we become aware of everything around us that is communicating its presence to us. We don't think of the past or the future: we are in the present. Breathing more freely helps us to let go of the need to do anything. Taking time to lie down for a few minutes during the day, or perhaps in our bed when we wake up in the morning, gives us time to be in touch with our body in a deeper way. We can feel that the mattress or the ground is supporting us. We can "let go" into the experience and feel the energy that comes with taking in a larger, deeper breath. A deeper breath also provides a larger intake of oxygen into our system and is invigorating and energizing. On the other hand, if we resist letting go into the present, it may indicate that we need to discover parts of ourselves that we have previously disowned.

The most valuable way of getting in touch with what is going on in our body, is through being aware of the breath. This provides a focus away from our mind and its many preoccupations. The breath establishes the flow between the heart, the brain and our body, giving us the space and time for this integration to take place. We can observe how our breath functions for us, where it flows and where it doesn't. We can access the "blocks" we encounter in our bodies. These blocks lie dormant but alive in our bodies, and it can be valuable to gain an understanding of these blocks over time.

The way we breathe tells us a lot about ourselves. There are many ways to breathe; some breathing techniques facilitate the flow of feelings; others seek to control and contain feelings. One way is to think of the breath as something originating via an intake of air through our nose, then an exhalation through the mouth. As the nose takes in the oxygen, the stomach is inflated. The air in the stomach is subsequently drawn up our torso, through the diaphragm, the heart area, upper chest, and throat. Finally, the air is exhaled through the mouth, and we get a sense of releasing and expelling the air down through the body, and out of the legs and hands and feet. This method creates a flow, an "in" and an "out", opening up a connection to the body. Being able to turn to a longer, deeper breath can be enormously soothing and focusing when we are stressed. It is a way to manage panic attacks, contain a reactive response, or pause before deciding whether to act or not. The breath focuses our energies so we are better able to find an appropriate response to an event, rather than a reactive one.

Observing our own and each other's breathing patterns can be quite illuminating. We may breathe into our stomach, the air going straight to the exhalation to bypass the heart area. This may be a way to avoid heart-felt or heart-broken feelings. We may allow some liveliness through the stomach but the fullness of painful or loving feelings may be muted. For others the breath flows well from the upper chest up into the throat, and out, but bypasses the stomach/diaphragm areas. This may mute the spontaneous/gut feelings that the breath does not touch so these feelings are not experienced.

Not many of us have a full flow of breath, so becoming aware of how we breathe is one way to tune into our blocks.

The throat may also contain emotional states, that is, all the things we have been unable to say but wish to say, so the muscles tighten and we are unable to release the words. The jaw also holds a great deal of tension, which is perhaps to be expected, since it is the area of the baby's sucking response. As a source of pleasure and pain, we can hold strong ambivalent feelings in the jaw. Sucking gives the pleasure, but when someone takes that pleasure away, we may feel an urge to bite.

The breath as a healing mechanism

We all have times when we feel disconnected from our feelings. At the same time, we can become aware that we are in a highly charged state, with a rush of emotions that have been inexplicably aroused. We know that something is missing, but we cannot connect our mind and feelings. At these times we need to return to the interplay between our mind and our body, and re-instate a sense of congruity. Enabling this process is a very basic part of healthy living and an essential outcome of therapy. The process is important to understand, so that we can reclaim our liveliness and bring to life aspects of ourselves that have been dormant.

The difficult task of being in touch with our feelings is made possible by becoming more aware of how our body works and through paying attention to the breath. The task is difficult because, as noted above, we have learnt to turn against our body and feelings.

If we are out of touch with our feelings, we need to become aware of the disconnection and piece together the story of why this is so. Most of us are aware that we are lacking in some way in our interpersonal relationships since it is usually this arena that motivates us to explore our internal states further. Gradually we can become aware of how our body reacts in certain situations. This is the beginning of articulating feelings that we have not previously explored.

We can begin by focusing the awareness on anger and how our body responds when we are angry. This is initially a task of observation, taking note of what is happening inside. The observational stance is the key element at this point, so we do not enact angry feelings, but identify them. Stepping outside ourself and watching develops a sense of curiosity about the self. Does your face flush when you are angry? Do your muscles tighten? Does the hair at the back of your head stand up? Does a fist form? Or does the blood pump more quickly through your system? Often we can note these states when we are driving or in the presence of authority figures. It can be gender based: we may respond to men or women differently. After beginning to observe ourselves, we can include other emotions: how do we react to a sad scene in a movie? Do we distract ourselves, look away or feel repulsed by the emotion? Where are the feelings located: in the heart area, throat, chest or stomach?

There will not be a seamless opening up to feelings, but we will gradually piece together an emotional life. Those who have an emotional life can find it difficult to understand how it feels to be disconnected in this way. In a disconnected state, we live with a sense of incompleteness, of living on the outside of what others seem to have. It is like seeing a family around a hearth from outside the door, looking in the window. It is a very solitary place and re-activates the lonely, unattended baby. Images are important since they form our earliest form of memory.

As we get in touch with our feelings, we may begin to get sick, and a number of physical symptoms can appear. The body is free to show its illness and express the overload of emotion in many ways. Once we have a rudimentary map of feelings, we can begin to wonder what other people may be experiencing. Gradually, we can work out when others experience similar feelings, or have different reactions. At this point, memories come alive and even those of us who recollect little of our past or childhood, begin to access states of mind that have been locked away. This process can open up to a new and exciting world alongside the painful and difficult feelings that we have activated.

Resistance to being in touch with our body and feelings

Some of us struggle to let our bodies go and remain rigid and unyielding. A young woman with quite disorganised thinking and high anxiety came to see me. She walked on the floorboards to avoid crossing the carpet for fear of dirtying it. She generally behaved as if she could not make a mark on the world. She lay rigid on the couch and commented with pride on how the cover was not disturbed by her lying there. Her mother had been married to a serviceman and was highly anxious every time he had to fly a plane. When she was pregnant with my patient, she decided she wouldn't worry about the risks he was taking and worked to allay her fears. On his next practice flight her husband, my patient's father, was killed. From that day her mother was unable to manage her grief. I wondered whether my patient had ever found a space in the world to occupy. It seemed she had never been able to imprint herself on this world and be fully born. Her mother was full of her own grief and not strong enough to manage the emotional states of her baby. It seemed that, in therapy, we would have to start with a pregnancy, in a psychological sense, before we could begin to think of a birth.

When we start to make contact with our feelings, it is natural to feel resistance. No one who has retreated from feelings did so without good reason. At some point we have been overwhelmed and forced to reject our feelings, and have absorbed the dismissive or rejecting attitude of those around us. We may have lived in an atmosphere where our parents looked down on our feelings either unconsciously or verbally: "You're pathetic, see, you are a blubbering mess," as if feelings are beneath us as humans. Those people who have become hyper-rational, treat those with an emotional life – something that they cannot attain – with contempt. Frequently we believe that feelings got us into trouble in the first place, so why would we want to explore them? Our feelings were too much for our parents and made them turn against us so why would we go there? By exploring these questions, we can find a space for feelings to feel welcomed, as opposed to rejected.

Many overweight people carry around the extra weight as a layer of protection against the baby inside, which is the more vulnerable, soft part of themselves. The protective layers of excess body weight act as a barrier to the tender parts of the self too fragile to expose to the harsh world outside. Additionally, there can be a connection between the words "weight and "wait". Often the protection lies around the painful feelings, of not being able to wait or of having had to wait too long in the past. Now they need support to be able to manage the feelings of waiting. Processing these feelings can lead to a natural weight loss as we address these issues as long as there is no underlying medical condition.

Meeting up with our body

When we begin to "inhabit" our bodies, we become more aware of the painfulness of being "out of touch" with our bodies. It is not pleasant to be out of touch, but we also learn that being in touch is also painful. It is like living between a rock and a hard place. In the beginning, growing this connection is very intermittent and fragile and we can easily lose it. If something in the environment triggers us, we will return to an old place of safety. It is like the tortoise; it exposes its soft parts, but when it meets something that may harm it, it will retreat. Poked or provoked it will return to the safety of the shell and hide away once more. Human beings are similar and it is helpful to be aware of this process occurring inside us. Once provoked, it is not just a matter of "will" to come out again, it will require a supportive presence to have another go.

Another human being, an event in our favour, the natural world, or "god" in some form, can all facilitate trying to reach out. I remember a radio broadcast in which an Aboriginal woman was discussing what kept her going in the face of abuse as a domestic helper, with very little support. She had been taken from her mother and father. She was asked whether she went to church on Sunday, the only day off she had each week, for decades. Her reply was that she didn't need to go to church; she would go fishing at a lake nearby and catch a fish for herself. She would enjoy the sun and the sound of the birds; that nature was her church and her God was to be found there. From this she could gain the sustenance she required for the next week.

Over time we become more aware of being disconnected. The previous adaptation of being "out of touch" shifts to the longing to *be* connected and "in touch" as much as possible. Crustacean dreams of lobsters and crayfish, or dreams of being in a castle with a drawbridge, which can be pulled up at any time, or of walls in a house beginning to come down, may be common at this time. We often become angry at our predicament and confused about where our anger belongs. Is it those who closed us off in the first place? Or is someone confronting us to open ourselves up? Usually there is anger at both: the first for creating the problem in the first place, and the second for disturbing the universe created to manage the problem and triggering painful states that we need to process.

Sometimes we can recognise early what we have to face. I remember an eight-month-old baby whose mother was very teary about feeding as her baby often pulled away from her during the feed and she began to feel that the baby didn't want her. She was beginning to think it would be better if she did not breastfeed her baby any more. We had a general discussion and all seemed to be well. She had fed her first child satisfactorily. Her husband supported her and they had a wanted a baby boy. We then talked about how the birth had been. The chord had been wrapped around the baby's throat and had begun to restrict the baby's breath. Together we used this information to understand why the baby might fear feeding.

The mother had very large breasts and firmly clutched the baby to her to help him attach, and held him against the nipple. We decided to see whether giving this baby boy more time to approach the nipple and slip on and off by himself would make him feel more relaxed at the breast, rather than arching and pulling away. Together we thought about what it would have been like for him choking and unable to breathe right at the start of his life. We wondered whether this might have made him highly sensitive to not having enough air, so that being firmly clasped against the breast, rather than being soothing as we might expect, was reactivating a sense of not being able to breathe. In fact, it could be reactivating a fear of dying. The mother began to approach the feeding situation quite differently, letting him take his time in attaching, and holding him more loosely. She also began seeing him differently, not as a baby who didn't want her, but someone struggling with a difficulty for good reason. The change was almost immediate. Within four or five feeds he began to relax. He began to explore his mother's breast with his free hand and to show initiative rather than fear.

Other emotions become more obvious after we recognise angry feelings. We may reject any positive comments, hate attention, or be hypersensitive to criticism, and experience the bodily response that these states elicit. For those of us who have been told who they are and what they think, it can be the first time we experience what is going on inside us. We can directly communicate with the body about something only we can know; no one else is more expert in how the body operates than we are.

Learning from our body

This work has a painstaking as well as a revelatory quality, as is the way of all new learning. It is, however, intrinsic to the process of connecting to our body. Until we have connected to our body, it is difficult to bypass our talking mind and make an authentic connections with others. It can be an explorative and unfolding experience for us all as we slowly activate an emotional world inside. A new world can unfold.

A comment made to me, as this process unfolded, was: 'I used to see the world in black and white, now it is in colour. I never knew what the world really looked like.'

To make these changes we face many fears and anxieties. As children our parents rejected our feelings, because they missed out themselves. We asked our parents for a response that they could not give, so we had to learn to adapt. We learnt to fear our emotions that were either stifled or became volcanic eruptions. However, as we begin to feel in touch with what is going on inside us, we can feel satisfied. Things link up and begin to make more sense. We are less left out in the cold, not knowing what is going on inside us, and less dependent on others to translate what is happening in the world. Once we are more connected, a range of feelings become available to us.

If we are in therapy, there will be a greater sense of two people in the room endeavouring to untangle the knots and unlock the secrets in the body together. A sense of a self grows like shoots in the soil of the relationship. All the old learned misunderstandings of course arise. 'If I open up to you, you will open up to me and overwhelm and control me.' 'Opening up only means that you will put all your unwanted feelings in me.' 'Letting you in will only mean a repeat of the hurt I felt from relationships on the past.' Yet beyond these understandable and predictable objections something else happens. The tentative tendrils of self-understanding, mirrored in the growth of new neuronal pathways in the relationships areas of the brain, begin to form.

Our own observations, or if we seek help, the mutual observations between therapist and patient, can reveal the restless legs that want to run away from what is being unearthed; the crossing of the arms that cover and protect a broken heart; the head turned sideways away in a gesture of 'go away I don't trust any human beings anymore, so don't come near me'. For each and every individual there is their own story, their own drama to unfold.

Chapter 6 The impact of prematurity: Sophia

Keep knocking, and the joy inside
will eventually open a window
and look out to see who is there

"The Sunrise Ruby," (Barks, p. 101)

One of my earliest adult patients confronted me with the painful work that needs to be done when early experiences have not gone well. I will only portray the initial parts of the therapy, as they illustrate the importance of those earliest experiences.

My patient, Sophia, was an attractive 36 year-old, who was tall and slim with curly blonde hair. Her blue eyes cast a look that was direct and unnerving. It seemed to hold two contradictory messages. One was as if she was permanently looking for something, and did I know something that would help her find what she wanted. On the other hand, she exuded a sense of foreboding. It was as if she was resigned to yet another failed experience, yet here she was coming to see me.

Sophia presented as a mess of shattered shards, splintered into many fragments and full of chaos. She became distressed immediately she began to speak, stopping to cry often, and she was unable to give a coherent account of what was going on for her. She appeared very lost and confused. Haltingly, she was able to tell me that she had recently broken up from a relationship. Her female partner had found someone else, leaving her devastated. It was painfully obvious that this had caused her to "break down". She felt like a skinned rabbit, porous and defenceless. A psychologist she had been seeing for counselling referred her, because she wanted to do "deep work". A precipitating event was that she had pursued her ex-partner and physically attacked her.

I pieced together her story. Sophia had been born five weeks prematurely and spent those weeks in a humidicrib. Her parents already had two boys aged four years and three years. After going home from hospital Sophia developed pneumonia, was vomiting and not feeding well. Within another five weeks she was back in hospital as a "failure to thrive" baby.

Neither parent had intact families. Sophia's mother's father left his wife to cope with his two daughters, and her father's father died when he was seven. Her father had migrated from Europe to Australia as a young man, where he met Sophia's mother and they married. Some relations (cousins) were living in Australia, but they broke links with Sophia's parents because Sophia's mother held different religious beliefs. Sophia remembered she had night fears up to seven years of age. Her father attended to her, because her mother had "bad legs". On Saturdays, she accompanied her father, who hand-delivered important items to his customers.

At the age of seven, she experienced a radical change when the family shifted house to another suburb and both parents became very involved in their work. Her father acquired a factory and his business grew rapidly. Her mother also became very involved in her own pursuits, which were also successful. From this time, to counter the lonely afternoons, Sophia joined a gang, all boys except her, in which she was the youngest. This gang was involved in petty theft, smoking, throwing rocks at trains or rival gangs and putting rocks on railway tracks. On Friday and Saturday nights they hung around milk bars. From seven onwards, Sophia became available for boys at school for genital inspection, in return for money, which she spent on lollies. It was also at this time that she began to "hang" her dolls from a curtain rod, beating them until the stuffing came out of them.

At twelve, Sophia began an ongoing relationship with the owner of the local lolly shop and heavy petting took place behind the store in his quarters. The shopkeeper was a widower with a daughter younger than Sophia, whom he was bringing up on his own. After three years, Sophia mentioned what was happening to an older girl at school who informed her parents. Sophia was locked up during the summer holidays following this revelation. Her parents never spoke about this incident again.

In high school, Sophia was in a class with students who were struggling with learning difficulties. She left school at sixteen to work in her father's office. At the time she was secretly drinking spirits from a flask (her father was a heavy drinker). While her mother was away on an overseas trip, Sophia threw herself in front of a car outside her father's office and was badly hurt. After weeks in hospital, Sophia spent a further six weeks alone at home recuperating.

Where does one start with such a history? I could only address how lost and confused she was. But when I look back, it was her symptoms that provided the greatest clue to what was going on in her mind. With the help of supervision, I began to wonder about her early experience in relation to her early birth and being placed in a humidicrib. I went to a neo-natal unit through a connection with a colleague and spent a morning there. What I confronted was very distressing; tiny babies with tubes from every orifice and machines that looked menacing, hard and harsh. Such vulnerability alongside life-saving equipment was difficult to process. The nurses did what they could to humanise the conditions for the tiny babies. They rolled nappies or put cushions around them, encouraging mothers to sit with their offspring. I was also able to discuss with an occupational therapist, the kind of treatment Sophia would have experienced. In the storeroom were old mittens that tied at the wrists to prevent the babies from pulling out the intrusive tubes. It was a salutary experience, but immensely valuable.

Much of the early stages of the therapy were spent reflecting to Sophia how lost and confused she seemed to be. She appeared to be communicating to me how no one was there to meet her when she was born and how the humidicrib was her home. At the time she was a newborn, nursing practices were such that nursing the baby was discouraged because of a fear of infection. There was less understanding of the baby's need for physical contact, so Sophia would have felt very alone. I needed to wonder about what it had been like for her. I felt that my mental and emotional preoccupation with her was not just reforming or filling in gaps for her, but was occurring for the first time.

We uncovered her belief that by paying me, I could "fix her up", that there was some way I could magically give her what was needed without any effort on her part. Together we discovered a part of Sophia that was deeply passive. What unfolded was that the life-giving intravenous drip that provided constant nourishment during the early weeks, while physically life-saving, robbed her of the natural rhythm of being in the arms of her mother for feeding, then sleeping, digesting and waking. Her circumstances disrupted her early learning. She did not get the opportunity to transition from having the constant umbilical cord feeding her, to being born and experiencing a natural feeding process of coming and going to her mother's breast. Instead, without her mother, Sophia took control of the feeding in her mind.

She needed warm enclosing arms, or even a blanket around her as she lay exposed in her humidicrib. This perversion of the normal feeding process had disastrous consequences for her development later, as she became the source of all she needed. Like all babies, what Sophia required was an emotional home with another human being. In the therapy, she had to relinquish her ownership of the intravenous drip, to learn about the normal baby-mother relationship, how to partner, then how to separate, followed by a shared reunion.

Sophia clung to her belief in herself as the sole provider to stave off the terror of being so alone, utterly helpless and unable to manage her states of mind. If Sophia had received sensitive, thoughtful care subsequent to her experience of the humidicrib, her sense of disruption could have been greatly reduced. However, she was left to carry these experiences until a much later time, when they could be understood. Only then could she express her grief at not being met.

Hospitals now try to approximate feeding times and no longer leave drips constantly running. The experience of feeling alternatively full or empty helps the baby accept the reality of the separation from the umbilical cord constantly providing all that was needed.

Sophia's experience had impoverished her personality severely. I had to be very patient and adapt my rhythm to her slower one. At times it was painfully slow. When Sophia and I first made contact the sessions, for a number of months, seemed to fall into two parts. At the beginning she would speak about her everyday life at a normal pace, then she would almost lock into a timeless, extremely slow pace where her unconscious thoughts appeared as disconnected thoughts, which did not always make sense.

Just before a holiday break, we had a session that showed Sophia gradually disintegrating, indicating how the session content was often less important in the session than the process that was taking place.

Sophia came in, lay down and spoke quite fluently saying, 'I've been thinking about all the packing up I have had to do preparing for the break. I usually fly, but because I am going by car it seems as if there really is a break.'

I commented on her capacity to find the space between being present with me, and not present.

Sophia then replied, 'Yes, that space seems more scary than the actual holiday. Going on the plane means it all happens so quickly' (at this point Sophia's voice trailed off and had a distant quality) '... there seems to be such a lot of feelings' (then more meaningfully), 'I don't want to be like the woman at the workshop... all the feelings just coming out of her... the feelings got shaken out of her... big changes take place...' (more desperate) 'it's all over the place... it all happens at once.'

I responded by talking about how she experienced being blown into bits and pieces inside when her feelings got too much.

Sophia went on to talk about 'having feelings when everything else was fixed up.' At this point, I didn't know what she was talking about, so I waited, then Sophia said anxiously, 'my hands feel big… there's pressure around them' (becoming a little panicky)… 'I can't see around them, they are getting bigger and bigger.'

I replied, 'How could I do it to you – how could I not see how terrified you are, and know how shattered you feel, but still go away and leave you.'

That response of mine was as far as I could get to in that session, but what subsequently unfolded were Sophia's "psychotic" anxieties before and after weekends or breaks. Her hands swelling began to make sense. Before or after weekends or breaks, her hands would feel as if they were swelling up to the point of exploding; her hands felt enormous and her skin seemed to be stretched tight. At other times, her wrists felt cut off and her hands felt cold and lacking circulation. Sometimes her hands felt as if they were set in concrete. Other symptoms gradually appeared, for instance, a pulse at the side of her head got quicker and quicker and more and more insistent.

When I was at the neo-natal unit, I had seen the mittens that would have been used at the time of Sophia's infancy. These were tied at the wrist and often attached to the sides of the cot to stop the babies from trying to remove the various tubes to which they were attached. Weekends and breaks seemed to Sophia to be literally times when I put her back in the humidicrib and left her with her hands tied to wait until she had human contact again. It was only much later that I realised the words I had been unable to understand at the time, about *having feelings when everything else was fixed up,* actually made sense. The mittens would have been put on after she had a feed and a nappy change and before being left alone to sleep.

Sophia wrote to the hospital where she was born for her records. In the records she was described as a "vigorous" baby, who frequently attempted to free herself from the tubes attached to her body. She was delighted with this description and its inference that she was a vital and lively baby. Her symptoms fell away as she better understood where the underlying feelings came from.

Sophia expressed other symptoms through her dreams. In the very early stages of the therapy, her dreams were not really dreams, but reflected more her state of mind. Her dreams were more like a stream of incoherent thoughts and experiences. As she realised she had a place to bring her dreams to and reflect on them, they became another way to understand her story.

One Monday morning I opened the door to Sophia, who looked at me strangely as if she didn't know me. She went and lay down as usual and began talking about whether her mother was loved, or not, when she was growing up. Sophia went on to discuss how, when she was growing up, she was fascinated by the Nazis and the Ku Klux Klan and had read everything she could on these two subjects.

Gradually Sophia's speech became very slow and she drifted into a semi-conscious state. 'The Ku Klux Klan... they stick things on you... like feathers... they leave marks on you... they wear masks so you can't see their face... the worst thing is it might be someone you know.'

I took this to mean, me, the torturer who had left her all weekend with her hurt feelings of being unloved, as she was once left in intensive care. In intensive care, she encountered life-giving, but tortuous treatment when nurses with masks on, prodded her with the various procedures and took anal temperatures to monitor her condition.

The constant working through of these anxieties demonstrates how central her early experience had been to her failure to develop. Importantly, she began to experience her rage at what had happened to her. Sophia then became the Nazi with dreams of attacking mothers and babies, with shootings and terrorist activities, as she got in touch with her rage at being so abandoned.

Another incident in her life also began to make sense. When Sophia was fifteen years old, she was on a bus sitting alone. At various stops, other people got on the bus, but everyone else was with someone. Out of nowhere, and with enormous force, she smashed the window next to her. She was taken away bleeding, to be psychiatrically assessed. This incident tells us how much she hated her humidicrib, how much she hated the distance it put between her and others and how enraged she felt at life for cheating her of so much. Why should she be so alone and not have a partner like everyone else? Without knowledge of her earlier experiences such an event would remain a psychotic symptom and indicate how disturbed she was. With understanding and connection, her action could be seen as meaningful and connected to her life experience. She was not "mad". As the symptoms fell away, Sophia was able to speak to me about her anger at our separations and the relief when we reunited. Over time she was able to look forward to a break, discuss what she might do while we were apart and return to share what had taken place. All of these were very normal experiences but they had eluded Sophia in the past.

As she began to build up the experience of my presence, she felt more secure. In the growing trust she went deeper into her painful experiences. This reactivated her early fears for her own survival.

This became clear in a weekend dream. 'I took an early flight up the north coast and was up there about 7am in the morning. I suddenly realised I had a session at 8.30 and I got very upset… I wanted to ring but it was too early to ring.' (Sophia at this point was having difficulty breathing but she went on). 'I tried to ring the airlines so that I could get back on the afternoon plane… I looked up the phone book but the letters were all jumbled… I couldn't see properly… I felt like screaming… I tried to ring directory assistance but my fingers wouldn't work.'

These terrified feelings reflect Sophia's early experience, her panic at being disconnected from me and being disconnected inside herself. The breakthrough was that these feelings could be shared, off-loaded and released, so that she did not have to carry that level of anxiety in her system any more.

There were many times when I felt the helplessness, the isolation and the rejection that Sophia must have felt. At times I felt useless to her, burdened with despair, and totally shut out by her. We went through difficult times, but we could begin to integrate the strands of who fed whom, who I was, whose anger it was, and her dependence on our partnership. Finally, she would be able to separate herself from me and realise she could survive on her own.

As her life began to improve she began to express her anger about, and grieve for, the early losses. One session before the Christmas break, she came looking a little dishevelled. This was something that hadn't happened for quite a while. She was nervous and noisily jangling her keys. When Sophia lay down she remained agitated and tense and pulled painfully on the skin of her hands.

In a broken hard voice (again not how she had been for a long while) she said, 'I had a dream last night. There were a couple of people working on a wedding painting in a house. There were soldiers outside going to shoot and they were insisting the people inside stop what they were doing. The soldiers also got the mother of the man inside to help them, because it had to be stopped. When they wouldn't stop they got this supersonic machine that was just like a space gun and it went into the house and made everything go away.'

There was a silence. I didn't speak because Sophia was so agitated, she wasn't in a state to be asked particulars about her dream.

Sophia then added softly, 'It feels just like it did when I was sixteen, at Dad's office.'

I said 'that was when Mum was away and you threw yourself under a car. What will you do these holidays to

124

yourself and to me?'

At this point, Sophia gradually decreased pulling at her flesh and said 'It's awful.'

Then Sophia's hand began digging into her solar plexus, her right hand resting on her stomach, so I asked her what her left hand wanted to do.

At this stage Sophia responded abruptly, saying, 'I am just going to hold on.'

Since more seemed to be happening I stated that it seemed as if she was digging in quite hard, as if she wanted to get something out.

Sophia then replied, 'it makes me think of a fantasy I used to have when I was making love to Janet. I used to want to get in and take out all my reproductive organs and get rid of them.'

She had to destroy the wedding painting representing their partnership; the pain of separating and being alone was so great, 'it had to be stopped'. This dream evokes in me the thought of the mass murders we hear about in the media. Get a gun and shoot everything in sight to eradicate the pain. The pain was so great for Sophia when her mother was away that she preferred walking in front of a car. Anything was better than experiencing the pain.

In our time together many issues arose that needed resolution. However, the centrality of Sophia's early experiences became clear when we began to work towards the final phase of the therapy and contemplate finishing. The earlier themes re-emerged together with an intense desire for a relationship with me, where she would be my daughter and we could be locked into a mutually loving gaze with each other. A remnant of Sophia seemed to be locked in a time warp, where she was forever seeking a mother to welcome her with a loving gaze, and make her life blissful forever. If only she had had those loving eyes of her mother to welcome her, or could capture it with me, all would be well and life would not be a struggle. Bit by bit, we dismantled the fantasy of living life constantly in this blissful state. There was a growing recognition of our work together and Sophia commented, 'It has at times been a long weary haul but it has been worthwhile.'

Sophia was very disappointed in me as she recognised that life was never going to be one long loving gaze, no matter how much she longed for it. I could never erase her original wound and its reality would remain. However, I had welcomed her, thought about her, felt with her and helped her to struggle with her rage at what happened. She had borne an enormous grudge about her beginnings and the lack of subsequent help to deal with her trauma. Sophia slowly accepted that all newborns experience a severing at birth, no matter what their family circumstances were.

Sophia taught me a great deal; that I needed to include the early non-verbal history if I was to get a full picture. The precipitating event for therapy was Sophia's recent break-up from her partner, so she came to me as a patient who was already breaking down. Her break-up had exposed her usual way of dealing with things. In this instance, our task in therapy was to put everything together again in a new way. For many patients it is the other way around, spending the time to excavate and chip away at the defences solidly built over the years to stop anything getting out.

Looking back, I can see that while I acknowledged the loneliness and isolation of the baby, if I had gone more quickly to this core issue, her therapy may have been shorter. I would have met her more directly and established the bond between us more quickly if I had sat with the lonely baby in the humidicrib. At the same time, I would have more actively built the notion of being partnered and held. Her underlying loneliness was a core issue. It was only through my exposure to the infant mental health work that I came to understand the depth of the loneliness and terror for the baby when she is unable to survive without someone else. I would also have contextualised her experience. The self-blame that a baby takes on for the failure of the relationship with the parent is deeply entrenched. It must be her fault.

This is something that therapists need to address and make right. I would now share more of what I know, so that Sophia could better understand her parents' difficulties, what had happened to her as a result of her experiences, and the processes involved in getting better. This leaves the patient in a solid position as they face the rest of their lives armed with a better understanding of how things work internally and externally.

Chapter 7 Developmental gaps: Kate

We listen to words
so we can silently
reach into the other

"A Dumb Experiment," (Barks, p. 328)

Working with children is different from working with adults. There is often an intense honesty in the room and if you don't know what you are doing, it is obvious. Once in the session there is not a lot of time to think and feel as a great deal happens. The transference feelings are very intense and overwhelming at times. A child's mood can change very rapidly and the immediacy of the moment is paramount. Outside support for the therapist, through supervision or peer discussion assists in enduring the ups and downs of the therapeutic process. Peter Blake (2008) has written a comprehensive and incisive book for those who wish to further explore the area of child and adolescent psychotherapy.

All of the statements above applied to therapy with a six-year-old girl brought to see me by her parents. When I spoke to them they described her as difficult. Her mother felt that Kate was very bossy, and overly jealous of her sister. She reported that Kate smeared her pants as a result of withholding her faeces, and at other times held on to her urine. Kate's mother experienced her as deliberately uncooperative. Medical checks had cleared Kate of any organic problems. Learning difficulties were beginning to emerge at school. Later, I learnt of her dermatitis/eczema problems. Kate was her parent's eldest daughter and she had a sister two and a half years younger. The parents were both professionals and had very demanding jobs. The mother was a partner in a firm and the father worked long hours, including time away from home. A nanny had cared for both girls since the birth of the second child and provided a consistent presence. Prior to that there had been several carers during her first twenty months.

Kate's mother dominated the first interview with the parents and wept continuously as she discussed her difficulties with Kate. Her father remained silent. Kate's mother felt Kate was obstructive. She complained that her six-year-old should know when she was supposed to take her medicine but refused to do so and would forget. The new baby was experienced as more accommodating and not as difficult. It was as if Kate was expected to be grown up and help her mother rather than be mothered. The mother's crying indicated that she had encountered early losses, but she was unwilling to discuss her family of origin.

It was important that Mum and Dad had their own support with a colleague at the clinic, so that Kate was not isolated as the "problem". They needed a place to discuss parenting issues at the clinic on a fortnightly basis to help find different ways to relate to Kate. Kate's parents were keen for her to receive therapy. It was agreed that I would have four assessment sessions with Kate, while they decided whether they could find the time to attend the clinic.

Kate had sharp features. Her face and body were angular and square. Her voice was direct, clear and clipped. Her hair was straight and cut in a short bob with a fringe. During the first session she seemed curious, responding to feedback I gave her, and she indicated she wanted to come to therapy. I gave Kate a box with coloured pencils, Textas, paper, scissors and sticky tape for her to use.

Shortly before the second assessment session was due to begin, I went to the waiting room to get Kate. She began speaking to me the moment she saw me and continued to talk all the way down the corridor to the playroom. Kate insisted that I had lost a tree she had drawn the previous week and that, because I had lost it, everything would be "spoilt".

As we entered the room and inspected her box, I said to Kate that she assumed I had forgotten all about her and had not looked after her things while she had been away. We found her tree drawing, but she didn't draw breath. Immediately she began checking things out and acted like a matron coming to inspect the clinic and myself, to see if we made the grade. Kate was highly critical. She criticised the blackboard as being old, the cup holding the chalks for having a hole in the bottom, and wondered about the pencils being good enough. These comments seemed to be her way of dealing with her anxiety and the expectation that I would *not* be good enough, to contain her and deal with her feelings. Clearly, she felt that authority figures had not done their job well enough with her and had not given her the time and attention she required. She now wanted to ascertain if I would pass muster.

At her third session, Kate entered the room saying, 'I'm going to talk to you about this today,' and she showed me a chart that had been prepared by her mother as a reward system for using the toilet. Kate clearly felt that she had to take control, that this was expected of her and that she had to do everything by herself, rather than receive assistance within a supportive partnership. Kate also tried to manage holding on to four pieces of chalk, the duster and a map she had prepared, all while drawing on the blackboard. You could feel her sense of being overwhelmed by the task she set for herself, but also her doggedness in feeling that she had to just get on and do it.

Feelings of rivalry with her sister emerged with comments like, 'She has everything', and when Kate saw her tree, she noted, 'I suppose Jane couldn't have taken it, she hasn't been here.' Kate expressed pleasure that she had me all to herself. A later comment was 'People have been coming in and stealing and burglaring things.' Kate clearly felt that she had missed out on something that others either had, or that something had been taken away from her, leaving her suspicious and watchful.

In the final assessment session, a sense of everything falling apart dominated our session together. Neither of us knew whether her parents would agree to continue therapy. Her tip truck kept dropping the toys, enabling me to say, 'everything is falling out with nowhere to go, if you can't come anymore.'

Her parents did agree to sessions with a colleague to be held in the evenings. They also agreed that I would see Kate three times a week at the clinic. Kate's mother would bring her the first couple of times, then the nanny would take over, because of the parents' work commitments.

Unfortunately, after a few sessions with the parents, my colleague moved interstate. No one else at the clinic was able to take them on so they began seeing me. A lot of early sessions with Kate centred on food, which was an obsession for her. When I asked about mealtimes, the parents said that in the evenings the nanny would feed the children and eat with them. The parents would return later and sometimes see the children before bedtime. On the weekend, they had more time and they generally got to eat with each other on Sundays. After a few discussions with the parents, they decided to increase the number of nights they had a meal with the children. They started taking family outings, like going to the zoo, on weekends.

Kate was a child who faced an enormous change to her life when her sister was born. In the early months after her sister's birth, primitive anxieties were activated that had not been worked through, as a newborn, because she did not have a consistent figure.

My experience with Kate indicated that the shock of the new sibling re-opened the old wounds of her vulnerability. How could she survive, not only the massive new intrusion and change in her life, but most importantly, how could she deal with re-activated, old unhealed wounds from the early period after her birth?

It was obvious from the start of the therapy that Kate was looking for a container for her undigested early feelings.

At our next session, Kate undressed a few minutes into the session to expose severe eczema covering not only her joints but her trunk as well. While Kate worked hard to prevent her nameless dreads and anxieties from surfacing, her skin worked overtime. Our skin can weep, itch and rage for us and Kate's skin did.

After nearly five months of work, and in the lead up to the Christmas holidays, Kate was able to speak about her vulnerable state to me when she drew a snail, commenting to me that 'the soft parts are inside'. This enabled me to comment that 'the shell is the one who says everything will be all right, but the soft scared part is inside', and Kate nodded.

More often Kate was intent on protecting her vulnerability, letting me know very early in our sessions that if she knocked herself, 'I don't cry, even if it hurts.'

She frequently hid behind my chair or lay curled up in a ball underneath the chair. This was a place she often used at the beginning of the session and became a place of refuge whenever things became intense or difficult. It felt as though Kate was returning to the womb – anything NOT to feel separate, alone or exposed.

Movement was another protective mechanism Kate used. To counter her nameless dread, Kate incessantly crawled around the edges of things. To quote from an early session:

> Kate began balancing around the edge of the sandpit
> (around the plastic rim) then jumped off. Next she
> went over to the windowsill and began walking
> along the edge of it (in a second storey room) became
> unbalanced and jumped off, got back up and walked
> along the edge again. A large truck was outside
> in the lane and the vibrations made an impact on
> the windows next to her. Kate was thrown and
> confused and clearly could not understand where the
> vibrations were coming from.

Gradually, we were able to make sense of these events.

In a session soon after, Kate went around the room on top of the furniture, starting with the windowsill, and avoided touching the floor at any stage. I commented on how hard she worked not to fall and be the baby who feels dropped. At this point Kate farted and got under the chair. I said, 'there are some feelings wanting to come out', and she said 'yes, but I want to hold it in.' Kate always retreated to behind or under the chair whenever there were farts, or any indication of movement in her bowel. Any movement of the bowel seemed to indicate a movement away, a separating and hence had to be controlled.

In time, Kate's movement could be put into words. A few months later, at the end of a session, when I had announced it was time to finish, Kate began to help pack up the toys but almost immediately went over to a chair and began jumping up and down. I talked to her about how her constant activity kept her from feeling scared.

Kate's reply was, 'I'm glad it's Friday because I get a cake.' (A cake after Friday's session was a practice introduced by the nanny).

I then said, 'you use the cake to fill yourself up so you won't be empty without me.'

Kate looked at me momentarily, looked sad, and said 'yes'.

The issue of rivalry, or threat from others, was a big issue for Kate. My reflections were that Kate had not had enough holding and time with a consistent carer after her birth and missed out on something important. Where the early vulnerability is not held, the baby feels exposed to creatures that threaten him or her. The arrival of a new sibling may arouse fears of attacking creatures. Dragons, gorillas, witches, ghosts and aliens populated Kate's world. In this primitive frame of mind other children or siblings are not children; they are monsters. They have such power in children's early minds that they feel threatened with death. In the primitive mind, these others take away from them what is needed to survive and leave them prey to death. Unless such anxieties are worked through, the child will always feel at risk, and it is imperative we handle these elemental terrors in the transference. Kate noticed every little piece of cotton, or fluff, or the smallest stone or a tissue in the garbage bin that identified that some predator had been in the room and was a threat to her existence.

Her sister was seen as all-powerful: 'Jane has everything, she always takes everything', 'she always has the biggest piece', 'she is always first', 'I am thin, she is round.'

After speaking to me about the other boys and girls I see, Kate asked whether I had children of my own. I commented that she was wondering whether I knew anything about looking after children. The question itself deflated her, as I noted how it made her feel. Kate then quite poignantly sang a song to me:

> Will there be a spring
> When we both can sing
> Will there be a time
> When we can say
> I love you

What Kate seemed to be asking was would there ever be a time without threatening rivals, when she could find her loving feelings and not the monsters inside, which made her suspicious and fearful for her survival and her well-being. Anything more than one, e. g. two drawings, immediately set up the cut-throat competition of who or what is first, who or what is best, in other words, who will survive in a world that is seen as having limited resources, and was not all-providing. While the more usual notion of rivalry, and who is best, played a part in my understanding of Kate, I thought it was important to hold on to and feel the more primitive mechanisms operating in her.

When a mother does not understand, empathise with and soothe the baby, it leaves the baby's body with an overload of tension that is not relieved. This overflow feels uncomfortable and may feel hard. This hardness is held in the muscles or skeletal system and operates as a protective shell. We can experience this "not me" as threatening, and it becomes the place that encapsulates the rage that is the accumulation of "not-me". This is the un-dealt with anger at not having what the baby needs or wants.

In the time leading up to her parent's departure on an overseas holiday, Kate and I had a first glimpse of some of that hardness now that she had a safe place for it to be let out. At the beginning of the session, Kate went behind the chair, then gradually crawled out and curled into a ball on the floor.

I said, 'baby-Kate is needing a hug.'

Kate then began moving around the room on the furniture while I said 'you feel you mustn't stop because you might feel your feelings inside.' Next, Kate went to the sandpit and lay quietly. She very gently poured sand on herself as I commented, 'you need peace and quiet and a nice cuddle, not all that rushing and moving around.' Kate then moved over to the other chair and lay like a baby, and I said, 'you need a mummy to look after you – but I make you go because it is Friday, and Mum and Dad are going away.'

On the floor was a tiny piece of red chalk and with this Kate went and made a mark on the wall, then looked at me anxiously. After making another mark she went and got the orange chalk saying 'this is what I am going to do,' and using the blackboard provided wrote 'I HATE YOU! DUMB HEAD, STUPID, FUCK.' Then she said, 'you won't like this one,' and wrote 'I DON'T KNOW YOU'. Finally, albeit tentatively, Kate was beginning to poo into the mental nappy I provided.

Months later she shouted 'I HATE YOU' – the day after this was the only time Kate was anxious about coming to the next session.

Once the hardness began to soften and let go, Kate started an extended period of attacking me. I was spat on, kicked, hit, punched (particularly aimed at my stomach and breasts) and she frequently threw sand at me. All of these attacks were aimed at me, because I would not stay "fused" with her. Kate seemed to feel that all would be peaceful if I colluded with her and let her go back inside. She sang another song about her wish to build "a world of our own" that we wouldn't have to share. If we did that, we would find "peace of mind" far away in that special world.

The separation from me threatened to make her disintegrate and she raged at how I exposed her to her feeling self. Vulnerable children are also preoccupied with having an extra bit to their bodies. This extra bit is usually a hard object like a truck or a buckle. I wondered if Kate's extra bit had been her hard poo. Perhaps it functioned in lieu of the firm upright inner core that she had not as yet developed, so she could not relinquish her poo control. Gradually, smearing her pants no longer occurred and 'going poo' began to take place every couple of days.

In a later session, Kate said, 'I did a poo last night – a soft one.' She looked very directly at me and said, 'I was so proud,' then added, 'I think coming to the clinic and seeing you is helping me.'

Of course the "poo" meant many different things over the period of time we were together. Very early, the poo was felt to hurt, to be "Spike" – "Spikey" being the nickname she made up for her sister. Gradually, it seemed to become the food that she would keep inside her for when she needed it. The poo also acted as a controlling mechanism – Kate couldn't stop me coming and going but she could stop the poo. Finally, it seemed to become something that if expelled, would leave a hole and make her feel empty. In other words, she would feel the separation between her and me. Perhaps her poo had been her last remaining barrier between her and a very floppy, totally helpless, dependent baby self, who felt unable to survive independently.

There was some evidence of this life and death meaning to her poo in a session well into the therapy, when Kate walked calmly down the corridor with me carrying a dinosaur.

Once inside the room, Kate walked over to the chair, sat down and said, 'do you know what'? I waited and Kate said, 'this is my dinosaur; this is Julie.' She then proceeded to speak for Julie as if she was a baby saying, 'who is this? Not Mrs. Gillies (her teacher) this is Mrs Rose, Julie.'

I commented that Julie was her mother's name. Her mother at the time was very distressed by her own recent separation from Kate's father.

Kate then sang a jingle 'open wide, suicide' and laughed. She repeated the jingle more fully, 'open wide, come inside – it's suicide.' I felt quite thrown but asked, 'what does suicide mean', and Kate replied 'going poo,' then I said, 'going poo is like killing yourself' (or alternatively she gets killed when she goes poo). After that Kate went and put her hand out the window, which was open enough to hang the dinosaur out and dangled it precariously. I felt quite distressed but managed to say that if Julie was "suiciding" she must feel a very frightened little girl inside – that she must feel afraid of falling or being dropped.

Kate put Julie on the table and hugged the dinosaur like a baby and I noted, 'you're being a mother to Julie when you are really a little girl.' Kate put some sand in a cup but it spilt so I said, 'you need a mummy to hold you together.'

With her back to me Kate said, 'can I tell you something? Mum said that if Dad doesn't come back by July we are going to live in Perth.'

I commented, 'now I can see why you were so frightened and worried.'

Almost instantly Kate asked, with a complete change of mood, 'Mama can I play with my dinosaur?' Then she added, 'can I build a house'? She began setting things up. At last we had a child in the room, who had communicated her worries and was able to get some relief. We can also conjecture that such a session revived long ago dinosaur memories of a Mum, who perhaps couldn't manage Kate's terrified feelings and was full of her own anxieties.

This interaction demonstrated the issue of Kate coming to grips with reality. Initially, the mother is required to provide a protective barrier between the baby and the world and then gradually introduce her infant to the world. If the baby becomes aware of too much too soon, that awareness may become unbearable. A premature and unprotected sense of two-ness can be too much. To tolerate this state, babies use various protective measures to deaden the awareness and avoid suffering. To act in such a way is to be out of touch with reality. They can shut off the outside world or grossly distort it and psychological integrations do not take place.

Kate, in most instances, turned the world upside down. At various times we entered her inverted universe to discover that she saw herself as an orphan. Throughout our early phase together, she believed that children could look after themselves. Initially none of the baby animals on the farm (in her sand play) had parents and later, when she built a house for herself, she was without parents. With time Kate became a child on the farm with parents on another planet and from there we were able to progress. Alternatively, Kate was the grown up and was the one doing the looking after. With time a mother/me appeared and she guarded our twosome jealously, but no dad was involved. Based on what she said to me, it seemed that Kate thought girls could make girl babies and that men were only needed to make boy babies. Additionally, little girls could have babies – she was adamant she had given birth to her doll. Her doll was like her; she thought she lived inside her mother Kate all the time. Little and big were consistently annihilated, as were differences between boys and girls, so that boys (or men) were unnecessary for conception. However, a dad was finally acknowledged and we were on the way towards an integration of a good working couple inside her and all the strengths that this entails. This had no doubt contributed to her capacity to do a soft poo.

Our working couple formed. In the outside world mum and dad also got back together. In this context, as Kate moved into the world as it really was, she began to control less and let go more. This allowed her to let things in. In conjunction with this, Kate's learning difficulties ceased to be a problem and Kate became a member of the top group in a high achieving school. The world was no longer a threatening and overwhelming place. Kate's spontaneity began to show. For someone who constantly hid under the chair and frequently had her back or bottom turned in my direction, she engagingly looked very directly at me more and more of the time. Quite a delightful sense of humour surfaced, and it was a real pleasure to see her feel free of her burdens and anxieties. For a child who had initially appeared sharp-edged and plain, she became softer, more open and attractive. Her mischievous streak made her even more endearing. For her last session, Kate wore a special dress saying, 'It is a special occasion.' She looked very pretty and very pleased with herself.

Kate's mother also softened and began to be more interested and engaged with Kate. After the period of the temporary separation, Kate's mother came on her own to our parenting sessions and continued to do so when her husband returned. During the earlier sessions she would look at me with a puzzled expression on her face as I discussed her child. In time she was able to see what I saw in Kate. She too could begin to express interest and joy in her personality and activities.

What Kate taught me, I was to re-learn many times over the years that followed with other patients. I experienced the return of her early developmental process as a gradual unfolding of her emotional and psychological development, in the same wonderful way that babies flow from limited vision to holding eye contact, from lying to sitting up. And on it flows, from fluids to solids, gradually crawling and then walking. This is the process of slowly building the idea of someone "being there" for them, and entering into a relationship with them that includes the storms and joys of intimacy, and finally the blossoming of a self that has an innate energy. It has its own trajectory, which will reveal itself if we provide the conditions for this unfolding.

Kate told the story of her unfolding in a graphic way. In the early stages, at the end of a session, she would roll on to her side in the foetal position and I would have to carry her out of the therapy room, down the corridor to her nanny (or occasionally her mother) and pass her over as a floppy baby, who couldn't walk or talk. Once in her nanny's arms, she would return to her six-year-old self. As the therapy progressed, she actually crawled on her hands and knees out of the room and down the corridor. Despite her own inner resistances Kate navigated the territory of her early developmental needs, catching up on what had not happened at an earlier time in her life.

Working with Kate also confronted me with the fact that young children can experience their own despair about life and have their own version of whether life is worth living or not. To see and feel such painful states in young children, is a very difficult experience. Yet we need to face the reality that the experience is very much part of some children's lives and share that pain with them. We need to let them know that another human being now understands what they had to go through.

Chapter 8 Emerging vulnerability: Ben

Quietness is the surest sign
that you've died
your old life was a frantic running
from silence

"Quietness," (Barks, p. 22)

Ben was a tall, good-looking, dark-haired, young man in his early thirties. He had a slight swagger in his gait, and his chest held high, exuding confidence. It was quite evident, however, that he was very anxious, and he was evasive with me throughout the session. He was the firstborn son of a religious pastor and an upper class European mother. His father, originally from central Europe, worked in Africa. When Ben was two his parents had his sister, at four another sister, then a brother when he was nine.

The issue of class pervaded the session and he questioned whether Australia was a sufficiently "cultivated" society in which to stay and make a home. Ben had lived in Europe and Africa and was contemplating going to another country, where he had never been before, if therapy didn't work out. Before that, he would climb the highest mountain he had ever tackled, as his next project. On the other hand, he did want to pursue therapy. Although he felt he had achieved all that he had set out to achieve, that is, to be rich and successful, he felt empty and did not want to wake up one day, at forty years of age, and find that life had passed him by. His father had been a teacher. This had been a bitter disappointment to his mother, but, in Ben's words, 'at least what my father did was meaningful to him.' There was, however, little closeness between him and his father, whom he remembered as speaking only in biblical terminology.

Ben's current employment required him to trouble-shoot in multi-national companies at any time, which meant a great deal of travelling. I commented that we would need to discuss quite a few issues before contemplating therapy and that we would have to take our time to do this properly, before we thought of proceeding. If he could not come consistently and reliably, we did not have the conditions for therapy.

Ben picked up the issue of "taking time" in the next few sessions, when I was given a clearer picture of his life – one of "firsts" and "precociousness". Taking time was something Ben did not seem to know about. He was born to doting parents and his mother lived her life around him. He felt treated like a "toy" when he was young and made the centre of attention. Servants were also on hand, so he seemingly wanted for nothing. Grandparents were also part of his life. Feeding, however, was done according to a rigid four-hourly regime. When his sister was born Ben spent more and more time with his grandparents at their home. Ben said:

> I loved to go every day to their place – I especially
> loved my grandfather. I was very close to him, he
> was retired, and we went everywhere together. He
> died when I was about five years old, when I was
> in my first class at school. It was really terrible. I
> thought then, never again, I'm not going to feel like
> that again. There have been other deaths; my sister
> was raped and murdered, on a beach holiday with
> the family. My family fell apart. I didn't cry; I just
> kept going. Others have died, my friends in the army,
> things that no one should have to know about, but I
> have never felt anything.

Ben hated boarding school because teachers and older students brutalised the children there. That his mother had agreed with his father to allow him to go was a deep grievance. He had always sided with his mother against his father, but she had finally agreed to him going away. Once there, he injured both knees in an unsuccessful attempt to force his parents to let him return home. Later, during military service, he struck discipline for the first time and hated it. Due to his abilities, he quickly moved up the ranks and was put in charge of supplies. Once there, he started appropriating goods for higher officers in return for an easier life.

After the army, Ben went to study at university in a field of work of which his mother approved. When he finished he became a researcher in a company and set out to make himself indispensable. When he had achieved this, he demanded a top job at a top salary, or he would leave. The firm agreed to his demand. Later, he left to set up his own business that was very successful. After a couple of years he sold the business and took on consultancy work and had to travel all over the world. The original reason for coming to Australia was to follow a former girlfriend he had met at university. This was a common experience: he could get whomever he wished to fall in love with him, but it was difficult for him to hold on to relationships since he would "take over" and was "too much" for his partners. At the time, he lived in a group house with two others who frequently left it to Ben to pay their rent, as they were not always employed. To come to therapy, Ben had to leave his job, which took him away constantly.

Essentially, Ben had no outer, but more importantly no inner, home, apart from the good memories of his grandfather. He had not acquired a capacity to work gradually and build up skills, having always managed to propel himself quickly and precociously into a top position. Coupled with this was little capacity for true reflection on the situation he was in, even though his mind ticked over constantly looking to manipulate events. To date, he had lived out his mother's idea of how his life should be, so he had little idea of who he was and what his thoughts and feelings were. Therapy's role was somehow to transform a body of sensation into a reflective, feeling person, with his own integrity.

Ben largely lived in an "auto-sensuous" state, where constant sensations assailed him, often accompanied by some kind of physical pain e.g. cramp, sharp shooting pains, itchy eyes, irritated skin and a tight jaw. The first eighteen months of the therapy were largely a dialogue between his body (a mass of seemingly disjointed sensations), his embryonic mind and myself, trying to piece together and wonder about what was going on. This does not mean that he was inarticulate. In fact, he was highly educated and verbal – his mind, however, seemed splintered. While he sought at times to control the therapy, so as to prevent an effective dialogue between his body and myself taking place, he also cooperated in the search for something meaningful to come from our explorations together. It was, however, his sensations that required understanding, and digestion, so as to establish the basis of an inner life and an emerging sense of self; his becoming "some-body".

In normal development, the mother's mind acts as a kind of womb for the newborn. At birth and in the early weeks and months, the mother is in a heightened state of sensitivity to her baby and within her attention the baby continues to experience itself as part of mother. Both mother and baby feel that, without the other, something is missing. In this way they maintain the illusion of the primal physical union. It is inside this protective, mental womb that psychological integrations begin. The adult Ben, however, still remained locked inside this illusion. The fantasy was that he was a combined figure with his mother "forced back inside" by experiences too difficult to bear.

This illusory state precedes a notion of bodily separateness. In this framework, there is a sense of oneness with the mother, and the baby has little internal psychic life. At this early point, the baby experiences an overflow of feeling, ranging from overexcitement to outrage. In normal circumstances, the mother can contain the feelings of excitement/pleasure/ecstasy and the baby is not overwhelmed. If not "held" psychologically, the baby will feel unbearable body tension if there are hunger pains, anxiety or being unwrapped. The baby will seek to protect itself in various ways to avoid suffering these intense feelings.

The enormous consequence of the baby needing to take such protective actions, is that he or she is out of touch with reality. The early omnipotent phase isn't gradually worked through and the baby retains the illusion that its movements, crying, urges, are the sole cause of what occurs. For many months Ben rang the buzzer on my side gate, as if by pressing it he made me appear; that he conjured me up. This implied there was a magical world where things appeared and disappeared at will. Paradoxically, it is the mother who reliably meets the baby's demands, who enables the baby to gradually find a sufficiently secure place in which to begin to realise this is not so.

If the mother cannot respond emotionally to the baby's highly sensitive states, there can be a mental and emotional shattering. As discussed earlier in relation to Kate, the baby's experience coalesces and solidifies the world into "soft" and "hard" experiences that cannot be integrated. Something hard then surrounds the softer parts of the personality. In the case of Ben, this took the form of a muscular and mental armour that protected the excessively tender feelings he was so afraid to experience. Because of this armour, Ben was unable to be nurtured – nothing could go in, or out. Development and growth was not possible. The only way forward was to re-experience the original psychological catastrophe. At some early point in his life, he was thrust into feeling his separateness before he was ready. The result is a precocious "as if", or a "false" self – the precociousness that he continued to repeat again and again.

Ben presented as someone whose psychological catastrophe had left him encapsulated in the illusion of having it all – of still being inside his mother, so therefore not in need of outside help. What then had gone wrong? Perhaps his mother was unable to bear his overwhelming early states, so she left him to feel alone and adrift, with dangerous feelings that were unbearable to him and to anyone else. He may have been the recipient of the worst of both worlds: a permissive, stimulating mother who failed to deal with her over-stimulation and fusion with her child, but was strict and rigid in her feeding regime.

Working with Ben meant I needed to enter Ben's world, to understand it from his perspective, but then to return to use my mind and feelings to find the context in which he was operating. I needed to reflect on his beginnings, his later experiences around the loss of his grandfather and his family falling apart after the death of his sister. These events cast him adrift.

In the early months of therapy, a very energised Ben would bound up the steps into my room, chest extended, dressed in a track suit top, shorts or some sporty outfit. He would have a big grin on his face as if to say, ' I'm here; you've probably spent all day waiting for me.' An enormous amount of energy went into this arrival, which also signified an enthusiasm for life. I felt as if it left little room or space for me. Because he filled the psychic space in the room, I had to make an effort not to let his energy overwhelm me and just succumb to his world. Ben had reversed the situation: he felt he gave to me, rather than needing something *from* me, namely my help to develop an inner life for himself. During this time the sessions seemed very short, and we had hardly started before it was time to finish. What we did together seemed like a drop in the ocean.

I worked hard to make our early period a cooperative one, when we could begin to explore the way in which his mind worked. It seemed necessary for quite a while, to talk with him about how he went about things, as his feelings were essentially remote. I needed to spend time thinking and talking about the structure of his therapy as being a firm "container" where he might begin to bring his feelings. In a session around this time, Ben entered the room, lay down on the couch, commented on the weather, then closed his eyes. He looked tense; his forehead was quite creased and he said:

'I suppose I want to ask a more intellectual question. I've been reading this book about therapy, and it was putting forward Jung's ideas and saying that it is quite common in people who have been successful to stop and question what it has done to them, like a spiritual malaise, and I was wondering whether this applied to me.'

I said: 'Are you saying to me that you don't know who you are, that you don't know your personal meaning?'

'Well, I've decided to really give it a go here, make this number one, to prioritise my life, so I've decided to start meditating. I'm also going to get into yoga. I already do physical exercise, and also to get into good eating. I've been successful and gotten what I've wanted from business by taking action, so I should be able to do this.'

'You seem afraid that unless you take action yourself, nothing will happen here, that there isn't another way to do things, that it can't be a cooperative venture here.'

'Nothing can happen if you don't take any action.' He then paused and spoke tentatively: 'I don't know what will happen here.'

'You seem to think that the only way is a full frontal attack on all levels; not that yes, you don't know, but that's OK, we can take it from there.'

At this point Ben visibly relaxed. 'My father was someone who never did anything; he avoided making decisions. I promised myself I would never be like that; I would take action. On the other hand, my father was very opinionated and he knew everything: I sided with my mother against him.'

'When did you decide to take action?'

'I was quite young, and then my grandfather died – that was, like, that was the end. What could I do, I was only little.'

'You get very frightened when you don't know what is going on, then you take action to deal with the problem, it's too frightening to stay with it and see what happens.' Something had obviously died in him when his grandfather died. He had lost good support, and with that his feelings, which he had closed down.

In addition to my coming to understand the way Ben approached things, we began to get tentative access to his feelings via his body. At this point in the therapy, Ben's body was the repository of his feelings. It was only in later sessions that Ben felt the possibility of a place or space in his mind for his feelings.

'I know when I have thoughts,' he said, 'and I know when my body hurts, but I'm just beginning to get the idea of something else.'

In the early sessions our only guide was his body. Ben came into a Thursday session (the end of his week) speaking as he lay down.

'I noticed your ferns on the front veranda, one of them looks very yellow and I was wondering whether you had it inside and now it's sick, or what. I was going to buy a fern today for inside.'

'You're worried that my fern, like you, might die under my care,' he smiled, 'because I might leave it too exposed.'

'I was just wondering what to do, but I have been wondering whether things are just all in our head or not. Philosophers are always trying to deal with the question is it possible just to contact our inner being and be complete, like we are already complete, and it is just that we don't think we are and it is just the way we think about it.'

'You want to be complete, then you can bypass feeling incomplete, maybe this is relevant because today is Thursday.'

'Why does it have to be that pleasure comes out of pain?' Ben said in an accusatory tone, then added, still in his philosophical, discursive voice, 'we all try and avoid the big problems, like we'll die; we all try and avoid our fear of death.'

I took the plunge and said, 'you're afraid that I might die, or you might die in the next three days before Monday, your fear of death is here and now.' I think he was also communicating the realisation that things do not go on forever.

At that moment, Ben took a very deep breath. 'I don't really feel that.'

I pointed out that he had filled himself up with a lot of air when I said that, but that since then he had stopped breathing.

'I have trouble with my breathing,' he said.

I responded, 'you fill yourself up with air so you won't feel empty and collapsed'.

'I've been trying this technique of expelling air.'

'So it is either held in your chest, or forced out, not a natural rhythm of in and out.'

'Yes, my breathing is shallow.'

'No deep gut breathing, no gut responses'.

Ben was thoughtful, then countered, 'but if I don't do something, nothing might ever happen.'

I then came back to our transference issue by saying, 'you are concerned I won't come and reconnect with you on Monday. I'll forget or just not come.'

'That reminds me that yesterday when I took a deep breath it gave me a pain in the neck.'

'It is painful for you to be in the dependent position of waiting and needing, and relying on me to come.'

To follow the philosophical talk would have meant abandoning him. I felt I needed to actively pursue Ben by connecting him to his body and thereby connecting him to his feelings.

On the other side of the coin, Ben subjected me to a barrage of his philosophy, on different occasions, on how the world should be run. 'Business should be able to do whatever it wished with no interference from the government.' 'Who were they to establish laws and regulations? If they did, the bastards should be got back.' 'Why should takeovers of whatever kind be limited by regulations? Who were these politicians who could tell you what to do and what not to do?' While I felt I was living inside the *Bonfire of the Vanities* by Tom Wolfe, and his sense of entitlement was on show, there were occasional cracks.

At this point Ben experienced strong feelings about authority and authority figures. These feelings unearthed anti-authority sentiments that were contrary to his normal belief system.

Ben dreamt that his endorphins were tricking him into believing that he owned a lot of property but in fact he didn't. Meanwhile his body spoke for the unspeakable feelings and fears more and more, with attacks of breathlessness, asthma, stomach pains, hernia and cramps often at weekends, holidays and ends of sessions. These pains and tensions demonstrated that he had nowhere else to put his infantile states of mind or his baby self, who was needy, anxious, fearful and outraged. The world seemed to be totally divided into "softs" and "hards". To be soft was to be "sucked in", "subsumed", "taken over'", or "lost forever". His only choice was to be hard and unyielding, and to protect or possess everything himself. I had the delicate task of supplying the active thinking container for his thoughts and feelings without taking him over.

Ben had a dream that aptly described his state at this point in the therapy. He recognised that there was something outside him, but the attitude that he should be able to possess it still consumed him. There was also the embryonic idea of the presence of a baby. In the dream, Ben went into a shop with a woman his own age and he asked for a special pie. This pie is "sweet and sour." The woman serving said, 'No, you can't have it. It is too hot. It is not for sale.' Thwarted and angry, Ben decided to wait until that shop assistant went out the back so he could try the other one. The second assistant also refused saying, 'It is not for sale.' Ben was furious and began to plot how he could destroy the business by blowing it up. At this moment, he saw another woman in the shop with a baby. If he rushed out of the shop he would fall on the baby. that, in his rush to charge out of the shop, he was about to fall on. Ben registered the concern on the mother's face for the baby and the fact that he might hurt it.

In this dream, we can see he wants to have what the mother has and realises that in destroying the provider/ shop he also destroys his own source of life and that he may be damaging something valuable. He is perhaps entering a phase of realising that he can't possess the source of comfort for himself and in attempting to do so, potentially destroys the mother-baby partnership. He is learning that relationships are "sweet" and "sour". They are good to have, but come with having to bear being apart from one another, and enduring that state before being reunited.

This tentative awareness lay alongside Ben's most primitive level that still functioned as the possessor of his mother's body to avoid the pain of separateness. He was still conjoined with her and attached to her body, without which he couldn't live. At the very least, he desperately needed unlimited access. In this state no separation existed at all. He had all that he needed.

When we were able to piece this fantasy together, I fed it back to him and it shocked him. Ben touched his face as if a blast of cold air had just hit him. He was quite overwhelmed. I was anxious that I had perhaps fed back to him what he was saying too quickly. The next day he came back to tell me that after leaving the session he had become so furious that he drove up the street and smashed his car into a parked car. This was accompanied by a feeling that he could have smashed the other guy's head into the ground. (He did take responsibility and left his details on the car). While he was telling me this, Ben began to get strong sensations of hot and cold throughout his body (the love and hate, the hot and cold "me" who comes and goes, who separates, rather than remains conjoined with him) and he felt that the circulation in his body wasn't working. His feet felt as if he was about to get pins and needles. When it was time to finish he had terrible cramps, and had difficulty breathing, as if breathing on his own for the first time. I was concerned and took an extra couple of minutes at the end of the session while he settled, then told him he could ring me if he needed.

The next day Ben was very subdued. The past couple of days had been a terrible shock for him, but he noticed that I shared responsibility with him and seemed to care about his condition. He also noted that even when he did need it, it had been difficult to accept my offer of help.

In the early phase of our work, Ben managed to find girlfriends for himself to help him bridge the gap whenever we had a holiday break. Once back in the sessions, he wanted to extricate himself from these liaisons. Gradually, we were able to understand his use of these women and Ben could begin to think about his needs, rather than act out this behaviour. He then directed some of this energy towards me. Before a holiday break, Ben arrived for the first time in a pair of tights, lay down and proceeded to talk about the wife of the guy at the tennis courts, who wouldn't let him play tennis without his shirt on and how unfair this was. It was important to suggest gently that maybe he felt I didn't sufficiently recognise his masculinity and that a sexual relationship would be the way around the problem of the holidays. That way he wouldn't need to separate from me.

The following term, these sexualised feelings began to recur. I became aware that prior to the weekend, instead of being more thoughtful, we would have a session where there would be an excited, sexual atmosphere in the room. I commented that this stirring up of intense sexualized feelings seemed to be a substitute for relating, to avoid feeling little and lonely. I felt some trepidation, as I was unsure how Ben would react to what I said.

'I know what you mean, that's how I got Rita,' (a girlfriend he had picked up during the previous holiday) 'and now it's all a mess.' Ben lay quietly saying, 'shit,' then much more softly, 'I can't keep it up,' and he cried. For the first time tears fell down his cheeks. This was a real breakthrough for Ben. 'I don't know who I am.' After pausing he spoke quietly, 'I am remembering a song the Beatles sang about a long time ago, when I was younger than I am now. It makes me think about how often I pushed help away… and my parents.' He added, 'it's all about manipulating – what hope is there?'

Here we can see a Ben who used his sexuality to avoid being someone who has feelings. He used his sexuality to give himself a form or a shape rather than a real identity. Later, Ben did speak to his sister about their early years and we were able to piece together a picture of a mother who perhaps did "over-stimulate" and "inflate" her child, rather than help him feel his ordinary valued self.

While Ben had some relief at not having to be "big" and puffed up all the time, he had enormous difficulty being little. We were able to glimpse the little child behind the façade, who needed a lot of attention and easily felt insecure. There was also a tyrannical infant who was never going to let me have time for myself and a Ben who desperately wanted to remain equal and not experience his difference.

We moved to a difficult phase that revealed other attitudes towards women. He wanted me to agree to his way of viewing the world. As his sense of entitlement and superiority became stronger, Ben himself was embarrassed by the depth of his push to get his own way. He found it difficult to show and own this narcissistic part of his personality, but it prevailed. Leading up to his Christmas break, Ben used every weapon he had to persuade me to agree with his decision to leave the sessions a couple of weeks early and go overseas to do a group course. He was enraged when I would not. This was a convenient time for him to go and he would take this opportunity. His mother told him he only had to handle women properly and they would always come around.

After the Christmas break, Ben arrived the first day very chastened and "softened". He came in and lay down, he was very teary and incoherent, and spoke with difficulty.

'I'm glad to be back, I-I need to be here. I saw a lot about myself while I was away, I-I-I can't get my words together.' He did calm himself and said, 'I was trying to impress everyone, be what they wanted me to be, so that they would need me.'

'Now you are dealing with who needs whom. You went to the course to avoid being the lonely, lost, confused boy.'

Struggling, Ben said, 'I don't know who I am.'

At that moment, I got a very strong, painful, restricted feeling in my chest and told Ben about this, adding that it felt that if I let go everything would collapse. (Perhaps it was also something to do with his broken-heartedness)

Again, somewhat incoherently, Ben said, 'I don't know what is happening, when you said that about feeling the pain in your chest I felt very strange, my head was spinning.' Then he added, 'don't you feel afraid?'

'I can feel how frightened you are; you seem to be wondering if I can bear the feelings that seem unbearable to you.'

The next day, I learnt that as part of the group process people were allotted tasks, and his was to do some weeding in the garden. Ben described his experience: 'Straight away I thought, I'm not going to do that, who can I swap with? Then I thought to myself, what would Lorraine say? Then I got on my hands and knees and did the weeding.' It was a very moving moment. For the first time I felt sure that Ben was attached to his therapy.

The following day, however, Ben began distancing himself from me and we discovered his fear that if I could get into him and feel what is going on, then I might dump a lot of things into him. What also re-emerged was his resentment over his mother, allowing his father to send him to boarding school. Ben's opening up to me was followed by a "hard" period, where we had to deal with his arrogance towards me. In this frame of mind, I was of no real help to him and he devalued the gains that had been made. These devaluations had to be consistently, and patiently, pointed out.

Ben also decided he was no longer alone and since he had help, it was now all up to me, he just had to turn up. Additionally, he could say and do what he liked in the session, since he was there for his own needs, and not mine. Even the fact that I was there to help him see the manipulativeness and the games turned into its own game; a bit of cat and mouse. Despite all this, some very tender moments began to emerge. Towards the end of this period Ben gently stroked the wall, and said softly, 'It's my perception that makes all the difference really.'

It was with some relief that Ben then arrived one Monday morning with a dream of a combined male/female figure and a monster fighting over his house. In the dream Ben felt some fear of the combined figure, but did prefer that one to the monster. Some "softs" and "hards" were being made into "firm" at last. In this session Ben began to really think there might be something called feelings. Finally, he spoke of his yoga teacher, how he liked what she said and how she helped people. He began to focus intense feelings around the yoga teacher, and as Ben stated, 'I feel sexual feelings and loving feelings mixed up.' This comment shows that we had created a framework where we could begin to look at the nature of this confusion.

We were able to clear some of the enormous confusions that limited Ben's capacity to engage in relationships. What Ben needed was the experience that all babies have a right to; a sensuous experience with a mother, who helps to contain and understand his early feelings. This sensuousness needs to operate within the parameter of sensuality *without* sexuality; a mother who assists her baby to understand her role and to clarify, who the mother is and who the baby is. The mother also carries the important task of introducing the baby to the "working couple", that is, her partnership with her husband, the baby's father. To not do this is to bring her "little man" in between her and her husband; it leaves the "little man" flawed and emasculated. This is a difficult inheritance and one that damaged much of Ben's life. How can he *ever* be who he can *never* be. Ben's mother possibly subjected him to over-stimulation and inflation and did not give him enough understanding and interest as a whole being. All of this acted in a perverse way, to cripple his capacity to relate in general and specifically, as a partner and potentially as a father.

What was the mix of factors that helped Ben move from a sensation-based way of operating to thinking, feeling, imagining and relating? First, I needed to understand and find the baby *behind* the false sexual identity and do the work that had not been done before.

Next was the context from which he came: what were his early experiences, and how had they shaped him? I needed to wonder constantly during our sessions, who we were in the transference, who was he today? Was he going to treat me with contempt to make me understand the lack of respect his parent's paid to his inner life? Am I being manoeuvred to act out the role of the harsh policeman and become his projection rather than reflecting on it? During any one session, I needed to consider which mother am I in his mind? The one who wanted to use him as a toy and manipulate him, or the one who was genuinely interested in his needs, his thoughts, his feelings and his on-going development?

Closely related to this is the issue of the "counter-transference". What experiences, as yet unconscious, was he communicating to me in other ways? I had the task of distinguishing between my own feelings and those that Ben was communicating. I needed to be open to receiving and processing those experiences and sort outing what belonged to me and what belonged to Ben.

Finally, to be alive with Ben in the transference and counter-transference meant being alive to the early infantile states in him and also in myself. This was not easy, but critical if I was to do the job he was asking me to do. I had to enter his primitive infantile world and to feel with him the early primitive connections he had made. Then, I had to return to my grown-up thinking self to understand and to communicate to Ben what I had found.

As his therapist, I had to be an active participant in Ben's growth and development, to be an active "container" on his behalf, who could place his needs, interests, and growth in a central position. I therefore had to protect him from my own needs and distortions. We had to work together in the task of enabling him to become *somebody*, so that he could take his part in life, and live his share to the fullest.

Being in the room with someone whose early needs have never been made central creates many sensations inside you as the therapist. You are sitting with someone, who is yet to be embodied and as yet lacks substance. It is like being with someone who is a leaf in the wind, blown here and there and unattached to anyone. They are adrift, a bundle of sensations reacting to whatever or wherever the wind blows with no central core. For highly intelligent people this is a type of torture. To not know who you are, you have to work hard to impress yourself on the world. Inside you know you are empty, apart from what you have cobbled together to appear to be someone. We need to provide a home for the wanderers, where they can find some understanding of their feelings. To live constantly in such a place is to be spun out forever, seeking gravity, the ultimate victim of outside forces.

Underlying this state, and because their first relationships have bypassed their interests, such people are ever fearful of relationships. Their only experience of relationships is to be hurt. They remain in a state of terror, forever watchful, like a sentry on guard duty throughout their waking lives. They can never fully relax; they have been burnt to a cinder by the failure of their relationships, and constantly fear that someone will attack them again. To avoid further damage, they are preoccupied with defending themselves at every moment. Only very gradually can they begin to consider trusting someone enough to let the sentry guard begin to rest.

Chapter 9 Recognising primitive processes

Crying out and weeping are great resources…
Cry out! Don't be stolid and silent
with your pain. Lament! And let the milk
of loving flow into you

"Cry Out in Your Weakness," (Barks, p. 127)

We all carry the responsibility to unearth the story behind us that makes sense of our choices, our patterns of behaviour and our sensitivities to certain events or ideas. It is important to use our understanding and knowledge to piece things together, to consider possibilities and to help activate them. By exploring our early history and our current behaviour, we can make some assumptions about how it might have been for us to live through certain experiences. This has the potential to free us from the hold these events have over ourselves and act from a position of choice. Then we are in the position to do this for others, in a natural ordinary way.

Where early experiences are involved, we enter terrain that is not for the faint-hearted. This is where the unconscious reigns. It is not an area that is easy to express in words. We are more likely to access it through our bodies. In certain instances, we may need a professional to help us in our explorations.

As noted in Chapter Five, the body is an important element in this process. I have also discussed the use of the breath to help us make contact with our body. In the arena of the unconscious, images are often more important than words, so we can begin by noticing images that come to mind and bringing them into consciousness, rather than letting them slip by. Dreams have a different sense of time and space and can help us connect with our unconscious selves.

The nature of the space we connect to through the primitive states, and through the baby, is quite profound. It is located in time yet carries a timeless and transcendent quality. It reinforces our connection to our roots: the roots of our humanness and the fullness of ourselves that is at odds with the constant striving, experiencing and wanting of our more usual selves. Staying in the moment puts us in touch with who we are and, therefore, we feel whole, not avoided, talked over, nor filled with innumerable thoughts; just there. It is from this place, we can touch areas where another human being has not been there for us, where we need to give time and attention. These states of mind are highly interconnected with each other. Each of us has a unique version of these ways of being and thinking.

Finn's parents brought him to therapy because he was struggling to adjust to starting school. This six-year-old boy came in a state of deep distress. One look at his eyes and furrowed brow showed he was in pain. He proceeded to throw pillows and hit out at the furniture in my office with a huge sense of rage and frustration. He then went outside the room to the garden and pulled up a couple of stakes.

I asked him to return to the room and said, 'Grownups don't always understand do they?'

He replied, 'The teacher is always telling us what to do and I don't understand, I don't know what she is saying.'

I spent time with the parents to ascertain his story. His parents had relocated from another state, set up a printing business in the front part of their home and did what they thought was best; combined business and home. The business had been successful and they were very busy after his birth, spending many hours working and building up their clientele. They told me that they had been there all the time throughout his early childhood, and couldn't understand why the boy was finding things so difficult. As the story unfolded, it became apparent that while his parents were preoccupied with the business, a number of child minders had attended to Finn and he had not had a consistent figure during this time.

Finn carried an overload of sensations in his body and was full of inexplicable events that he had never been able to make sense of cumulatively over the years. Starting school had finally tipped him over the edge. He was already full to the brim with experiences that others had never understood. Now he had many new things that he needed someone else to listen to and comprehend. He needed someone to slow things down and to begin to make sense of the whirlwind of sensations and feelings that assailed him. Once he had gradually processed these, there would be room to let new experiences in and then he would be all right.

Another child once helped me understand how terrifying it is when thoughts and feelings overwhelm them. A five-year-old girl spoke to me about the numbers in Sesame Street. In the numbers segment, the numbers would go from small to large on the screen. It felt like objects being thrown at you all the time. They don't stop. When a child is having an experience that is new, or needs to be understood, it registers in their body and they look for someone to help them make sense of it, so they can find some resolution and "file it away". When the child is constantly alone with experiences that they cannot process, the child feels constantly assailed; they don't have an "off" button. All the chaotic sensations and thoughts swirling around them torture them. This is close to the feeling that they are going mad. Sometimes the only way out is to shut down and emotionally turn off.

It does seem important to contact our own earliest fears, anxieties and terrors. We all suffer from the burden of the "living death" aspects of ourselves that have not come fully alive. In these areas, we are constantly avoiding certain feelings and do not allow ourselves the freedom to fully embrace life. Our task in life is to join in, and engage in the life we have, while we have it.

The most important issue is whether we have been partnered in our emotional life: when we have been and when we have not. Many of us have had parents who cared for us well physically, supported our educational needs and looked after us in a general sense, yet they did not understand or support our emotional needs sufficiently. This can impair or prevent our psychological birth.

What is crucial to understand from infant mental health work is that the baby in the person, child or adolescent who has not had adequate care, feels alone and unsupported in his or her efforts to connect and has little understanding of the emotional world. The whole neurological system at birth is almost totally oriented to seeking and finding the other. The parent needs to help the baby to know, gradually, that it is possible to live in a world where you can be met and understood emotionally. Forming a partnership and alleviating the aloneness is a crucial part of what a mother and baby do in the early period of their relationship. To be alone and unmet is an enormous assault on what is meant to be a natural process of finding someone else, and it can set the course of an unfulfilled life.

An associated feature for those who have been left alone with sensory experiences is a sense of working hard, with a corollary of doing it all on our own. If this has been our experience, we feel we are carrying two roles. In the absence of the father and mother we do our own "holding", plus being with parents who are unable to manage their feelings, or alternatively, closing off feelings. Both these scenarios leave no room for the experiences of babies, who must do their own holding and struggle with unprocessed experiences. This is clearly an impossible task, so we carry the world on our shoulders and stagger through life, reliant on a false omnipotence, and forever in danger that the load will crush, or expose, the emptiness inside. In this paradigm everything, even small daily tasks, can feel like climbing Mt Everest. Without an alternative, we are doomed to the grinding relentlessness of everything being too much and manically trying to keep up.

If this has been our experience, we grow into adults who are not even aware that someone else should be involved in our lives. Everyday tasks can seem overwhelming, since past experiences overload us. Often we feel put upon and resentful, but we cannot afford any time to contemplate something different, because that is the way it has always been and we must endure it.

Because these early experiences are so embedded and inaccessible, in most instances we unconsciously enact them in later life. We need to tune into the way we feel and behave and see how we are re-enacting earlier traumas in everyday life. If we are repeating negative scenarios with our superiors, our children, relationships, or friends, it may be time to explore what is embedded in our psyche.

Maria, in her late twenties, came to see me in a highly distressed state as the result of a traumatic experience and was in the midst of a psychotic breakdown. She not only needed medication and a deep understanding of the experiences leading to the trauma, she also needed basic support that grounded her in her everyday reality. Day/night differentiation, sleeping and eating routines, how to plan what she needed to do; all became part of the picture. All of these elements needed to be "held", while establishing some basic ground on which she could stand.

Later in her therapy, when she had achieved some self-regulation, a remnant of her early experiences was reactivated. She had been successfully working for a couple of years in a satisfying job, but was beginning to feel she might look elsewhere for work. Out of the blue, someone reported her to her manager for a minor infringement. Suddenly, she lost all perspective and was back in a world where everything was in turmoil. She was unwanted and needed to get in first by putting in her resignation. Once more, she was re-living the experience of the unwanted baby and she needed, for a temporary period, daily phone contact to help hold her in her current reality, when she could discuss a minor infringement at work and connect with the original feelings. The intensity of the trauma permeated her initial response, but with support she was able to slowly differentiate between past and present. She was able to manage her feelings and handle the exchange with her boss. She remained successfully and happily in the workplace until a few months later, when an opportunity for another job came up. Without extra help she might well have sunk into a further repetition of her trauma and left the workplace before working through the experience. Over-reactions to minor events can have intense and traumatic elements of a pre-verbal nature embedded in them.

The baby born to narcissistic parents, whose own needs have never been processed, never gets to first base. The baby in this situation is wronged. If we have inhabited this space, we carry a deep sense of injustice underneath the veneer we have adopted because something is profoundly wrong; someone should pay, and someone should be responsible for the depth of that injustice. We feel that fate, even god, has mocked us. We have been given life, but not the means to live it fully. Many of us, who outwardly appear to be functioning, carry this experience inside.

All parents have a degree of narcissism, but when it is the predominant quality in the relationship the baby misses out. Babies can only be born into a space that belongs to the parents. If their unmet needs already fill the space, they cannot acknowledge the baby's integrity. If we are in this position, we have never received the welcome that is necessary for a psychological birth of our own. When we are born into such a vacuum, the only option is to fuse with a parent, because there is no space of our own, as was the case with Ben, in Chapter Eight, who fulfilled all his mother's dreams and aspirations but never had his own. My patient Sophia, mentioned in Chapter Six, allied herself with the intravenous drip and internally carried it with her all the time, never needing anyone to help her until she broke down. Her desperation lay side by side with a notion that she had it all. Often when we are in this state we can present as arrogant and difficult, perennially unhappy, and nothing is right or good enough. On the surface the complaints can seem trivial, and we seem intent on making those who might help us feel useless, with nothing of benefit to offer.

Underneath, however, if we are able to go deeper into our mind, body and feelings, we find a part of ourselves that is disassociated from our feelings, and have no real concept of who we are. We live outside ourselves and inside some unrealistic and omnipotent notion we have had to manufacture, in lieu of a genuine idea of how we work, and how the world works. We hang on ferociously to this construction in a life and death way, out of fear of the emptiness underneath. We perceive anything outside our construction, anything new or different, as a threat. Inside is an unmet baby, full of envy and rage, resistant to all attempts to soothe and settle. We have enormous envy towards others because we feel shut of out of the world of relationships, with no way to get in. No matter what we do, we don't have the "technology". We are denied it until someone will be there for us, to give us the key into the world of relationships. Underlying everything is a deep, envious hatred of those who have what we were unable to obtain. We are the "have-nots".

In *The Life of I: The New Culture of Narcissism*, Anne Manne (2014) has eloquently discussed how severely narcissistic individuals avoid at any cost revisiting this ignoble place. It is, however, necessary to return to these places because otherwise we remain limited and constrained.

If we are able to persevere through the "excavation" involved when returning to these places, we meet a baby whose parents never validated their baby's integrity. Here the most authentic part of us has never been born and the outrage at this offence is enormous. This outrage, while deeply personal, includes a broader quality. We rage at our fate or destiny;

a generalized rage at life. It feels profoundly wrong to be born physically, but not receive the means to be fully born into our uniqueness. We experience this as the deepest insult and the cruellest offering that life can give. Life represents a fundamental betrayal. Not only have our parents deprived us of the opportunity to be fully who we are; they have also placed us in an invidious situation. We turned against ourselves, and became what we had to be to survive. We turned against our own authenticity to remain alive, in the hope that some day something else may come along. This state is soul destroying. We have lived a lie, because we have lost our authenticity. Those who are supposed to give physical and psychological life gave psychological death.

This is an intensely painful psychic space. If we can never get our parents to provide the foundations that will enable us to form relationships and feel the richness of being loved and loving, we are alone and barred from the fullness of the human condition. We are left to scavenge what understanding we can of the world by observing what others do, copying, living inside others, pretending and making it up as we go along. There is a profound sense of betrayal. Our parents and fate let us down and the unfairness is palpable. We need to understand before we can let go of our deep sense of injustice and injury.

A patient of mine tried to explain to me the depth of her fear. The experience she related was not a dream, or an actual experience that she was remembering, but more like an hallucination, or an articulation of how she had felt throughout her life. On the surface, she was impeccably dressed, attractive and amiable; but she carried deep emotional scars from both parents, who themselves had not been well cared for, but all presented as part of a perfect normative family. Whenever she sought to express herself she felt annihilated. As a result she had had to adopt a "false self" and, while parts of her personality operated well in the world, other parts were undeveloped.

She described being in a swimming pool. 'There is a foot on my head holding me under the water and the life is draining out of me… it is… murdering me. I am being drowned over and over again. I am pushed under, I come up for air then I am pushed under again.'

At this point this patient was terrified and feeling she *was* being murdered. Her breathing was laboured and this was frightening, because she has had asthma throughout her life. She *had* to struggle to be alive or she would die. The paradox was that, as she continued to struggle to stay alive, she was experiencing a slow death. She was dying because she could not let anything in. While she struggled, she could not see anyone there to help her or envisage a way out. What she feared, the letting go, is what will set her free, but her terror was huge. The letting go, in this instance, is in fact a movement towards life. This is a feature of these places that are psychotic in nature, where black is white and white is black. Things have been experienced the wrong way round so that to attack oneself is good. To not attack the parents on whom they rely for survival has been the imperative. Setting things right is a difficult but rewarding process.

A related element is feeling "stupid"' at a very profound level. Patients who perceive themselves as "stupid" carry an inner sense of this notion at an elemental level. This flows from the fact that at a primitive level the baby feels unable to attract the mother sufficiently so that she will engage emotionally with them. The baby sees this inability, usually related to the mother's inability to be available, as an enormous gap or hole in themselves; something is wrong with them. Blaming oneself in this circumstance, is the preferred option to the terror of realising that you are reliant on someone, who is not up to the task of doing the job.

If we have had this experience, then this becomes the reason why we are not responded to: we are inadequate; we don't know what we are meant to do to make the relationship work, so we are unlovable and not interesting.

For whatever reason, we feel responsible for the breakdown in the relationship. How could we be so ill-equipped to live life? How stupid is that? It is experienced as an intrinsic phylogenetic fault. How stupid am I that I am alive, yet I am unable to do the most natural, primary thing I should be capable of as a living human being, which is to draw another human being to myself? There is no greater stupidity than that.

In this situation the baby becomes the one who has to "know", because there is no alternative. When the baby takes responsibility for the failure of the relationship, the internal voice is harsh and merciless: 'Why didn't you know?' In such a situation, we can only sit with the misery and outrage and understand the enormity of the situation. By having someone with us in the present, we can commence the long way back to becoming capable of forming a connection and an attachment, and finally becoming a full member of society.

The sense of stupidity is closely related to the self-loathing that is part of turning against oneself and incorporating a sense of worthlessness. The sense of the rejection of the self, the intimate, feeling self, is so unbearable that it is preferable to live the lie of "it must be me" than to face the truth of our predicament: that we are unable to get what we need from this person. Hope is maintained at a great cost to the self. We can only see what happened in the past and differentiate that from the present. Perhaps now it is possible to be accepted for who we are and the reality is that our feelings are not "too much," "too messy," or "unwelcome". In fact, we are a normal healthy baby, with normal feelings, but we feel we are loathsome because of those early needs not being met.

Those whose parents were severely depressed, drug addicts, or addicted to alcohol, have a similar experience, but in these cases the emphasis is on what has been missed out on in terms of needs. We are not born into the mindset of the parent, as with narcissistic parents, but we are born into a vacuum, an empty space where something ought to be. If the neediness of the parents comes first, our desire for partnership is met with a wall of needs in the parent. We have drawn a short straw. Born with a bundle of healthy needs seeking to find a responsive home, our need is rebuffed. Instead of a kind response the feelings come back at us amplified rather than reduced. Our systems are constantly overloaded. We carry these early needs into our current life, so that new experiences can be overwhelming rather than new and exciting.

In these situations, we are profoundly alone. Someone is there, there is "an other," but they are utterly inaccessible. Our needs are so strong that we will have continually knocked at the door of the parents, but no one will answer. The wall of the parent's need cuts them off and is impregnable. We long to be met, but the loneliness of the gap between the two is immense.

I was working in a clinic in a session with a young child while a therapist in another room in the clinic was seeing a child who proceeded to wail in the most primitive way I have ever heard. It was not a human sound but rather like an animal baying at the moon, the sound utterly desolate. I had to stop the work with my child and discuss how upsetting it was to hear such a sound. Later, I asked my colleague what was happening. This child was experiencing the impact of a drug-addicted mother and what it felt like when she would be passed out, there but not there, and unreachable. There is a profound loneliness when the need of the baby is unmet in this way.

We absorb a sense of worthlessness. The unprocessed old needs of the parents, their depression, the bottle, the drug, is more prized than we are. It is humiliating and degrading that we are of so little value and importance. Later, we may direct the denigration and disgust onto the parent, or therapist, or be dismissive of others. We need to revisit the feelings of not being valued, by reliably experiencing someone being there for us; someone who helps us find the words for what we have not understood before. With consistency and reliability and a rhythm of presence and absence, like the mother and the baby, we can repair the rupture and the wound.

Hopelessness, despair and the desire to die are states that our society does not find easy to relate to. Yet they are crucial states to experience in order to clear early hurts, disappointments and angers. When a baby, or a child, is utterly dependent and suffers physical or emotional abuse there is an enormous impact on the psyche. To be abused in these ways means that the role of the parent has been lost and the parent is out of control. For the baby or child, it is like being hit by a tsunami over which they have no control. At the moment of abuse both sides are de-humanised. Who they are is annihilated.

If this has been our experience, the child's needs no longer exist in the mind of the abuser who acts within the law of the jungle, where their survival is paramount and the rights of the abused are erased. The powerlessness, humiliation, and degradation make the victim a piece of dirt under the heel of the attacker. The parents themselves may feel under threat to come up with capacities they do not have. Having a child may activate their own past hurts so they too are victims. The tragedy of these mutual early experiences between parents and babies, or children, is that people can assign early experiences to the unconscious with the vow to never be in that position again.

Dianna Kenny (2013, p. 271) writes movingly of this state:

> Bendit (2011) has proposed that chronic maternal misattunements during infancy are coded first implicitly, and, later, as language develops, in semantic memory as facts of the kind "nobody cares" or "nobody responds", "I'm not important" or "I don't matter." (p. 26). These experiences thus coded cannot be consciously remembered, and, therefore, are unlikely to be responsive to cognitive therapies such as cognitive reframing. These semantic memories cause intense emotional pain. If the pain is unrelieved and unmitigated over time,

suicide becomes an option. Subsequent experiences
of emotional pain trigger the original unbearable
self-state without any recall of their origins, thus
giving the present situation the same emotional
intensity as the original experience against which the
person-as-infant felt helpless. Any form of emotional
unresponsiveness from important people is likely to
be sufficient to trigger the original abandonment/
annihilation fears produced in the original situation
during infancy.

Repeated rejection of our deepest needs leads easily to
the desire not to be born; the wish we had never been born.
We can often trace suicidal feelings back to early states of
mind where life was *not* worth living. We need to agree.
It wasn't. What happened was wrong, there was betrayal,
and it would be true if life stayed that way. However, there
are other opportunities for something new to grow, the
possibility that gradually life can change and get better.

*Where there is trauma, or unbearable memories, we will find
disassociation.* When we have unbearable memories we find
an adaptive way to conceal these memories. These moments
of disassociation will take place in the body and we, or others,
can begin to notice the changes that occur. There may be a
precipitating movement like shaking a foot, looking away
into the distance, moving a chair, all ways to get away from
what is too much to bear. It can also be a thought that we
need to cut off, because it will take us where we don't want
to go. The head can become disassociated from the body
and thoughts and feelings are disconnected. Gradually, in a
supportive environment, connections will grow.

When an overwhelming experience is split off, we
lose something. In this state we cannot live with our full
truth, we are forced into denial. This creates an uneasy
sense of something not being right. Life gets lived, with
us unconsciously working around anything that may be a
triggering event. We may turn to self-medication through

drink or drugs so that a more "peaceful" state of being can be achieved. Often, though, insomnia, restlessness, and agitation become a companion.

Because trauma is so often made physical, the use of deeper breathing is important, as discussed in Chapter Five. It is important in getting the body flowing, rather than holding, and therefore enabling memories to surface. It is also important as a resource to turn to when thoughts and feelings threaten to overwhelm us. Sometimes resistance will arise as we connect to why we had to cut off in the first place. The resistance will urge us to continue to stay cut off. 'Why would I want to go there?' 'I promised myself I would never let myself ever have that experience again,' 'It is not going to change anything so why open up a can of worms?' 'I am too afraid to go there, I will never be able to function again,' 'If I begin to cry I will never stop.' These are examples of how we can speak for the part that has never spoken.

We need to challenge our underlying beliefs about the world. With early trauma it is not hard to wonder whether life is perverse. That is what it is like. Why be born when life is continuously bleak and disaster on disaster creates the picture? This is a perspective that 'the world is totally fucked!' This is where the desire not to be born is not a difficult internal state to understand. We come ready, equipped, wanting to be born, only to be met with hostility or indifference at a vulnerable time. If nobody comes to us and we need someone to make our lives worthwhile, why wouldn't we want to die?

If we have had to split off our feelings, we often feel like a fraud, or live with the anxiety that we will be found out to be one. We live with a form of psychological death and an empty hole, where the connections should have grown, in the relational areas of the brain. When we first confront the world of feelings, numerous doubts and anxieties arise. The question is: why let in feelings, why have them when they are so painful? At this early point we are not able to deal with having emotions, as we have never had the opportunity to explore them with someone. It is akin to learning to run a marathon. You start with the first kilometre and build from there. Each training session can gradually help to grow muscle and strength, and over time we can build the capacity to run the long race. The same can be said for learning to tolerate our feelings. This time, however, we need to feel that we have someone on our side. This time it will be a shared task with someone there to receive and understand what is going on inside.

Allowing feelings that have been split off is not just a wonderful flowing experience. Feelings can feel like attacks, like a sharp sword slicing into the psyche that has rejected them, to protect us from reality. They can disrupt our carefully constructed world that sealed off unpleasant experiences. To reverse the vow never to return to our painful states takes courage and persistence.

We need to allow ourselves to be in a state of not being able to relate. Of course, all of us are relating to people, but there may be areas where it is difficult. Exploring our notions concerning relating can be fruitful. Digging deeper to clear out misconceptions can be confronting, in a healthy way. We need to create the conditions that enable us to grow new neuronal pathways that open up the relationship areas of the brain.

Many of us have a distorted view of relationships. Some misconceptions are:

- A relationship is one person listening to the other only, without an exchange

- Being in a relationship means to be enmeshed, rather than being two separate individuals who relate to each other

- A relationship requires us to assume the burdens or troubles of the other, or be responsible for them

- The outcome of a relationship is that someone controls us

- Relationships mean that someone will completely understand us and will support us at all times

- There should be no friction or pain in a relationship.

We need to dismantle these misconceptions. Understanding our underlying beliefs about relationships is important, as they form the bedrock of how we go about relating to others and the world.

A sense of repair is something that is an important part of healing old wounds. Repair is an important part of learning to be in a relationship in the early years, as discussed in Chapter Two. If we are fortunate, we had parents who were able to repair the inevitable ruptures that must occur at times. Engaging with an understanding of normal developmental processes and reconsidering the developmental needs that were met or unmet as a child is itself a reparative process.

This means that when no one has partnered us, we seek a partner. When no-one holds us, we find someone to hold us. When we have felt alone, we find a companion in our journey in life. In this process we sort out need from greed. We look to meeting our needs and moving from being a "have not" in whatever areas that are relevant to being a "have". Then we can take our place in the world as a grown-up who is able to relate and be a responsible citizen.

If we can begin to repair old wounds, we can arrive at a sense of the beauty and wonder of the world, as well as a sense of joy about our existence and the existence of nature. With repair there is a lightness of being and a sense of "settled-ness". If we have looked at our earliest experiences and come out the other side, we have nothing to fear.

Many of us carry the underlying belief that no one will be interested in us. It has been inconceivable to believe that someone would enjoy giving us the time and attention previously denied to us. Hence we are suspicious when someone is bothering with us now. We need to bear these suspicions but move on to understand the ordinary normal process whereby a mother enjoys taking care of her baby, to understand that the process in itself is rewarding. The smiles, responses and growth of the baby express the growing relationship and are intrinsically satisfying.

Facing realities about life is important, because early difficulties lead to early misunderstandings we need to clarify. Reality needs to intrude into the distorted fantasies that have grown in the absence of proper care. We all have to abide by the human condition and how it operates. Fate, god, destiny, whatever it is, operates in a particular way and on this planet we need to breathe oxygen through our lungs, live with the laws of gravity and within the framework of how relationships work. Others will understand us enough, but not completely. We have to learn to be with others, and to be separate from them – that others will bring pleasure and also sorrow. Conflict will be part of life. None of this is negotiable; it is just the human condition.

Our deepest longing is for our parents to be the ones who gave us our early nurturing. Often we keep knocking on that door long past the time it is reasonable, in the vain hope we can turn back the clock. This is understandable. But a new loyalty has to be developed: a loyalty to our own life force and what we need. This painful reality indicates the first shoots of growth and the possibility of healing.

If this growing connection includes a therapeutic relationship, the space between the two becomes more crowded in a good way. Once we connect with a therapist, two therapists and two patients begin to inhabit the space. As a potential working couple begins to form, the therapist will divide into the one who provides warmth, is welcoming, listens and understands and soothes. The other one is the hard one who sees their client out the door, makes them wait and confronts them with the reality of the world. Corresponding to this are the two parts of the patient: the grateful, relieved and pleased patient who has found someone who will take their interests to heart, and the other who is angry, dissatisfied and suffering. As all of these aspects are evident, a slow digestion takes place when all these parts gradually become part of the self and the relationship. The growth in complexity, richness and nuance of the relationship becomes mutually rewarding, providing the possibility of a full birth.

PART 3

The family, community, and global society

Chapter 10 The family and society

There is a community of spirit,
join it, and feel the delight
of walking in the noisy street,
and being the noise

"A Community of Spirit," (Barks, p. 3)

The family

Family can be a group of people affiliated not only by birth or marriage, but also the group responsible for the socialisation of the offspring in the family. Family structures include blended parents, single parents and same sex partnerships. The notion of "family" can be defined as the group of people surrounding an individual who have long-term roles and relationships with them. Members of the family group have enormous power over each other and their unconscious dynamics have a powerful impact on each member of that unit. This makes the family group very potent.

When babies are born, they come with their own psyche, open to be responded to and ready, in most instances, to interact with and meet the world. But the world into which they are born is peopled. The space is already crowded. Intergenerational factors come into play. The experiences of the parents include the family issues that the previous generation grappled with; what happened to grandmother and grandfather and subsequently mother and father is important. The unresolved experiences of the previous generation will come to inhabit the psychic space of the baby.

A useful analogy is one of space junk. Objects in space do not break down as the atmosphere does not generate the conditions for disintegration, so they continue to float around in space, with no prospect of being cleared away. Something similar operates for us psychically. Old hurts and grievances, as well as creative capacities like musical, physical or intellectual aptitudes persist. At least psychically, there are conditions under which we can modify the less helpful inheritances. If the parents are able to break the unhelpful patterns of previous generations, the next generation benefits enormously. To do this we need to explore the stories of the previous generation and reflect on the impact they are having. A crying baby, in many instances, also carries the traumas and difficulties of the parents.

Knowing oneself involves knowing how we operate in the family in which we are embedded, both in the present and in the past. As individuals, it is helpful to learn the roles we play in our family of origin, and remain attuned to whether we re-enact these roles in the family we create, react against them, or create our own version of family. In all instances, rather than being in a reactive role, it is helpful to find who we are and how we want to behave as freer agents. The family needs to be seen in the context in which dramas are played out. It is the family in our mind that is important to get to know.

Family Therapy

The advent of family therapy brought a new way of understanding and explaining human behaviour. It involved engaging with the whole family system as a functioning unit and allowed for communication, social factors and relationship issues to have special importance. Family therapy, as a branch of psychotherapy, began in the early 20th century. It was initially associated with the earlier social work movements, but its formal development dates to the 1940s and 1950s. Various groups independently contributed to its development. John Bowlby used an attachment model in the United Kingdom while Gregory Bateson and Don Jackson introduced general systems theory in the United

States. Later, Virginia Satir, known as the mother of family therapy, developed her conjoint family therapy model, which downplayed theoretical constructs and emphasised subjective experience and unexpressed feelings. Initially, there was a strong influence from psychoanalysis and social psychiatry through Nathan Ackerman and later from learning theory and behaviour therapy. While there were diverse influences, all agreed that the family was more than the sum of its parts.

In the early 1950s, Gregory Bateson's studies led to the view that family problems arise out of the systemic interactions within the family, rather than from individual members. The studies pointed to the notion that the identified patient, or presenting problem, manifested, or was a surrogate for, the family's or even society's problems. By the mid-1960s, there were a number of distinct schools, for example, systems theory, brief therapy, strategic therapy, structural family therapy, the psychodynamic model, and the Milan model. By the late 1970s, steps were taken towards integrating the various schools. There was a growing movement toward a "generic" family therapy model that sought to incorporate the best of the accumulated knowledge in the field and that fitted many different contexts.

Holding all the members of the family in mind

I have seen a number of families when all the members of the family have been present, but this does not have to be the case for family therapy to take place. It is possible to do family therapy with subsystems of the family unit if that is assessed as being appropriate. Bringing together whomever is willing to come has rich potential as unspoken material can be made manifest. A newly separated mother brought her two girls, aged five and two, to a session. Her former husband, the children's father, did not wish to attend. I asked the mother how she was going. The mother stoically stated that all was well, even though it was obviously not the case. Her five-year-old stood next to her as if to hold her up and be her support. I noticed that the two-year-old kept building blocks into a tower, then using another block to ram into it and knock it over. This was normal behaviour for her age, so initially I didn't take much notice. However, she began to be very emphatic in her actions and wanted me to watch her. I noted that maybe she was trying to tell me something. The five-year-old then said, 'Mum crashed the car into the garage door yesterday.' Her mother began to show more of the distress she was carrying and began to cry. The five-year-old, with her mother now engaged with another adult, went over to the toy box and looked for something to play with. She was able to turn to her own activities now that the reality of what was happening was allowed in the room.

Parents from the previous generation may be psychically present in the room, even if they are not physically there. I remember a mother coming to see me when her son was experiencing a great deal of difficulty at school and was being so violent and disruptive that his school had asked him to leave. This mother wanted to discuss what she could do with the boy and the possibility of my seeing him. Once we began talking things became clearer. This was a mother who had had a girl and all had gone well. During the second pregnancy, the mother learnt she was having a male child, and from then on, had experienced many physical difficulties in the pregnancy. Relationship difficulties continued when he was born.

Exploring further, we were able to ascertain that this mother's father had been violent to her in her childhood. At times he had been close to her, but also violent towards her, verbally and physically. She had chosen a partner who was supportive and not violent, but this had not been sufficient to heal her past experiences. Once we were able to connect her fear of her son (as well as her love), her son began to thrive and they began to get to know each other better. At his new school he did well, was popular and began to take a leadership role. Many of her fears about him fell away and she was able to fully meet her real son for the first time, without the static of her history preventing her from having a real connection to him.

What this mother saw was not the son that was born to her, but someone who was likely to harm her. Because of the past, her image of him was at odds with the reality. I felt that their arguments were often attempts on his part to get her to see him as he was. There was sadness on both sides, she feeling alienated from him and he feeling he could not get her to see him; a tragedy for both. Thankfully, she began to let her projections fall away and what emerged was a boy quite different from her expectations. A true meeting was able to take place.

Where possible, it is important for the parents to be involved in the repair of any events and ruptures that may have occurred. It certainly strengthens the family if this is the case. With children, I also feel it is important to get away from the notion of the child bearing the responsibility of being the designated problem. A child presenting for therapy has needs but I do think it is important to look more broadly at what the child is telling us about a larger issue in the family, either in the previous generation, or in the history of the parents.

A young mother came to see me about her first-born, who was having difficulty starting school. She was an intelligent woman, able to articulate her feelings, and married to a caring partner. She told me of the year following the birth of her first child, a son, when she had fallen into a postnatal depression and felt nothing. It had been a most distressing part of her life, but her life proceeded, and she had another child and she was better with the next one. We talked a great deal about her first year of feeling "apart" from her son and the possible connection to his sleep difficulties and his current struggle to separate from her and go to school. Talking about these issues, we wondered whether he was trying to repair this part of his relationship with his mother before moving on and being a more grown up boy at school.

Once she had dealt with her sadness and anger about that time and had found a way to talk about her experience, we decided that she and her partner would work together to make sense of this period with their son. If it didn't work then the son could come for some sessions. They would set aside one night a week to have special time with him and get out the family albums that showed him and them from the time of his birth. Mum explained that she had been unwell at that time, and hadn't been able to look after him as she would have wished, and how upsetting that had been for her. She also discussed with him that what happened must have made him as a baby very sad and angry, and that time must have been very hard for him too. Subsequently, the little boy discussed what might be going on for the baby in the photos. He identified an early photo as one where the baby was feeling "sad". The parents discussed how dad used to come to the hospital to see them both during her depression. Dad also spoke to the boy about not knowing how to help mum at the time. He also talked about how busy he became because of this. Initially, their son was very keen to get together with his parents for their special night and have these discussions. Finally, after about five evenings, when they got up to get the photo album, the boy said, 'I think the baby is happy now mum, we don't need to do this any more.'

Families can divide rather than stay whole

Families manifest themselves in many forms. When couples are unable to work together in the task of bringing up the children, the family often splinters so that one child is allied to one parent and another to the other parent. Parents not pulling together around childrearing can create anxiety in the family. This does not mean that parents need to agree at all times, but they do need to discuss the underlying tensions around how they rear the children. Families can also notice the level of engagement in the family of the (mostly) eldest child. When there are conflicts, the oldest child can become too embroiled in the marriage difficulties and try to hold the couple together. With one family, I saw it was going to be difficult for the couple to break their old pattern of communication. So I pointed out to the young adolescent that she could remain over-interested in her parent's troubles, or she could get a life for herself with friends from high school. Subsequently, she did so. Her siblings too, benefitted from seeing her making a choice to break away from her old role.

Families have enormous potential when they want to tackle their issues. It requires, however, that the parents be open and have some understanding as to what they carry from their own families and how this impacts on their children. I prefer to do some preparatory work with the parents before tackling these issues in front of the child or children. If parents take the time to come to understand the influences they are operating under, then they are engaging in an important transformative experience. Even when parents have caused great distress, children remain very forgiving if the parents explain the origins of the difficulties they have had. Parents taking responsibility is enormously relieving for children, as they carry the burden of wondering whether they were the cause of the problem.

The family and society

Given the importance of the family unit, it may be valuable to reflect on the context in which parents operate. As noted in the early chapters, it takes more than the nuclear family to create a working unit. The family needs support from grandparents, friends, and society at large. The amount of support society offers varies from country to country, depending on the level of poverty or wealth, and the values of the society. We all play a part in creating the culture of our country through our traditions, history, outside influences and the style of leadership we have supported. All of these need to be assessed, and at times re-thought, if they are to be aligned to the real goals of the community.

Some years ago, the Nordic model of government was seen as likely to fail in international economic circles. Now, while Europe and the rest of the world struggles, these Nordic countries are performing highly and have the lowest unemployment rates in Europe. Denmark, Norway and Sweden have, in recent years, achieved what might be regarded as the holy grail of a healthy economy and society: very high wages and productivity, flexible working arrangements, and the world's highest rate of workforce participation, especially among women. The three countries boast workforce participation rates of almost 80% and female participation rates of 76%, according to OECD figures. Female participation is a full 6% ahead of that which prevails in Australia, the US and Britain. In Norway, a key element of success has been the combination of 12 months' paid parental leave, with subsequent universal access to childcare at highly subsidised rates.

Norway's high taxes, levied on oil companies and individuals alike, pay for these generous benefits. The success of the system reflects a political consensus that places a high priority on family-friendly policies, in particular, those that encourage the nurturing of children through workplace flexibility. Norwegians can have 46 weeks of parental leave at 100% of pay, or 56 weeks at 80% of pay. The father can take up to 14 weeks of this leave. If he doesn't take the leave it is forfeited as it is for him only. Norway's social welfare spending is 22% of GDP, while Australia's is 18%. As a proportion of gross domestic product, the cost of Norway's social welfare is not that much more than Australia's. It just appears to be more targeted towards child-rearing, and the needs of the individual and the society. Australia could achieve what Norway has achieved if we had the collective will to do so.

Paul Cleary (2013) reports that Norway's Deputy Finance Minister, Hilde Singsaas, praises the fact that workers typically leave the office from 4pm. Although Norwegians work short hours and part–time, they work effectively:

Many people, especially women work part-time. On average we don't work a lot, but productivity is high. Most Norwegians go home to their families in the afternoon about 4–5pm. That is the Norwegian way of living – we want people to combine working life and their family obligations.

It also creates social cohesion, because the mothers, fathers and children are in the parks socialising and forming informal networks of support for each other on a daily basis. Norwegians appear to have absorbed the idea that attachment networks do matter to our overall health. The government gives every child a basic crib at birth free of charge, together with several layettes of clothes, enough for the early months. As a society, they are proud of this arrangement and most Norwegians use their gifts. These acts reinforce a sense of families being in it together: the parents feel supported and that all the children are "our" children. This contrasts with the growing sense of competitiveness that is taking hold in our society in Australia. Here there is a tendency to pit families against each other and a push to get an edge for your child over another, as opposed to a socially inclusive model.

Singsaas says a key part of the strategy has been the mass expansion of childcare centres. However, these centres are different from the long day care centres operating in Australia. We are the only country in the Western world that officially accepts six-week-old babies into this form of care. Often those babies are there from 8am or earlier, until 6pm in the evening. Centres in Norway accept only one- to five-year-old children because for the first year the family is fully supported at home. Singsaas says:

> We manage to combine high fertility rates and high employment among women, mainly due to the family policies of government since the 1990s. In the 1970s, there were not many kindergartens and the majority of women were housewives. We have now what we call total coverage. You have the right to

access the kindergarten from the age of one year, and at the same time we have paid parental leave for one year. This is a doubling since the end of 1980.

The importance of political will

Support for these practices has been a high priority for Norwegian politicians, enabling women to combine family obligations with working life. Childcare figures are high, with 90% participation rates of children from one to five in Norway, while Australia averages 42%. Contrary to the general experience in Australia, business and companies in Norway are highly flexible in their work practices. This built-in flexibility leads to a high rate of productivity. This outcome is seen as one of the impacts of having a good welfare system. In Norway workers know there is a decent health plan, there will be a good school for their children, and a pension, even if you lose your job. Having this safety net means not staying working in a job you feel unhappy with, or underperforming in, or with an unprofitable company.

In Sweden, parents receive 480 days parental leave on the birth of a child, including 390 at around 80% of their salary for each parent. Europe is slowly catching up. Germany allows new parents to take up to fourteen months of parental leave on 65%of their salary. In Britain, from April 2015, parents are able to share 12 months of leave after the birth of a child. Under the UK plan, new mothers must take the first two weeks, but the rest of the leave is based on the decision of the couple. Both parents could take 25 weeks together. The first 39 weeks are paid at the statutory minimum. The policy is not as far reaching as those in Norway, Sweden and Iceland, which have adopted a so-called "daddy quota" that reserves part of the parental leave period exclusively for fathers. If dad does not take his allotted period of leave, the family loses it. While gaining ground in Europe, the shared parental leave policy, which aims to help women return to the workplace and men to become more involved in caring for new babies, is unknown in much of the world. Some large countries, China and India, for example, allow no leave, paid or unpaid, for fathers.

After the pre-school period, the next major question for parents in rearing their children is education. In April 2000, at the World Education Forum in Dakar, 164 countries pledged to meet a set of six targets by 2015 with the Education for All Initiative. The agenda called for expanded and improved early childhood care and education and stipulated that school attendance for children should be compulsory, free and of good quality. These millennium goals launched at the turn of the century, also called for every child in the world, boys and girls alike, to receive a full course of primary school education by 2015. While there has been progress, with around 7% more children registered by 2007, the ideal of universal enrolment remains elusive. Unfortunately, donor funding by western countries or private institutions for education has been declining since 2010.

What was once considered as a universal right is beginning to be re-interpreted under the weight of market forces. Capitalising on the inability of governments to cope, or having the will to cope, with rising demands on public learning, private education providers are mushrooming and seeking funds. Following the May 2015 Korea World Education forum co-convened by the World Bank, participating countries set targets to widen access and promote domestic spending on education. However, questions have arisen about the Bank's agenda for global education. The most contentious issue is not what the goal or size of the financing will be, but who will deliver the goals. Under consideration is the role of the private sector, as the World Bank and the United Nations have increasingly different visions of how the education goals should be met. Education needs to be a government and community responsibility and making money and market forces are not the answer to *the universal right to a free education.* A strong education system is a fundamental basis for establishing a fair and equal society. A universal, well-resourced government system better meets the needs of the community.

In recent times Australia has put more money into the private education system than into the government system. There are tentative steps to return to a needs-based model, but it remains a two-tiered system. No other country has funded private sector schools to this extent. Private means private and those schools should fund themselves. The capacity and talent in a society is not only found in wealthy families. For a society to maximise its resources, it needs to provide an equal opportunity for all those in the community to develop their abilities. Some parents feel they must work long hours to pay school fees for children, because they think that the system provided by the State does not meet their needs. But working longer hours is mostly not in the interests of children and family life. Families now have less time to spend together because of educational policies, costs and work practices.

Taking the view of the common good, communities develop and prosper where there are local schools with easy access and where supportive networks can form. Opening access outside the local area has had many repercussions for the quality of life for parents and children. Those children are less likely to meet other children in their neighbourhood and so establish friendships that can continue outside school hours. Open access has meant a loss of quality of life in terms of time, demands on parents to drive their children and clogging up road systems. All children being able to attend local schools was probably one of the main reasons, in Australia, that the educational system was able to assist in integrating immigrants into the community in the past. Universal access to good quality education is one of the best indicators of the values and intentions of a society.

Regressive and progressive society

Societies, too, can be discussed in terms of their mental and emotional states, and observed in terms of what makes a society healthy. There are numerous social theorists who offer valuable insights as to how and why our societies function the way they do. Postmodern theories take differing views from critical theorists, but these cannot all be covered here. As a starting point to a way of looking at a broader perspective on society, it is helpful to consider the work of a group of diverse professionals, who have explored different societies in a variety of situations.

In 1987, the University of Virginia School of Medicine established the Centre for the Study of Mind and Human Interaction that drew on cross disciplines such as psychoanalysis, psychiatry, history and political science, as well as former diplomats. To give an insight into their work, I will give an example of what they do. After the Iraqi invasion of Kuwait and the subsequent retreat of the Iraqis in the early 90s, a team from the Centre interviewed 150 Kuwaiti citizens to ascertain the impact that this event had had on their society. What emerged, among other findings, was a shift in attitude among young men, most particularly in regard to women and their perception of their fathers. Many of the young men who had fiancées or girlfriends lost interest in them. The rape of some Kuwaiti women by the invading forces generalised to all women and many withdrew from their relationships.

Before the invasion, Kuwaiti fathers had been perceived as strong. After the invasion, when many young boys witnessed, or knew about, the humiliation of their fathers by Iraqi forces, these sons lost respect for their fathers. The fathers themselves became withdrawn and more distant in their relationships with their sons as a result of their humiliation. The end result was the formation of gangs of youths who roamed the streets and stole cars, a previously unheard of phenomenon in their society.

The founder of the Centre for the Study of Mind and Human Interaction, Vamik Volkan, writing in his book *Blind Trust* (2004), discusses how, in the normal course of events, a well-functioning society operates so that our sense of our large group identity is very much in the background of our consciousness. He postulates that in times of fear and anxiety, if the society is not helped to deal with the anxiety, citizens will shift to identifying at the large group level of the society.

When governments manipulate us we identify with our large group to the extent that we give over our personal reflective capacities to the leader. Identifying at the large group level does not bring out the creative energy of a society. In this regressed state, the leader dominates and citizens become passive. In uncertain times, reality and fantasy can be confused and anxiety raised rather than lessened. Leaders and governments can exaggerate people's need to have enemies or allies. In these circumstances, they are generally pursuing their own self-interest, rather than working in the national interest. They may magnify the dangers, increase anxiety and help the group to remain in regression, which in turn will have further societal and political consequences. In times of crisis and terror, leaders can heal or poison their people.

Manipulation can occur by creating confusion around the concepts of nationalism and patriotism. Nationalism includes the desire to be more powerful than other nation states. Patriotism is the notion of pride in one's own country, but it is not coupled with a need to laud it over others. The leader can take advantage of this confusion to use the flag as a rallying point and make scapegoats of some groups in the society. Autocratic and narcissistic leaders seek to put all the focus on themselves, so that the power is concentrated at the top of government and inclusive discussion is not encouraged. In this climate there is an attempt to undermine a basic trust in institutions and other sources of power, leaving the citizens to turn to blind trust in their leader. This in turn leads to the loss of reflective thought in the members of the society. We can also assess regressive societies in terms of the degree of truth and reality that they permit. Such leaders may resort to violence, but violence should always be the last resort in a democracy, because democracy is supposed to be based on negotiation.

Under the guidance of a healthier leader, the regressed large group can move to function in the interests of the people. Such a leader will separate fantasy from reality and the past from the present, to minimise disruption and conflict. Further, he or she will not seek division or fan an attitude of "us" and "them" or "evil" and "good". In a healthy society there will be support for families to raise their children with a sense of basic trust in the society in which they live, where freedom of speech and the rights of women are valued. Well-functioning civil institutions form part of the web of this trust and include a fair legal system, humane mental institutions and well-run prisons, together with strong unions and medical organisations that serve the members of the society.

An individual's large group identity is intimately connected to his or her personal core identity. Volkan (2004, p. 33) points out that:

> As a result, serious threats to large-group identity,
> such as shared helplessness and humiliation,
> are perceived by members of that large group as
> *individually* wounding and *personally* endangering,
> psychologically speaking. They induce a collective
> response of anxiety or terror and shared defences
> against the fragmentation of the self, above and
> beyond each individual's specific personal defences.

Volkan shares a very moving example of how "the group", at a micro level, can become the meaning for individuals, when they have no other option. He visited an orphanage in Palestine. As he entered the courtyard he noticed a small group of young boys playing soccer together, kicking the ball to each other in a seamless way. Later he asked to speak to one of the boys who, when isolated from the others and asked individual questions, became angry and antisocial and was unable to cope with the interview. The background of these boys was that they were part of the two Palestinian refugee camps that the Lebanese Christian Militia, with Israeli forces, had attacked in 1982, killing nearly 3,000 people. The women hid their babies under the beds or in garbage cans to save them. They were later transported to the orphanage. These boys stayed together during the day and appeared happy in each other's company. Alone they were unable to relate, having not had enough experience of one-on-one care. While their days appeared happy, nights brought bedwetting and night terrors. Perhaps it is this loss of a personal identity and not knowing who you are, which leads to being open to manipulation.

Re-orienting society: becoming citizens

Perhaps it is time to return to the developmental process discussed in the beginning of the book to recall the stages we are asked to traverse. How do we grow into healthy citizens and how do we become mature adults, taking our part in the society in which we live?

The context for our development is establishing relationships with those around us, usually parents, grandparents, extended family and social context. However, our first relationship is with our main carer, often the mother. Within that context, we begin to learn about ourselves, starting with the sense of our own body and where our mother's body begins and ends and where our body begins and ends. This is the beginning of developing a sense of self, and this gradual learning is the foundation of building a more sophisticated sense of who we become over our lifespan. Our interdependence means we must learn to rely on someone else to tend to our needs. For this to happen we have to learn to wait. The umbilical cord is no longer there to supply all our needs on a constant basis. We begin to learn that we need to be patient, that not everything we want or desire is just magically there for us, but hopefully our basic needs will be satisfied.

In this framework, we grow into more complex relationships and form attachments initially with our mother and then with our father. We fall in love with those who are providing us with loving care and commitment. Those loving feelings towards the one who cares for us, however, bring other feelings like possessiveness and the beginnings of envy and jealousy. This possessiveness leads to feelings of anger and frustration that the help and the support we need is not always there. While they are loving, they are also a source of frustration, because they come and go and leave us on our own and we experience ambivalence towards them.

These encounters with feelings of love and hate, desire and frustration, in relation to the ones we love, are something we will continue to grapple with throughout our lives. They are also the birthplace of real love, as we accept those who love us as they are, not just how we would like them to be. We grow in appreciation of their totality and their uniqueness and not just because they provide us with what we want. The reality of who they are forms the basis of a more authentic love and appreciation of them.

This includes the realisation that the mother/carer is not just in a twosome with us, but comes with their relationship with the other parent and people around her. The parent's partnership, or other helpers, provide the support needed to do the job of caring. With time, the child can observe these partnership(s) and how they work, so that at a future time they can establish relationships of their own, which are likewise interdependent and supportive.

These experiences also provide the basis of learning how to be on our own and to have our own thoughts and interests. We grow the capacity to hold in our mind the experience of care and support. By taking this in we feel content with ourselves and do not continually need attention from someone else. This enables us to be part of the family group and to experience both what we receive from that group and what we contribute. It is also through this initial partnership we see the world as a place to be explored, enjoyed and offering the adventure of living. The excitement of learning about the beauty of the world and how it works and how to care for it, flows from the interest and care we receive.

What are the capacities and characteristics that are being nurtured at this time? The sense of oneself as being important and of value is critical at this time. This valuing sits together with the sense that we are not the centre of the universe, but part of something. We become a member of the family and ultimately a member of society. Learning to wait to have our needs met means we gradually appreciate what we receive, so the one who cared for us is also valuable and important. That mutuality leads to a realistic love about what they can and cannot do for us. Hence we forgive our parents or partner for not being able to be all things to us and we love them even though we can be disappointed in them as well. Likewise, we are not able to be all things to them and are accepted for who we are. There will always be the tension between our own needs and the needs of the group.

In addition to an extended family, pre-school or childcare will provide a larger world for the child. Starting school marks a shift in the development of our capacities to deal with others in a social and cooperative way, handle conflict, test our skills and ascertain our strengths and weaknesses in the outside world. It is an enormously challenging time and we have to adapt to new circumstances.

Adolescence is a turbulent time during which we deepen our knowledge of how we function in the world, particularly at the emotional level. Self-knowledge now includes facing the tempestuous, less likeable side of our nature that emerges and needs our understanding and integration. This deepening is imperative for us to gradually manage the more diverse experiences we encounter. Working through these issues enables us to come out the other side with a clearer perspective about ourselves, including our limitations and greater resilience in handling the world around us. In late adolescence, we take on some tasks of citizenship as we exercise the right to vote, begin to pay taxes and enter into mutual relationships with government and social institutions.

Forming a partnership, settling down and having children heralds the next cycle of development, as we become responsible for the next generation. This provides an opportunity to re-work our own early experiences and further shapes the decisions about our choices in life. Contributing to the wellbeing of the family and our work can be a source of satisfaction and a realisation of our greater capacity to be part of the world.

Finally, in our later years, freed from earlier responsibilities, we are able to explore deeper understandings of the human condition. This enables us to experience a sense of the links that bind us together with a greater empathy and a sense of mutual sharing of the joys and travails of living. It is at this time we fully become citizens of the world and are able to embrace the larger notion that our shared humanity extends to all cultures and creeds.

The above processes, if sufficiently traversed, enable us to become part of society and enter the mutual responsibility that is shared between governments, leaders, organisations and fellow citizens as we decide how we wish our society to operate. Each country bears some responsibility for dealing with the particular issues that impact on that country and creating the conditions under which citizens can play a role. This is a collective as well as an individual responsibility. We all have a role in re-orienting our society towards what is in the best interests of all of us. A major outcome of our individual developmental process is to find our own way to express our involvement in our society.

Community participation can be at the individual level, embraced by the society as a whole, or take place through involvement in projects that impact on the community. It is important to consider alternatives to the current paradigms under which we operate, to help the community to be a vital part of the landscape of the society.

An example of an *effective citizen's campaign* is one being waged by Shen Narayasamy against Transfield Services. Transfield Services was renamed Broadspectrum in 2015 and then taken over by Ferrovial in 2016. Originally, the organisation had been operating the Manus Island and Nauru camps on behalf of the federal government. As a private citizen, Shen Narayanasamy helped create a group called No Business in Abuse (NBIA) that drew support from religious groups, unions, progressive law firms and human rights bodies. As reported by Richard Baker and Nick McKenzie (2015), NBIA had been meeting investors, banks, superannuation funds, institutions and analysts. In those meetings, the group sought to highlight the instances of alleged rape, violence and other adverse incidents that it claimed showed the company's complicity in human rights abuses. Shen Narayanasamy also wanted to put the release of children at the top of the organisation's mind. The campaign asserted that the company's role in these adverse incidents was a legal, financial and reputational threat that could impact on its shareholders. Several big investors have now withdrawn their investments, while others are reviewing their holdings.

A case example of a *society changing over time* is Denmark in response to the problem of climate change, a defining issue for all countries. To tackle this problem, Denmark has moved, since the 1970s, from being a country that was entirely dependent on fossil fuels to its current position. Connie Hadegaard (2015), the former European Union Commissioner for climate change, spoke at the Citytalks series run by the City of Sydney Council. In this talk (available on line), she told the story of Denmark where, since 2000, the green energy sector has experienced 7% growth rates. There are days in Denmark when alternative energy is their sole energy source.

It is also the case that 2014 was the first year in which renewables overtook fossil fuels as the primary source of energy for the world. This makes it harder to justify fossil fuel industries receiving five times the subsidies available to renewables worldwide. The societal change will be predicated on our behaviour in shifting away from the worst of consumerism towards binding targets and agreements at the international level. The China and US agreement broke the stasis of waiting to see what other countries do first before tackling climate change, so that business as usual is no longer viable and will end up being more costly if climate change is not tackled.

Participation of citizens in their societal structures has growing support from people at grass roots levels across the globe. One measure of involvement is participatory budgeting, which allows citizens to decide how to allocate part of municipal or public budgets. It allows citizens to identify, discuss and prioritise public spending projects and gives them the power to make real decisions about how money is spent. The first full participatory budgeting process was developed in the city of Porto Alegre, Brazil in 1989.

An example in Australia is a People's Panel, which the City of Melbourne Council initiated. This panel was established as a representative group making recommendations to Council on where and how it should spend its money for the next decade. The newDemocracy Foundation, established by public policy advocate Luca Belgiorno-Nettis, oversaw this initiative to provide better community input into government decision-making. It designed the program, ran the selection process of ratepayers and oversaw the project. The City of Melbourne sent 6,500 letters to randomly selected businesses and households inviting them to apply to join the panel. A further 1000 invitations were sent to students living in the City of Melbourne. From those responding positively, a further random draw was conducted that broadly matched the City's census profile by age, gender and ratepayer mix. The final group of forty-three citizens met over a three-month period and was given open access to information, expert opinion and financial data and made recommendations to Council on priority projects, initiatives, revenue and spending, as part of a Ten-Year Financial Plan. The council integrated almost all of the recommendations into the plan.

The newDemocracy Foundation also assisted Penrith Council in Sydney's west, which is facing rapid changes and pressure on finite resources, while providing opportunities for the future. To assist the council, the Penrith City Community Panel, with thirty-five randomly selected citizens, met six times between September and December 2015 to provide Council with a set of recommendations on what services and infrastructure should be paid for.

Modern democracies, where politicians are seen as being out of touch with their citizens, need to find ways to engage their citizens and make them part of the process. Disengaged citizens turn to populism and demigods to be heard, creating instability and undermining the democratic system.

Chapter 11 The global society

Gamble everything for love,
if you're a true human being
if not, leave
this gathering.
Half-heartedness doesn't reach
this gathering.

"On Gambling," (Barks, p. 192)

The first part of the book examined the importance of exploring our history in order to embrace the future. This chapter will give some background into the evolution of the most recent economic and social models western society has been using nationally and internationally, to assess whether our society and these models align with the needs of its citizens and families. I will also look at ways to reform this system, where it is not supportive of the better functioning of society as a whole.

The second part of the chapter will address issues that are topical in the world at the moment, but impact on the wellbeing of individuals and societies. These include the effect of inequality on society, war and immigration, and the importance of leadership and the leadership-citizenship social contract. The notion of leadership will include government and corporate institutions that hold powerful positions in society.

Background

Prior to World War I, in 1914, there was entrenched inequality across the world, with aristocracies, colonisation and deeply divided societies. This war, which wiped out a lot of capital assets, paved the way for communism, which was tried and failed as an alternative. In the United States, Roosevelt initiated the New Deal in response to the Great Depression, which was the most widespread depression in the 20th century. Many believed that corporate greed and mismanagement had caused the Great Depression and they turned to governments to provide regulation. (The corporations referred to were the large Anglo-American publicly traded businesses, not the small not-for-profit organisations.) Debt had spiralled up and general economic thought was that governments needed to keep the total money supply and aggregate demand on a stable growth path.

Despite corporate leaders' claims that they were capable of regulating themselves, in 1934 President Roosevelt created the New Deal that curbed the powers and freedoms of the corporations. Roosevelt's New Deal focused on the three R's; relief for the unemployed and poor, recovery of the economy to normal levels, and reforms of the financial system to prevent another depression. Corporations at the time were angry, and a few even plotted a coup to overthrow his administration. For fifty years following its creation, the New Deal prevailed. There was an era of cooperation between the people and government. This meant that there was an offset of the power of corporations by the expansion of government regulation, trade unions, and social programs. The British economist, John Maynard Keynes, put forward the idea that the government needed to play a role in stabilising the economy. He overturned the idea that the free market alone could provide full employment and advocated that governments needed to intervene in periods of crashes and booms to counter cyclical movements.

In the United Kingdom, men and women returning from World War II sought recognition for having given so much to their country. Governments were generally committed to building fairer societies, financed by progressive taxation and trade unions were strong. In the late 1940s the National Health Service was established. During this time the growth rate was high due to infrastructure re-building.

Many governments believed it was a valuable goal for countries to work together. The United Nations, an intergovernmental organisation, was established in 1945 to promote international cooperation and preserve world peace. The General Agreement on Tariffs and Trade (GATT) was set up 1948 to facilitate the reduction of tariffs and trade barriers, to eliminate trade preferences and create a reciprocal and mutually advantageous way for nations to trade. In 1994, the World Trade Organisation (WTO) replaced GATT in the Uruguay Round of Agreements in Marrakesh.

In his book *Australia's Boldest Experiment,* Professor Stuart Macintyre (2015) discusses this kind of cooperation in Australia in the years after World War II under the leadership of Ben Chifley. Chifley, along with public servants like Nugget Coombs, reformed Australia by establishing commissions, for example, the Rural Reconstruction Commission and the Housing Commission. These commissions toured the country getting people's views to better understand current issues and provide information on which policy could be based. These changes heralded the beginning of a long period of uninterrupted growth.

Another moment of cooperation in Australia occurred when Prime Minister Bob Hawke established the Summit, which included business leaders, government, the unions and welfare organisations. The Summit resulted in "The Accord" between the government and the unions in 1983. Under the leadership of Bob Hawke and the treasurer Paul Keating, the parties to the Accord accepted lower wages on the basis that the social wage of Australian workers would improve as a result of government reforms in health, social welfare, superannuation and taxation. The Accord itself succeeded and the unions and the people accepted a social contract. The period after the Accord saw the greatest increase in executive earnings Australia had ever experienced and reflected a worldwide trend.

The growth of a new model

Throughout the period of cooperation between citizens and government, the corporations regrouped. A new convergence of technology, law, ideology, the advertising industry and the process of globalisation gradually reversed the trend of cooperation. The advertising industry turned to psychological techniques and we moved from being people who purchased on the basis of "need" to those who bought on the basis of "wants" and "desires". We became "consumers". Satisfied citizens are not the best consumers. In the 1970s, many advanced countries suffered both inflation and slow growth, that is, stagflation. Monetarism became the new school of economic thought, which meant targeting the growth rate of the money supply. When Margaret Thatcher became Prime Minister of Britain in 1979 and Ronald Reagan President of the USA in 1980, their governments embraced neoliberalism and New Deal ideas and policies ended. The neoliberal era after Reagan and Thatcher undermined this earlier period of greater cooperation and growth, with an emphasis on the deregulation of the markets, privatisation and a smaller role for governments.[4] Creating incentive became more important than maintaining fairness, on the assumption that there would be a "trickle down" effect if those at the top prospered. According to Bakan (2004, p. 21), 'Over the next two decades governments pursued neoliberalism's core policies of deregulation, privatization, spending cuts and inflation reduction with increasing vigor.'

Communication through technology improved. The introduction of the internet allowed corporations to produce goods and services at locations outside their home jurisdiction at substantially lower labour costs. With this greater access they could now dictate the economic policies of governments. Economic globalisation enhanced corporate

---

[4] Maclean, N. 2017, *Democracy in Chains*, Scribe, Melbourne and London, provides ten years of research detailing how US institutions have been systematically undermined in the US, altering democratic governance. These processes parallel what has occurred in Australia.

power. John Perkins' (2004) book, *Confessions of a an Economic Hit-man,* a *New York Times* bestseller, is a graphic account of some of the excesses of this era and helps to explain how we have reached the level of instability we experience now.

After World War II, leading corporate figures, politicians and bankers began engineering the massive power shift away from national, state and local government and communities. Western countries entered into an agreement called Bretton Woods to align all of the world's formerly separate national economies behind a central formula to develop *corporate-led economic growth.* The three major global institutions, the World Bank (WB), the International Monetary Fund (IMF) and the World Trade Organisation (WTO), were created to express these economic rules.

With the creation of the WTO in 1993, the deregulatory logic deepened. The WTO required nations, under threat of punishing penalties, to change or repeal laws designed to protect environmental, consumer or other public interests. The WB funded large-scale projects, promoted structural adjustment policies and dominated the development debate through its research department. The IMF introduced similar economic "reforms" through short–term emergency loans. The WTO set the rules for global trade and investment. They worked together to ensure that all countries adopted identical visions, policies and standards and kept to them. In the early years, these systems worked to the benefit of developing countries and their citizens, but that changed over time. As the corporate sector grew in influence, these three bodies became known as the "unholy trinity" or the Washington Consensus reflecting the USA's dominance.

Since the 1980s, these organisations began to share the overall goals of deregulating corporate activity; that is, to privatise whatever is public, to prevent nations from protecting natural resources, labour, safety laws or standards, and to open all channels in every country for a free flow of investment and trade. The thrust of those policies is perhaps most dramatically revealed in the structural adjustment programs that the IMF and the WB imposed on low and intermediate income countries. Structural adjustments, which I quote from Cavanagh and Mander (2004, pp. 55-6), required governments to do the following:

- Cut government spending on education, health care, the environment, and price subsidies for basic necessities such as goods, grains and cooking oils.

- Devalue the national currency and increase exports by accelerating the plunder of natural resources, reducing real wages, and subsidizing export oriented foreign investments.

- Liberalize (open) financial markets to attract speculative short-term portfolio investments that create enormous financial instability, and foreign liabilities, while serving little if any useful purpose.

- Increase interest rates to attract foreign capital that has fled its country, thereby increasing bankruptcies of domestic business and imposing new hardships on indebted individuals.

- Eliminate tariffs and other controls on imports, thereby increasing the import of consumer goods purchased with borrowed foreign exchange, undermining local industry and agricultural producers unable to compete with cheap imports, increasing the strain on foreign exchange and deepening external indebtedness.

Yet it was possible to resist, as the people of Cochabamba, Bolivia, did in 2000. The Bolivian government, under pressure from the World Bank to privatise water utilities, contracted Aguas del Tunari, the major shareholder of the Bechtel subsidiary of International Water Ltd, to run the water system of Cochabamba, a water-starved region in central Bolivia. When Aguas del Tunaria took over they tripled the cost of water and began charging peasants for water they drew from their own wells. The government, in compliance with its contract with the company, passed a law that prohibited people from collecting water from local lagoons, rivers and deltas or even rainwater. The company confiscated people's alternative water systems, without compensation, and placed them under its control.

These actions, including the rate increases, which imposed severe hardships, were justified by the company as necessary to meet contractually mandated profit levels. After bloody confrontations between the citizens, when police and military inflicted much damage and in which five people died and many young people were badly injured, the company finally left. The corporation was returned to the people of Cochabamba. The non-profit corporation now has a board of directors composed of local officials and representatives from unions and professional associations. It is transparent, just, more efficient and encourages participation in solving problems. When Bechtel left it filed a $25 million dollar lawsuit against Bolivia for lost profits under the Bolivia-Netherlands investment treaty, which mirrors the former North America Free Trade Agreement (NAFTA) rules.

The above was not an isolated incident. By 2003, the golden era of corporate-driven economic globalization and the dominance of the USA model of economic and political affairs was over. In Cancun, Mexico, WTO talks gathered to revive the shattered trade talks in Seattle in 1999. However, the talks collapsed. Months later, the Free Trade Area of the Americas (FTAA) discussion broke down. The poorest countries were listening to the voices of their people.

The next part of this chapter will cover inequality, war and immigration and the leadership-citizenship contract, as areas needing our attention if we are to tackle the issues of our time. This is part of a discussion on what role we have to play as citizens, and what role do our structures play in creating a world that includes our needs and fosters our human interests. All of these issues impact on our individual wellbeing and the level of functioning of our society. Climate change was referred to in the previous chapter. Reflection on these issues provides an opportunity to promote change and alleviate suffering.

Inequality

Inequality is regarded as the central marker of a civil society. Growing inequality in countries is bad for growth and for sustainability and inhibits the generation of creativity among its citizens. A civil society relies on good working structures and the separation of powers as the context in which governments function. This requires a system where the law prevails over both leaders and citizens and where checks and balances keep the system working as a functional democracy.

The three powers in a parliamentary democracy are the legislature, the executive and the judiciary. The fundamental value in this system is that we are all equal in the eyes of the law, as Aristotle says:

> It is more proper that law should govern than any one of the citizens; upon the same principle, if it is advantageous to place the supreme power in some particular persons, they should be appointed to be only guardians, and the servants of the laws." *Politics* 3:16

The *Oxford English Dictionary* defines "rule of law" as the authority and influence of law in society, especially when viewed as a constraint on individual and institutional behaviour. This is the principle whereby all members of a society (including those in government) or who are powerful in the community, are equally subject to publicly disclosed legal codes and processes.

The rule of law is considered a key dimension that determines the quality and good governance of a country and is essential to democracy. Democracy is a system of government in which power is vested in the people, who rule either directly or through freely elected representatives. It requires four key elements: a political system for choosing and replacing the government through free and fair elections; the active participation of the people as citizens in politics and civic life; protection of the human rights of all citizens; and a rule of law, in which the laws and procedures apply equally to all citizens.

What has happened, however, since the 1980s, as a result of neoliberal policies, is that *inequality went back to where it was in 1914*, bringing with it the inevitable impact of social problems. The neoliberal view that giving incentives to higher income earners produces the "trickle down" effect has now been rigorously challenged. The work of Piketty (2014) is important here. His specialty is researching economic inequality, taking a historic and statistical approach. He painstakingly disproved the "trickle down" effect which, in fact, had the impact of concentrating wealth in the hands of a few. His central thesis is that inequality is not an accident, but rather a feature of capitalism, and that regulation and intervention through, for instance, progressive tax policies, helps to mitigate the situation. Piketty's view is that unless there is reform, deregulated capitalism, or neoliberalism, will compromise democracy, and vest greater power in a few. With inequality heightening in the last thirty years, we are heading for what he calls patrimonial capitalism, in which a few families control most of the wealth. He observed how the fruits of the economy are distributed, looking at the income from capital and the income from labour. He shows that the wealthy accrue capital, and that capital creates capital, while poverty creates poverty.

Amartya Sen, writing in his book *Inequality Reexamined* (1992), explores the notion of inequality in relation to how class, gender and communities can limit human freedom and lessen citizens' ability to function fully in their society.

After two decades of imposing structural adjustments on 90 developing countries, the WB and the IMF abandoned the program, replacing it with the Comprehensive Development Framework, because the whole scheme had been highly unsuccessful and destructive to participating countries. Slowly, and against opposition, these institutions are beginning to work their way toward a more realistic view of what needs to be done. The IMF released a report in June 2015 by five of its economists, stating that there should be money incentives to the poor and the middle class if governments and countries are to have growth. The recommendations included progressive income tax laws, so that payment relates to what has been earned, tackling tax avoidance and evasion and applying taxation to capital and property ownership. This report was not widely reported and those who have been benefiting under the old system resisted it.

After the 2008 financial crisis, governments were quick to recapitalise and add liquidity to the broken banking system. The poor and middle classes had to pay for the mistakes of the rich and the results have been devastating. The consequences were felt around the world. According to Cunningham (2015, p. 150) *In the Age of Selfishness:*

> In 2009 some 47 to 84 million people in developing countries were thought to have fallen into, or become trapped in poverty as a result of the financial crisis. A further 120 million people who were living just above the poverty line were put at risk of falling into extreme deprivation. In the developed world there was a significant deterioration in child wellbeing, in areas that include health and safety, education, housing and environment. Spain was particularly hard-hit by the crisis, more than 2.2 million children are estimated to have fallen below the poverty line, with many families having to cut down on basic necessities.

Subsequent protests in Spain lead to the gradual evolution of the 15M Movement, named after the demonstrations on 15 May 2011, when a coalition of groups responded to the government's austerity measures. Spain was suffering massive unemployment of nearly five million people at the end of March 2011. Youth employment was over 43%. Harsh housing policies evicted people from their homes, even though the banks had originally encouraged borrowing. Once evicted, they were forced to pay 40% of the cost of the house back to the bank. All of these events fuelled mass demonstrations. According to statistics published by RTVE, the Spanish public broadcasting company, between 6.5 and 8 million Spaniards participated in these events. ABC TV Foreign Correspondent Sally Sarah (2015) reported, under the banner of "Yes We Can," that members of 15M were elected to office in Barcelona and Madrid in the municipal elections. Their platform is for citizen participation, employment, anti-corruption and opposition to welfare cuts.

Bakan (2004) has made several suggestions for reforms to restore balance to societies. In his view, government regulation should be rethought in order to bring corporations under greater control, so they will respect the interests of citizens, communities and the environment. At present, they have a legally defined mandate to pursue relentlessly, and without exception, their own self-interest, regardless of the harmful consequences to others. He also states that governments should be more effective by providing adequate staff, appropriate fines and strengthening the liability of top directors and managers, for unethical and illegal behaviours. Finally, he supports barring repeat offenders from government contracts and suspending those that persistently violate the public interest.

These are small movements in reform in this direction, but it is obviously extremely difficult to achieve reform. Cunningham (2015) reported an early attempt in the European Parliament to combat tax fraud and avoidance. This resolution was supported by all the major European Union countries, except the British Conservatives and the United Kingdom Independence Party, who voted against the measures. Further studies have looked at the impact of tax evasion. A European Parliamentary Research Service (EPRS) by Dover *et al.* (2015, p. 4) studied per annum losses:

> We estimate that revenue losses for the EU as a result of corporate tax avoidance could amount to 50-70 billion euro representing the sum lost to profit shifting. We think this figure represents a lower-end estimate of lost revenue, If, however, we include other tax regime issues, such as special tax arrangements, inefficiencies in collection and other practices, we estimate that revenue losses for the EU due to corporate tax avoidance could amount to around 160-190 billion euro, again a conservative estimate. On an assumption of no base from sources other than shifting, then this figures jumps to 160-190 billion.

The charity ActionAid (2013) published figures which showed that, of the top 100 companies listed on the *Financial Times* Share Index UK, only two did not use tax havens as a tactic to avoid paying corporation tax. Corporations use the "Double Irish and Dutch Sandwich" to shift multinationals' profits to tax havens; that is, jurisdictions that impose very low or no income tax at all. These actions create systemic inequities, whereby some individuals or organisations pay tax and others do not. The Australian Government brought in the *Diverted Tax Law* 1 July 2017, which begins to address this by closing loopholes to ensure the profits of multinationals are taxed here. Further inequities need to be addressed and properly regulated if real reform is to be achieved.

In Australia, the National Centre for Social and Economic Modelling was commissioned by Anglicare Australia to look at inequality. This was reported by Judith Ireland (2015). The gap between Australia's richest and poorest was found to have grown by 13% over the past decade and is projected to jump by a further 10% over the next 10 years unless policies are changed.

In Australia, the looming problem of money laundering is another example of poor regulation. This impacts on society and further distorts the market by creating further inequities. As reported by Michael West (2015, p. 2):

> A Swiss NGO went public this week with allegations that the family of prominent Malaysian Taib Mahmud had laundered $30 million through an obscure Australian company called Sitehost Pty. Ltd. Sitehost owns and operates the Adelaide Hilton.
>
> There is a sea of black money swishing about in Australian property markets – with a blind eye conveniently turned by our elected representatives and the bureaucracy…

According to West:

> Austrac [the money laundering regulator], has identified that laundering illicit funds through real estate is an established money laundering method in Australia; criminals are drawn to real estate investment in Australia because it is possible to purchase in cash, it offers reliable returns and it is possible to disguise ownership, and criminals also use professional facilitators such as lawyers and accountants to help them seem legitimate.

Governments promised legislation for 10 years before beginning to consider the issue. Such activities distort our economy and corrupt the systems that are meant to operate in the interests of the citizens of the country. These distortions create instability and others will have to pay the cost, usually those with fewer means.

Other reforms suggested by Bakan (2004) are to strengthen political democracy by phasing out corporate donations, introducing tighter regulations on lobbying and controlling the flow of personnel between government and business. The status they have endangers the democratic process and their influence should be scaled back to be similar to other organisations, such as unions, environmental and consumer groups and human rights advocates.

Electoral reform could include proportional representa-tion and re-engaging disaffected citizens who feel left out of the power structures. We need to have a healthy public sphere to discuss how to counter the prevailing presump-tion that no public interest exists beyond the accumulated financial interest of individual corporations, consumers and shareholders. Bakan also discusses the need to chal-lenge neoliberal ideology and corporate power as they are our own creations. He reminds us that they have no powers and no capacities beyond what we give them through our governments.

Stiglitz (2003) writes of how the International Monetary Fund and other major institutions put Western interests ahead of poor countries. He has said that it is not just economic problems that arise from inequality. He takes the view that the few will have too much sway in the political process. Our institutions are under attack, like the unions where casualised labour undermines their role. The lack of values exhibited does have an impact. When corrupt behaviour is more profitable than honest hard work, it puts the whole of society at risk, leading to disconnection from the system. Stiglitz argues that, in an egalitarian government, we would have good policy, a good health system, pensions, progressive tax (including inheritance tax and land tax), closing tax loopholes and no negative gearing.

Consultation can achieve change, for instance, a recent aged pension reform in Norway is the outcome of listening to the relevant institutions. Norway has combined pension flexibility and active workforce participations. The country recently introduced an automatic increase of two-thirds of a year in the pension age for every one-year increase in life expectancy. Employees can retire at sixty-two, but this choice reduces the benefits paid later in life. This reform was achieved without conflict. Cooperation between strong trade unions and government achieved this reform without strikes or demonstrations. Having a fair share and cooperating are key indicators of success. Fairness leads to fewer strikes and fewer mental health issues when it is egalitarian in nature.

Leadership-citizen social contract

In recent times the relationship between leaders and citizens has been breaking down. People view politicians as being out of touch with the people and there has been a corresponding rise in populism. People see banks and large corporations as greedy, pursuing the profits at the expense of the common good. Both sides have lost their role in the relationship. Leaders, political and corporate, have treated people as consumers of the political and social process and not as active participants in a relationship. Citizens have felt angry, but powerless to respond. It is valuable to explore the growing research on leadership to learn what makes a healthy leader over one who cannot put the interests of the society central to decision making. Being sufficiently informed is the role of the citizen. This knowledge includes exercising judgment of the psychological profile of our leaders, to look beyond what they say and to assess their capacity. As citizens, we are responsible for voting or appointing our leaders, so we need to be well informed.

Unfortunately, there is a lack of proper leadership by the media, nationally and internationally. Non-public sponsored media often behaves as if it is free to do what it wants because it is privately funded. However, there are ethical considerations around the use of the media, because of the special role they have in our society. They are expected to present information to the public, not just present the proprietors' views. The Leveson Inquiry (2012, p.5) into the culture, practices and ethics of the press in the UK, reiterated the place of the public interest and concluded that the political parties in the UK national government had developed too close a relationship with the media:

> The Press operating properly and in the public
> interest is one of the true safeguards of our
> democracy… [the freedom of the press] is one of
> the cornerstones of our democracy… With these

rights, however, come responsibilities to the public
interest: to respect the truth, to obey the law, and
to uphold the rights and liberties of individuals. In
short to honour the very principles proclaimed and
articulated by the industry itself.

Unfortunately, deregulation has reduced the regulatory
strength of bodies that are meant to oversee the proper
workings of the general media and they are unable to
perform their role robustly, against major conglomerates
with immense power. In *Rich Media, Poor Democracy*, Robert
McChesney (1999) of the University of Illinois has compiled
an important set of statistics and analyses on global media
concentration. As of 1999, only eight giant global corporations
owned over 70% of *all* global media. This included television,
newspapers, magazines, radio, satellite systems, cable, book
publishing, film production and distribution, and theatre
chains. Since then, the rules of the WTO organisation and
domestic policies within countries, have only increased the
concentration. This concentration is not always apparent,
because many affiliates continue to operate under other
names. The influence of a few corporations on government
officials and public policies throughout the world is immense.
As pointed out by Cavanagh and Mander (2004, p. 233):

> Given such a situation, one might ask if there can
> possibly be a free enough flow of information for
> real democracy to survive. It would be difficult
> to overstate the impacts of these few powerful
> corporations on public opinion when major issues
> are in play, whether concerns with the environment,
> social policy, or national elections.

In fact, some in these powerful corporations are actively
engaged in attempting to destroy public broadcasting, which
is seen as a competitor, rather than an independent source
of news. *The Conversation* has carried articles by Professor
Julian Petley (such as "How the Murdoch press has waged a
relentless campaign against the BBC (and why it's worked)"

(2015). Ben Goldsmith (2013), in *The Conversation*, wrote of the "The Foxtel-BBC deal; implications for Australian television and content" and the ending of a 50-year partnership between the BBC and the ABC. Under the new deal, Foxtel will host a new BBC channel that will screen first run, "fast-tracked" British programming, meaning ABC viewers will no longer have free-to-air access to many popular shows. The deal came into place in July 2014. Foxtel subscribers will pay an additional fee for the premium, first-run BBC drama, comedy and lifestyle productions and receive "fast-tracked" programs, available within hours of their first screening in the UK. Free-to-air viewers will have to wait for at least a year to see the same programs.

Taking a contrary view to power through dominance and control, the then President of the Business Council of Australia, Catherine Livingstone, delivered an impressive speech, available online, to the National Press Club in Canberra on April 29, 2015. When discussing leadership in Australia in a subsequent *Saturday Extra* program on the ABC, she noted the need for *reflective leadership*, where problems are faced, and worked through in a partnership of stakeholders. She is a strong believer in connectivity, because ideas flow through interactivity. She pointed out the need for governments, business and unions to get together to discuss the issues we face. This requires leaders to acknowledge they do not have all the answers, but they should try to resolve the issues collaboratively. Without proper dialogue, business and government fail to anticipate and deal with genuine problems in the future. She also mentions a major cause of concern, that is, robots displacing workers from jobs. Robots will take over not just repetitive jobs, but routine cognitive labour as well. Currently 400,000 young people in Australia neither work, nor are in a study program. Davos (2015) reports that international leaders at the World Economic Forum meeting started to realise that the rate of change of technology and the implication for jobs was a massive looming problem. This will put pressure on governments to manage the adaptation to the increasing use of robots.

Failure of leadership

The perceived failure of leadership is not just about one person at the top of the pyramid, but all the other levels of leadership from heads of corporations, layers of management and public service administration in general. The public service in Australia formerly had a tradition of providing advice without fear or favour. This system served both sides of politics and enabled more areas of policy to be bipartisan in nature and achieve more satisfactory outcomes. The public service is now politicised, with governments of both persuasions replacing existing employees with their own exponents. Ideologically driven policies skew reality and distort the possibilities available for consideration, and so produce poor policy.

Over the past 20 years, the academic psychological literature on leadership and management derailment (or what constitutes poor management) has grown enormously. A research project by Webster and Brough (2015) looked at the issue of toxic leadership in Australian workplaces and its impact on employee wellbeing. In Australia, workplace health and safety legislation effectively holds employers responsible for ensuring the emotional, psychological and physical wellbeing of employees. When they perceive an employer has breached this responsibility, affected employees may lodge compensation claims for stress. The research found that mental stress claims have increased by 25% from 2001 to 2011 according to Safe Work Australia (2013). A Medibank Private study (2008) on work-related stress, including stress caused by poor relationships with superiors, reported that in 2007 the direct cost to employers was $10.11 billion.

The study also researched the impact of toxic leadership on employee wellbeing. Seventy-six self-selected respondents to a survey across Australia and New Zealand reported experiencing behaviours consistent with toxic leader behaviour typologies. The main industries represented were education, healthcare, professional services and financial services/accounting. Forty-two respondents no longer worked for the organisation where the reported incidents had happened. Respondents identified the most common toxic behaviours exhibited by managers to be: needing constant praise, taking credit for other's work and winning at all costs. These managers micromanaged staff and took away decision-making capacity. They were also critical of others and the work done, while ignoring requests and not fulfilling promises of action. Behaviourally, they used charm and manipulation and played favourites. They exhibited mood swings and temper tantrums, often lying, bullying and abusing others.

Other studies describe how so-called "dark-side" leaders emerge. This is discussed in Furnham (2015), who nominates three national and corporate cultural factors that facilitate this outcome. First, individualistic cultures more than collectivistic cultures value personal achievement over group success. Thus, it is more natural to look for and select people who have significant self-belief. Second, when people perceive an imagined or real and significant threat to their wellbeing and livelihood, they are often drawn to the "superman/heroic" leader who promises that he or she can save them. People are drawn to the rhetoric, the self-confidence and the bravado of leaders who can mobilise them and give them confidence. Third, all organisations, for not only historical, but also legal reasons, have processes and procedures which can, in effect, facilitate or frustrate the emergence of a dark-side leader. Some place serious restrictions on an individual's power and freedom to make decisions. Others have strict rules about group decision-making and record keeping, while others are more relaxed.

The modern literature, based on both psychological and psychiatric theory, suggests that underlying all leader derailment (and all personality disorders) there are three very fundamental markers. According to Furnham, they concern issues of empathy, intimacy, identity and adaptation. The first marker or query is whether the person can establish and maintain healthy, happy, long-term relationships with various sorts of people. What is clear from the work on personality disorders, and "dark-side" traits is that, for different reasons, those with these disorders have difficulty with relationships. One recognised reason for management failure is lack of emotional intelligence. The next question is around self-awareness and whether the person has a capacity for insight. The bottom line is that most derailed leaders are poorly informed about their strengths and weaknesses. They do not understand how they come across and their effect on others. This is potentially a serious issue. The final marker or need is for adaptability, learning and transition. Senior leadership is often about dealing calmly and rationally with ambiguous, threatening and uncertain situations. The inflexible and non-adaptive executive cannot change their mindset and grow to meet changing circumstances.

Rosenthal (2007), quoted in Furnham (2015 p. 199), notes a number of problems that are inter-correlated with dark-side traits and the leaders with whom they are most associated:

- feelings of inferiority

- an insatiable need for recognition and superiority

- hypersensitivity and anger

- lack of empathy

- amorality

- paranoia, seeing enemies everywhere.

Such leaders are narcissistic. Their long-term disadvantages outweighed short-term advantages, because the narcissist's persistent efforts are aimed at enhancing their self-image, leading to group clashes. They bring "costs" because of their need to distort reality into a form conducive to self-enhancement. As a result of their inability to acknowledge failure, or even mistakes, they are unable to learn from experience. Overall, they favour judgment over analysis and they often seem to have little time for "mulling" over a decision. This leads to a lack of rational analysis, prolonged contemplation or regular dialogues with others. There is no room for "doubt", which they see as a sign of weakness or dithering. Lack of introspection and reflection completes the picture.

An important feature here is that the people who work around narcissistic leaders are complicit. It is said that we get the leaders we deserve and our complicity needs to be accounted for. Often, particularly in situations of crisis, people at work have unrealistic expectations of their leaders. If our expectations are unrealistic, we tend to be disappointed. We want them to be superhuman and to ensure success and continuity. Followers, according to Kets de Vries (2006a,b), quoted in Furnham (2015, pp. 204–5) encourage two types of behaviours in narcissistic leaders, which are very bad for both leader and follower:

> First, there is the process of *mirroring*, where
> followers use leaders to reflect what they want to
> see. Narcissists get the admiration they crave and
> there occurs mutual admiration. The problem is that
> managers can take their eye off the ball, being more
> concerned with policies and procedures that make
> them look good, rather than serving the best interests
> of all stakeholders. Second, there is idealisation, in
> which followers project all their hopes and fantasies
> onto the leader. Thus, leaders find themselves in a
> hall of mirrors which further decreases their grip on
> reality.

War and migration

Conflict is part of our lives, but the human and economic cost of conflict means that engaging in war is a decision of significance. Leaders and nations bear an enormous responsibility when making such a decision and the consequences need to be well worked through beforehand. Exploring conflict implicates all of us, both leaders and citizens, to better understand motivating elements that may lead to war.

While we are not just the sum of our early experiences, I want to make a direct link between unresolved experiences as babies or children and later manifestations of rage and fury. I will quote from a colleague's experience of a child in therapy, who is learning how to handle his intense feelings about her absence. This child had begun to connect with my colleague, as he had been unable to do so with his mother who had her own struggles:

> After a holiday break in his therapy, a four-year-old boy showed me, in words and play, my fate after a holiday infidelity. First he made a figure in plasticine, and told me *it's you*. The plasticine me had a round head and eyes, nose, mouth and ears, and a round body with a hole he called a belly button; there were no arms. Then slowly and fiercely he tore off my legs and my ears, gouged out my eyes, nose, mouth and belly button, and he said, deepening the holes with his pencil, *fill them up with pees!* He then glanced up at me and screamed. Clearly at that moment the me he saw was the me he had mutilated; his mind's eye view of me obscured his physical view. Gradually he quietened, and was able to look at me, a "me" who could survive and understand his murderous rage. We talked about his feelings towards his mother and the new baby that was coming. When he left the session he did not take only a damaged, revengeful me in his mind but he felt that his own rage had been understood.

Feelings that we have not dealt with remain embedded in the archives of our memory, our unconscious, until later experiences activate them. Activation can be of incidents like domestic violence, beating children, attacking authority figures, vandalism, corruption, theft and war. The more the community is aware of these early processes, the more they will be understood and held in the "mind" of the community.

Former President Richard Nixon was the second child of a struggling family that frequently faced death, separation and financial hardship. For Nixon, those struggles began early, with his mother taking many weeks to recover from her pregnancy. His mother then took in a newborn nephew when Richard was only six months old. A few months later his mother returned to hospital for an operation and went to her parent's home to recuperate. Soon after returning, she was pregnant again and moved back to her parent' place to give birth. At twelve he was sent away for five months to live with his aunt, and at fourteen his older brother contacted tuberculosis and his mother moved to a sanatorium to look after him.

Volkan, Itzkowitz and Dod (1997) have written a psychobiography of Nixon, taking into account his formative years and explaining why Nixon was prone to extreme reactions when he sensed that someone or something humiliated him.

Blema Steinberg (1996), a political scientist and psychoanalyst, suggests that the US bombing of North Vietnamese sanctuaries in Cambodia in March 1969 and subsequent invasion of Cambodia in 1970 were Nixon's personal response to shame and humiliation. According to Steinberg: 'Attacking Cambodian sanctuaries ostensibly enabled Nixon to demonstrate US resolve; but his use of violence was a way of restoring his self-esteem.' (p. 177) The result of these decisions was the invasion of Cambodia, and the beginning of a fully-fledged civil war that devastated Cambodia, killing more than a million people.

The actual cost of war and the weapons required to wage it falls on the general population, whose work generates the taxes that pay for them. This implies some responsibility on us as citizens to have a say about that spending, given its reach. Accumulation of arms is a burden on every country involved because it wastes colossal sums that could otherwise be spent on raising the standard of living of those in need. According to the Stockholm International Peace Research Institute (2017), world military expenditure in 2016 amounted to $1.69 trillion. The insanity is evident when two-fifths of the world's population lives on less than $2 a day and a billion are hungry. Imagine the difference that could make to the destitute and hungry people of the world if these sums spent on wars, arms and military bases were instead directed to the worldwide distribution of food, healthcare and education. According to the United Nations, $300 billion a year could lift those who are under the poverty line of $1 a day to above the poverty line. This is less than a quarter of the global military budget in 2011.

The United States has the highest number of arms sales, followed by the United Kingdom, together worth around five billion dollars a year. Buyers of arms have consistently been autocratic regimes in North Africa, the Middle East and sub-Saharan Africa. The UK's arms sales to repressive regimes in Arab countries increased 27% between 2010 and 2011. This is a cause for shame, as Feinstein's (2011) book, *The Shadow World: Inside the Global Arms Trade,* shows. He argues that governments should regulate this destructive industry that goes unscrutinised.

In times of conflict, countries mobilise collective opinion to justify attacking or retaliatory behaviour by dehumanizing or demonising the enemy. The conflict is presented simplistically, polarising other groups and designating them as enemies. Strategic lying and fear mongering that promote national interests has long been part of the repertoire of political leaders. They promote the belief that their cause is good, while the other side is evil. This interferes with our capacity to think and feel our way through the issues to find other solutions. The fear and hatred involved in current conflicts also activates memories of older conflicts, going back many years. When atrocities are committed on both sides, the immediate impulse is to avenge them, which makes it almost impossible to contain the survival instincts that are aroused.

The war in Afghanistan (2001) began as retaliation for the bombing of the twin towers in the United States, and Australia and other countries joined the US. Afghanistan today reflects the horrors of war, and generations to come will suffer the consequences. Mahboba Rawi was interviewed by Paul McGeough (2015) after a trip to Kabul. She graphically spoke of the experience of returning to her country. She went to oversee the work of her organisation there. She set up Mahboba's Promise in 1998 in response to a plea for help from the victims of the war in Afghanistan. Mahboba was an arranged bride who came from a refugee camp in Pakistan to settle in Australia. She was happy here, but in 1992 her six-year-old son Arosh, and six other members of their extended family, drowned when a freak wave struck them as they stood on rocks at the Kiama blowhole south of Sydney. After years of grief, she promised that she would not allow children to die from poverty or sickness. Having lost a child, she would save a child. She started with a small orphanage and community education centre in 2002 called House in Kabul, but she also established schools, medical centres and programs for children and widows.

Mahboba always found reason for hope, but, after her 2015 visit to Afghanistan, she locked herself away and cried for two weeks in despair. McGeough (2015, p. 23) reported what she saw as she entered Kabul International Airport, fourteen years after the war started:

> The poverty was unbelievable... I was shocked
> because after 10 years there seemed to have been no
> improvement – the road was full of kids begging,

women sitting on the roads, wearing burqas. They
crowd around, ten to fifteen at each car. They run
alongside, saying things like "I haven't eaten" and
"my children haven't eaten for many days"... Afghan
men don't cry... these days they do – and when a 45
year-old sobbed as he told his story, others waiting
in the futile hope for work at a Kabul labour pick-up
spot, dissolved into tears too. "Tell the president (to)
kill all poor people," he told her. "We don't want to
die slowly like this – put us out of our misery."

Over a decade and a half later, this is the forgotten
state of Afghanistan, a country that is forced to endure the
intolerable.

The Iraq War began in 2003 with the United States
invasion of Iraq to topple the government of Saddam
Hussein. In October 2013, the results of a new study on the
number of victims of the Iraq War since 2003, published by
the professional medical journal PLOS *Medicine*, stated that
half a million people died, noting that this was a conservative
estimate. This war displaced between 4 and 7 million people,
who became refugees. Traumatised and injured people,
witnesses to the destruction, and the children, were left
to bear the scars. The winner of the Nobel Prize for Peace,
and the author of *The Age of Deception: Nuclear Diplomacy in
Treacherous Times*, Mohamed ElBaradei (2011, p. 85) raises
substantive issues in relation to this war:

If the community of nations seeks to live by the
rule of law, then what steps should be taken
when violations of international law result in
massive civilian casualties? Who should be held
accountable when military action has been taken
in contraventions of the law as codified in the
U.N. Charter, or worse still, when military action
is found to have been based on information that is
deliberately selective treatment of information, or the
promulgation of misinformation.

For ElBaradei, this war was about bringing democracy

and change to the geopolitical landscape of the region. It defies rationality and any form of common sense to *invade* a country to establish democracy.

Democratic freedoms

Many western countries, including Australia, are increasing executive power at the expense of basic democratic freedoms. As noted by Mark McKenna (2015, p. 10):

> Much has been written about the government's cavalier attitude toward the rule of law, its determination to control the flow of information and silence criticism, and the dramatic increase in state surveillance and detention powers. Judging by the proposal to allow the executive rather than the courts to determine evidence of an offence when revoking citizenship, as a society we would fail question 15 of the government's own practice citizenship test, and come to threaten the very fabric of Australian democracy.

The work of Steve Killelea, founder of the Institute for Economics and Peace, supports a more *inclusive* approach, as well as beginning to focus on what is involved in having more *equality* and a more *peaceful* society. This Institute published its ninth Global Peace Index in 2015, using 23 indicators to rank 162 countries, covering 99.6% of the world's population. Steve Killelea, interviewed by Hamish McDonald (2015, p. 9) and reported in *The Saturday Paper*, notes that stopping violence is different from maintaining peace. This led him to the concept of positive peace as:

> ... the attitude and institutional structures that can sustain peaceful societies. Countries that are strong in positive peace perform better on a whole lot of other things: strong business environments, measures of wellbeing, [less] gender inequality, a [healthier] environment and many more. We are describing an environment that is optimal for human potential to

flourish. Nations high on positive peace have fewer
civil resistance movements. [These movements] exist
for less time, they're less violent, their aims are more
moderate, and they're more likely to achieve their
aims. That shows the adaptive qualities of positive
peace, and societal resilience.

The global peace index also includes a terrorism index,
which indicates that terrorism is associated with being
alienated from the rest of the society. Killelea adds:

In France, Muslims make up 8 to 9 per cent of the
population but 60 to 70% of the people in jail. This is
a bit like the Aborigines in Australia. We need more
inclusive societies.

A painful running sore for Australia is our treatment
of asylum seekers. The *United Nations Report on Mandatory
Detention* shows that Australia contravened the *International
Covenant on Civil and Political Rights* and the *UN Convention of
the Rights of the Child*. Instead of a humanitarian response to
refugees, they have become a widening political issue while
men, women and children live in intolerable conditions
on Nauru and Manus Island. There was and is abuse of
children, who live in appalling conditions, as well as sexual
harassment and assault of women. The centres are shrouded
in secrecy and journalists are unable to visit unless they
support the government's policy. Doctors and healthcare
workers, contrary to their professional ethics, cannot report
on what is happening unless they are prepared to face legal
consequences.

In her article "The Long Journey to Nauru," Julie Macken
(2016), shows how there is no real discussion on this issue
in human and resources terms. She quoted the following
report:

The 2014 Commission of Audits report reveals that
Nauru and Manus cost Australian taxpayers 10 times
more than allowing asylum seekers to live in the

community while their refugee claims are processed.
It costs $400,000 a year to hold one asylum seeker
in offshore detention; $239,000 a year to hold them
in detention in Australia, and $100,000 a year for an
asylum seeker to live in community detention. It
costs about $40,000 a year for an asylum seeker to
live in the community on a bridging visa while their
claim is processed.

Countries need to deal with their individual issues and therefore assist the workings of the world at a global level, where there is a growing need for international cooperation.

Another story sums up the beginning, middle and end points of this discussion. I attended an international group conference in 2001 and was discussing, with a fellow colleague, the work I was doing with couples in a group during the time of the wife's pregnancy. He responded by talking about a program with which a friend of his was associated. The Tavistock Clinic in the UK had been running a program to assist Palestinian refugees remain alive to the bonding process with their young babies, despite the difficult conditions they lived under in the Palestinian camps.

After some time the leaders of the community came to speak to the workers, saying that while they appreciated the work that was being done and that while it was very successful, they were concerned that if it continued they would no longer have an army to call on once these children had grown!

Chapter 12 Where to from here?

Being humble does not diminish. It fills.
Going back to a simpler self gives wisdom

"Father Reason" (Banks, p. 146)

At this point in the book, we have surveyed the developmental processes that all of us experience as humans. We have engaged with what the science has to offer. We have also explored how our development can go wrong and how we can heal. Further, we have discussed possible ways of observing our society to ascertain its relative health. Finally, the views of four people are offered, people who have grappled with our nature and the human condition. These people have all attempted to look at the overall picture of where we are and where we need to go.

Carl Jung, the founder of Jungian Psychology, or Analytical Psychology, was deeply aware of our need to be in touch with our unconscious drive for power and dominance. He pointed out the obsessive need for control that affects so much of the way governments and corporations conduct themselves in the world, their relationships with other nations and the people they govern.

Jung articulated both a personal unconscious and a collective unconscious. The *personal unconscious* holds all our repressed feelings from our parental and cultural conditioning. This includes the fear, guilt, anxiety and rage that come from our early traumatic experiences. Importantly, Jung also considered that the unconscious holds the creative potential of our being; the ideas, longings and creative gifts that are waiting to be expressed, when we free ourselves of our blocks, and/or when there is a cultural "container" to receive and develop them. The *collective unconscious*, quoted in Baring (2013, pp. 249–50) was his notion that:

> … the world has an inside as well as an outside, that
> is not outwardly visible but acts upon us in a timeless
> present, from the deepest and apparently most
> subjective recesses of the psyche – this I hold to be
> an insight which, even though it be ancient wisdom,
> deserves to be evaluated as a new factor in building a
> world view.

Jung defined sickness as a state of incompleteness and health as a state of wholeness, brought about through connecting our conscious mind or ego with the unconscious through dreams, synchronistic events and making contact with our inner selves. His view was that only insight into our own nature and its power to both create and destroy, can change our deeply ingrained habits of aggression and, therefore, our suffering. What Jung offered was not a new belief system but one that was spiritually grounded in self-knowledge, including an awareness of the shadow, the dark side of our nature and freeing ourselves from it. This he felt could lead to a greater sense of ethical responsibility towards life in all its aspects, seen and unseen.

The Jungian perspective discusses the instinctual aspect of the self, which is so cut off from inside us and not sufficiently understood, even though it contains the source of our creative life. Our deepest feelings and instincts are the tools of our creative imagination. Facing our terrors and anxieties allows us to unlock our creative potential. This should be a major motivation for us to engage in our inner exploration. Perhaps our hesitancy to confront these aspects is because it also contains all our old habits, where our aggressive and predatory habits lie. *Anne Baring* (2013, p. 263), also a Jungian analyst, sees the seeds of hope in a growing awareness of these behaviours when she says:

> Becoming aware of this dimension, and the immense
> range of relationships and experience it embraces,
> constitutes an evolutionary advance. For, until we

learn how to relate to it, and know to integrate it with our more familiar focused ability to think, we remain immature, living on the surface of life, falling prey to events which we bring into being because we are unaware of the habits that compel us to repeat the mistakes of the past. We are then easily manipulated by political and religious leaders who think in terms of accruing power to their own particular group or ideology, rather than in terms of what truly benefits the people they are meant to serve and the wider needs of the planet itself.

Jung (1964, p. 94) spoke often of the cost of having a merely intellectual dimension, but not exploring the instinctual or emotional elements of our being:

Modern man does not understand how much his "rationalism"… has put him at the mercy of the psychic "underworld". He has freed himself from "superstition" (or so he believes) but in the process has lost his spiritual values to a positively dangerous degree. His moral and spiritual tradition has disintegrated, and he is now paying the price for this break-up in world-wide disorientation and disassociation…we have stripped all things of their mystery and numinosity; nothing is holy any more.

In a BBC interview with John Freeman in 1959, Jung made the statement, 'A man cannot stand a meaningless life'. He begged us to become more aware of the psyche, so that we could understand the events of our time more intelligently. Jung foresaw dangers for humanity if we did not tackle the task of gaining insight into our nature through self-reflection. Only self-knowledge could help us to avoid destroying the planet and the real danger is man himself. Jung is quoted in Baring (2013, p. 258):

It is becoming ever more obvious that it is not famine, not earthquakes, not microbes, not cancer, but man himself who is man's greatest danger to

man, for the simple reason that there is no adequate
protection against psychic epidemics, which are
infinitely more devastating than the worst of natural
catastrophes. The supreme danger, which threatens
individuals as well as whole nations, is a *psychic
danger*.

He took the view that, without our consciousness, there
would not be anyone to perceive the world, reflect upon it
and interact intelligently with it. This made us indispensable
for the completion of the creation. If we take this view, it
seems that potentially our individual lives may affect the life
of the cosmos and the unfolding of evolutionary intention
on this planet.

Baring (2013, p. 252), like Jung, points out the dangers of
the supremacy of the rational mind coupled with our lack of
knowledge of the instinctual life and connects our individual
and civil journey in life. She, however, believes that, as these
elements drive us more and more, we will:

> … fall victim to secular and religious ideologies and
> utopian goals which could ultimately lead us to
> destroy ourselves. The paramount goal we need to
> focus on is reconnecting our conscious mind with the
> deeper dimension of the soul… this unconsciousness
> is reflected in the difficulties and conflicts in our
> relationships with each other, whether within a
> nation or as nation states, and in the fact that we
> repeat the same patterns of behaviour without any
> apparent ability to prevent ourselves doing so, or
> even any awareness of what we are doing. We need
> insight into ourselves to get out of the hubris we
> have created.

This helps us to have a greater understanding that the
consequences of hubris are that we will attach ourselves to
religious ideas of a more fanatical kind, or adopt ideologies
that help simplify life and its complexities, rather than
sustain reflective thought.

Pope Francis's appeal to the world, through his encyclical *Laudato Si*, July 1, 2015, was a plea to all of us. The encyclical is available online.

> The urgent challenge to protect our common home includes a concern to bring the whole human family together to seek a sustainable and integral development, for we know things can change… humanity still has the ability to work together in building our common home… I urgently appeal, then, for a new dialogue about how we are shaping the future… Never have we so hurt and mistreated our common home as we have in the past two hundred years on our planet. We need a conversation which includes everyone since the environmental challenge we are undergoing, and its human roots, concern and affect us all. (par. 13, 14).

The Pope enunciated The Principle of the Common Good: '… the sum of those conditions of societal life, which allow social groups and their individual members relatively thorough and ready access to their own fulfilment.' (par. 122). He extended this principle to include future generations, so that justice would occur and our current actions would not penalize future generations. The process for working through these principles would be one of dialogue and transparency in decision-making.

The Pontiff also noted that, if everything is related, then the health of a society's institutions has consequences for the environment and the quality of human life (par. 142). His encyclical covers a discussion of those displaced by climate change, the issue of water as indispensable to human life and the loss of biodiversity (including oceans and reefs). By exploring the decline of the quality of human life and the breakdown of society the Pope contextualizes these difficulties. He emphasises global inequality and notes the international community's lack of response.

He further points out that technology has become disconnected from human responsibility, values and conscience. 'The predominance of the market has wreaked havoc, and in reality there is not an infinite supply of the earth's goods.' The consumerist vision of human beings has a levelling effect on cultures, diminishing the immense variety that is the heritage of all humanity.

The technocratic paradigm dominates economic and political life. The economy accepts every advance in technology with a view to profit, without concern for its potentially negative impact on human beings (par. 109). The specialisation that belongs to technology makes it difficult to see the larger picture. The fragmentation of knowledge… often leads to a loss of appreciation for the whole, for the relationships between things, and for the broader horizon, which then becomes irrelevant (par. 110). The time has come to pay renewed attention to reality and the limits it imposes. This in turn is the condition for a more sound and fruitful development of individuals and society (par. 116).

The Pope considers that consumption doesn't bring happiness and it destroys familial ties and family cohesion while instilling greed, instant gratification and the idea of no limits. He laments that we are encouraged to compete, and not cooperate, and in all this 'lost-ness' people are driven to a frenetic 'busy-ness' (par. 6). He notes our tendency to evade and not tackle issues, pretending nothing will happen. We are warned, like we were by Jung, that:

> Our freedom fades when it is handed over to the blind forces of the unconscious, of immediate needs, of self-interest, and of violence. In this sense, we stand naked and exposed in the face of our ever-increasing power, lacking the wherewithal to control it. We have certain superficial mechanisms, but we cannot claim to have a sound ethics, a culture and spirituality genuinely capable of setting limits and teach clear-minded self-restraint. (par. 105)

Despite all these realities, the Pontiff is not unhopeful about the future and sees that there is an underlying natural desire to reach for our fulfilment. This was noted by Robert Manne (2015), who spoke in his blog of the encyclical as '… the marriage of a critique of contemporary post-industrial culture with the most profound and sincere democratic beliefs and instincts'. Manne quotes the Pope:

> "An authentic humanity … seems to dwell in the midst of the technological culture, almost unnoticed, like a mist seeping gently beneath a closed door."
> He believes we can transcend our mental and social conditioning… [because we are] born for love.
> "No system can completely suppress our openness to what is good, true and beautiful." He further says, "A sense of deep communion with the rest of nature cannot be real if our hearts lack tenderness, compassion and concern for our fellow human beings."

Another figure who has thought about the state of humankind, our nature, and how best to deal with a crisis in humanity is the Dalai Lama. It is his view that in today's secular world, religion alone is no longer adequate as a basis for ethics. Any religion-based answer to the problem of our neglect of inner values, can never be universal and so will be inadequate. For the Dalai Lama, what we need today is an approach to ethics that has no recourse to religion, and can be equally acceptable to those with faith and those without, that is, *secular ethics*.

The Dalai Lama has studied a great deal of the neuroscience and our early primitive experiences. He concluded that we are all, by nature, oriented toward the basic human values of love and compassion, without depending on religion. His secular ethics, discussed in his book, *Beyond Religion: Ethics for a Whole World* (2012, p. 19) implies an inclusive and impartial attitude to all religions and includes nonbelievers. Basic spiritual wellbeing does not depend on religion, but comes from our innate human nature as beings, with natural disposition toward compassion, kindness and caring for others. The two pillars for secular ethics are the recognition of:

> ... our *shared humanity* and our shared aspiration
> to happiness and the avoidance of suffering; the
> second is the understanding of *interdependence*
> as a key feature of human reality, including our
> biological reality as social animals. From these two
> principles we can learn to appreciate the inextricable
> connection between our own wellbeing and that of
> others, and we can develop a genuine concern for
> others' welfare. Together, I believe, they constitute
> an adequate basis for establishing ethical awareness
> and the cultivation of inner values. It is through such
> values that we gain a sense of connection with others,
> and it is by moving beyond narrow self-interest that
> we find meaning, purpose and satisfaction in life.

He concluded that for humans, with our prolonged period of nurture, the concern for and affection of others is crucial to our survival and wellbeing. The observation that our concern for others contributes to our own wellbeing is supported by scientific research. There is now increasing scientific evidence that love, kindness, and trust have not only psychological benefits, but also observable benefits to physical health. Similarly, negative emotions such as anxiety, anger and resentment undermine our ability to combat illness and infection.

The Dalai Lama believes that indulging in violent instincts by pursuing revenge is misguided and not in anyone's best interests, as it will sow the seeds of further conflict. Also, destructive emotions distort our perception of reality. These feelings cause us to narrow our perspective, so that we fail to see a given situation in its wider context. In intense anger, almost 90% of the quality of repulsiveness we see in the object of our anger, is an exaggeration and a projection. This makes us incapable of rational judgment. When you dwell on the harm someone has done to you, there is an inevitable tendency to become angry and resentful, which destroys your peace of mind. To forgive others, therefore, has an enormously liberating effect on oneself.

In his book, the Dalai Lama (2012, p. 55) distinguishes compassion and empathy. He says that:

> Empathy is characterised by a kind of emotional resonance – feeling with the other person. Compassion, in contrast, is not just sharing experience with others, but also wishing to see them relieved of their sufferings. Being compassionate does not mean remaining entirely at the level of feeling, which could be quite draining. … compassion means wanting to do something to relieve the hardships of others, and this desire to help, far from dragging us further into suffering ourselves, actually gives us energy, and a sense of purpose and direction. When we act upon this motivation, both we and those around us, benefit still more.

In his terminology, "compassion" does not mean surrender in the face of wrongdoing or injustice. Maintaining an attitude of calmness and nonviolence actually shows strength, as it is the confidence that comes from having truth and justice on one's side. Further, a compassionate approach should inform the exercise of justice.

In his chapter "Ethics in our Shared World," he discusses how we now have a global responsibility, because our shared problems did not fall from the sky, but are the products of human action and human error. He notes that when we see greed as acceptable, even praiseworthy, there is clearly something wrong with our collective value system. He also wonders whether, with the challenge of technological progress, it is possible that our responsibilities are now growing too fast for our natural capacity for moral discernment to keep pace.

The way through, in his view, is mindfulness. His sense of mindfulness is that of "recollection," so that mindfulness is the ability to gather oneself mentally, then recall our core values and motivation. He considers that patience, contentment, self-discipline and generosity are an integral part of our basic outlook on life. Further he concludes that engaging with these feelings will have far-reaching effects. At the level of the individual, doing so will bring about greater happiness and provide a real sense of purpose and meaning in our lives. At the level of society, as more and more of us do the same, there is a real chance that we will move decisively in the direction of a culture that is less materially focused and instead pay closer attention to our inner, spiritual resources. The benefits of doing so will be shared by all. As a result, we increasingly accept the oneness and the interdependence of humanity, giving some basis for optimism. He calls for the education of the heart, that one day it could be part of the school curriculum, focusing on the indispensability of inner values such as love, compassion, justice and forgiveness.

Conclusion

As Gerhardt (2004, p. 10) puts so well:

> The human baby is the most socially influenced
> creature on earth, open to learning what his or her
> own emotions are, and how to manage them. This
> means that our earliest experiences as babies have
> much more relevance to our adult selves than many
> of us realise. It is as babies that we first feel and
> learn what to do with our feelings, when we start to
> organise our experience in a way that will affect our
> later behaviour and thinking capacities.

For our development and to enhance the neuroplasticity of our brain/mind complex, we first need secure relationships. This allows us to acquire an optimum level of physiological arousal for functioning. Following this, we need to meet the challenge of balancing our emotional and cognitive processing and of constructing a coherent narrative about our relationships and our world.

Every stage of our development is important in shaping who we become. Each stage can either produce distortions or bring us to fulfil our potential. What we have now learnt is that the earliest years shape our relationships in the future. The primacy and intensity of our earliest states imprints on us because of our utter dependency at this time. We can change the neuronal pathways initially laid down in the beginning, but it requires effort, consistency and the will to do so. Bringing our pre-verbal selves into consciousness is now more possible as we grow in our awareness of its functioning. The implications of this will take time to evolve, but a better understanding of this period, means we can incorporate our pre-verbal selves into a general understanding, or collective awareness of our nature and our needs. These parts will then be more readily available for our thought and reflection rather than re-enactment. It is another piece of the puzzle of who we are and therefore of managing ourselves in our community, society and environment.

The helplessness and vulnerability that are inherent in the primitive processes we experience in our early years touch at the heart of our current struggle with our narcissism and connect with the state the world is in. If we were more in touch with, and sensitive to, these parts of ourselves, we would not be able to be as destructive as we are to our environment and to mother earth. Being disconnected from these states is the only way we could have reached a point that, within living memory, the planet could become uninhabitable. Further, we would be unable to wage war in the way we do if we were connected, as we would think through consequences first.

In our society, where we prize independence highly, we are less attuned to the early response to dependency needs that is required to develop a truly independent being. Neoliberal policies, when examined, reveal an inherent attack on who we are as human beings with inherent social needs. These policies also attack the civil society and democratic values. The lack of humanity inherent in the neoliberal approach to the world, is evident in our adherence to deregulation, privatisation, materialism, consumerism, monetary costs and technology as the major determinants of policy. The onus of proof is on those who adhere to such a view to show how greed, rapaciousness, selfishness and corruption contribute to our wellbeing more than cooperation and sharing. Government, corporations, unions, and civil institutions need to work together, and proper regulation should be established to maintain balance. Where only a few amass more and the many have less, we need to re-examine whether our structures need to be realigned to better accommodate our humanity.

This is not a matter of a "left" or "right" political divide. John Hewson (2017, p. 17) a former leader of the Liberal

Party in Australia, writing in the *Sydney Morning Herald*, "Wanted: an economy that benefits the many, not just the fortunate few", says:

> Sometimes we seem to forget that in the design and implementation of public policy and reform we are attempting to improve our society, not just our economy. … Do we want to build a society where we consciously create an underclass … a group of people who cannot hope to share in the life, ambitions and achievements of the rest of society? … In policies such as privatisation we have transferred economic power and privilege from the public to some in the private sector, in a quest for greater "economic efficiency". However we need to first set the necessary regulations to limit the use of that power … Competition policy has clearly failed when we have allowed the concentration of economic power in essential services to result in the bulk of our society being ripped off … No, I haven't suddenly woken up a socialist. I am still basically an economist. I believe in markets, but I want them to work for the great benefit of our whole society, not just to benefit a few.

The "technology" of the social, the human technology we have discussed, is the technology of which we need to be mindful. We now have sufficient information to know what to do to create a healthier self and a healthier society, so it is up to us to make the choices. We understand how we learn to love, how we learn to think and reflect and how we socially engage and share. We also know that these experiences lead us to feel satisfied and fulfilled. Further, we know how to tackle the tasks that take us through to maturity. We now have the option to live in a connected world, where we realise that we are all one and connected by our humanity.

Internationally, we face major issues that cross national borders. We will need to cooperate and to look beyond national interests to global ones or we will not be able to deal with substantive issues like climate change, the impact of inequality, manufacturing of arms, drug production and distribution, sex slavery of women and children and domestic violence. We need the capacity to work through issues over time. As we have seen, it was the only way that the stories of individuals told here were able to have positive outcomes. They worked through difficult and complex problems and stayed with difficult emotional states inside them until those issues were resolved. At a community level, we need to do the same. Citizens and leaders need to stay with and work through difficult and complex issues until they find some resolution. We are all part of a body politic at the national and international level. Each of us is a cell of that body and responsible for the health or otherwise of that cell and responsible for the part it plays in the whole. To do otherwise is to disavow our nature.

It would help if we could collectively cultivate a greater acceptance of suffering and difficulties, alongside our pleasures. It would help, if as a community we could accept the reality that pain and suffering are an integral part of living and support each other in that reality. If we do not accept this, we carry a lot of inner dissatisfaction, anxiety and unrecognised vulnerability beneath our outward affluence.

The reality is that when individuals are well responded to and live in favourable enough environments they flourish. They are cooperative and respect themselves and others, including the planet. Such people are loving and thoughtful towards themselves and others and are content to be who they are, not constantly comparing or wishing to be someone else. They also possess a capacity to manage their inevitable states of anger and frustration. To achieve this state requires consistency and commitment but brings with it an underlying sense of being an integral part of the world and part of an on-going learning process that is bigger than ourselves.

I started with a sense that as individuals and members of a society, we were losing our way and losing our capacity to reflect on what are the best conditions for us all to thrive. I also wanted to address how we maintain our humanity in times of turmoil and stress by staying committed to our developmental process.

To some extent, I have found some answers to the questions of what our challenges are as we live in the human condition. But I have also found that there can be pleasure in the fact that the meaning of life and the universe is also greater than me and bigger than what I can know and envisage. In the end, so much of it is a mystery and therefore remains continually intriguing. The more I know; the less I know. Some of our experiences – seeing a sunset or observing an act of human kindness – or the tenacity with which we hold on to life, can transport us, temporarily, to another place, yet these experiences are in this world; the mystery of life remains just that.

In a sense, we are back to the beginning of the book. We are born social and die social, whether with others or not, because people are around us and inside us. To be alive is to honour our social nature and our interdependence as our greatest asset. We have a striking example of this in Australia, in our history. In World War II, both Australian and British soldiers were prisoners of war on the Burma Railway. Later it emerged that the Australians had a higher survival rate than the British. Researchers discovered that, while interned, the prisoners were paid a pittance as prisoners of war, the officers receiving slightly more. The difference was that the British individually kept their money, while the Australians pooled their resources and fared better. One wonders whether this would be the same today, but the point is made. As humans our survival and lives will be better off if we cooperate, rather than compete, or remain isolated. All these lessons reverberate back to our earliest beginnings.

References and further reading

Introduction

Hitchcock, K., "Too Many Pills: On lifestyle diseases and quick fixes," *The Monthly*, September 2015, accessed 10 October 2015, <https://www.themonthly.com.au/issue/2015/september/1441029600/karen-hitchcock/too-many-pills>

Chapter 1

Barks, C. *The Essential Rumi,* 2nd ed., New York: HarperCollins, 1995.

Tracey, N., ed. 2000. *Parents of Premature Infants: Their Emotional World*, London: Whurr, 2000.

Further reading

Raphael-Leff, J. 1993, *Pregnancy: The Inside Story*, London: Sheldon, 1993.

Chapter 2

Stern, D. 1985, *The Interpersonal World of the Infant,* New York: Basic Books, 1985.

Further reading

Gerhardt, S. *Why Love Matters: How affection shapes the baby's brain*, London and New York: Routledge, 2004.

Lieberman, A. *The Emotional Life of the Toddler*, London: The Free Press, 1993.

Mares, S., Newman, L., & Warren, B. 2005, *Clinical Skills in Infant Mental Health,* Melbourne: ACER, 2005.

Rose, L. *Learning to Love: The Developing Relationships between Mother, Father and Baby during the first year,* Melbourne: ACER, 2000.

Chapter 3

Agazarian, Y. M., "Theory of the Invisible Group Applied to Individual and Groups-as-whole Interpretation," *Group*, vol. 7, no. 2, 1983, pp. 27–37.

Bion, W. *Learning from Experience*, London: Karnac, 1962.

Bion, W. *Attention and Interpretation*, London: Karnac, 1970.

De Mare, P. *Koinonia: From hate, through dialogue, to culture in the large group*, London: Karnac, 1991.

Grotstein, J. *Bion's Transformation in "0" and the Concept of the Transcendent Position*, 1997, accessed 20 February 2016, <http://internationalpsychoanalysis.net/2015/05/11/bions-transformation-in-o-and-the-concept-of-the-transcendent-position/>.

Hillman, J. *The Soul's Code*, New York: Warner Books, 1996.

Maslow, A. H. *The Farther Reaches of Human Nature*, Penguin, USA, 1980.

Ralston Saul, J. *The Unconscious Civilization*, New York: Simon and Schuster, 1995.

Waddell, M. *Inside lives: Psychoanalysis and the Growth of the Personality*, London: Karnac,2002.

Wilbur, K. *No Boundary*, Boston and London: Shambhala, 1985.

Further Reading

Neven, R. *Emotional Milestones*, Melbourne: ACER, 1996.

Obholzer, A. & Roberts,V. *The Unconscious at Work*, London: Routledge, 1994.

Chapter 4

Cohen, J., Campbell, S., Matias, R., & Hopkins, J., 'Face-to-face interactions of post-partum depressed and no depressed mother-infant pairs at 2 months', *Developmental Psychology*, 26, (1), 1990, pp. 15–23.

Cozolino, L. *The Healthy Aging Brain: Sustaining Attachment, Attaining Wisdom*, New York: WW Norton & Company, 2000.

Gerhardt, S. *Why Love Matters: How affection shapes the baby's brain*, London: Routledge, 2004.

Grof, S. 2000, *Psychology of the Future: Lessons from modern con-*

sciousness research, Albany, NY: SUNY, 2000.

Mercer, J., 'Attachment Theory and its vicissitudes: Toward an updated theory', *Theory and Psychology,* Sage Publications, vol. 21, no. 1, 2011, pp. 25–45.

Odent, M., 'Prevention of Violence or Genesis of Love? Which Perspective?', Presented at the fourteenth International Transpersonal Conference Santa Clara, California, June 1995.

Odent, M. *The Caesarean,* London: Free Association, 2004.

Pert, C. *Molecules of Emotion,* London: Simon & Schuster, 1998.

Schore, A., 'Attachment and the regulation of the right brain', *Attachment and Human Development,* vol. 2, no. 1, April 2000, pp. 23–47.

Stern, D. *The Motherhood Constellation,* New York: Basic Books, 1995.

Further reading

Bowlby, J. *Attachment*, Attachment and Loss, vol. 1, 2nd ed, New York: Basic Books, 1999 and 1969.

Bowlby, J. *Separation: Anxiety & Anger*, Attachment and Loss, vol. 2, International psycho-analytical library no. 95, London: Hogarth Press, 1973.

Bowlby, J. *Loss: Sadness & Depression*, Attachment and Loss, vol. 3, International psycho-analytical library no.109, London: Hogarth Press, 1980.

Bretherton, I., 'The origins of attachment theory: John Bowlby and Mary Ainsworth', *Developmental Psychology*, vol. 28, no. 5, September 1992, pp. 759–775.

Cozolino, L. *The Neuroscience of Psychotherapy, building and rebuilding the human brain,* New York: WW Norton & Company, 2002.

Articles on "neurocardiology" available online include:

Pearce, J. C., 'Waking Up to the Holographic Heart: Starting over with Education', Interview, *Wild Duck Review*, vol. IV, no. 2, 1998, accessed 19 June 2016, <https://ratical.org/many_worlds/JCP98.pdf> .

Pearce, J. C., 'Expressing Life's Wisdom: Nurturing Heart-Brain Development Starting with Infants', *Journal of Family Life*, vol. 5, no. 1, 1999, accessed on 19 June 2016, <https://ratical.org/many_worlds/JCP99.html>.

Chapter 5

McDougall, J. *Theatres of the Body,* London: Free Association, 1989.

Miller, A. *The Body Never Lies,* London and New York: WW Norton & Company, 2006.

Ogden P., & Minton K., 'Sensorimotor Psychotherapy: One Method for Processing Traumatic Memory', *Traumatology,* vol. VI, no. 3, 2000, accessed 25 June 2016, <https://www.sensorimotorpsychotherapy.org/articles.html>.

Wilbur, K. *No Boundary,* Boston and London: Shambala, 1996.

Winton, T., 'Havoc: A Life of Accidents', *The Monthly,* 10th ed., 2014, accessed 20 June 2016, <https://www.themonthly.com.au/issue/2015/may/1430402400/tim-winton/havoc>.

Further Reading

Cornell, W. *Somatic Experience in Psychoanalysis and Psychotherapy,* New York and London: Routledge, 2015.

Chapter 7

Blake, P. *Child and Adolescent Psychotherapy,* Melbourne: IP Communications, 2008.

Chapter 9

Kenny, D. *Bringing Up Baby: The Psychoanalytic Infant Comes of Age,* London: Karnac, 2013.

Manne, A. *The life of I: The New Culture of Narcissism,* Melbourne: Melbourne University Press, 2014.

Chapter 10

Baker, R. & McKenzie N., 'Investor Campaign has Transfield Edgy', *Sydney Morning Herald,* 19 September 2015, p. 7.

Cleary, P., 'Norway is proof you can have it all', *The Australian,* 15 July 2013, accessed 4 November 2015, <http://www.theaustralian.com.au/life/norway-is-proof-that-you-can-have-it-all/news-story/3d2895adbace87431410e7b033ec84bf>.

Hadegaard, C., 'The Politics of Climate Change: Towards the

Paris Climate Conference 2015', *CityTalks*, 2015, accessed 27 August 2015, <http://www.cityofsydney.nsw.gov.au/council/news-and-updates/global-issues-ideas-and-conversations/city-talks/the-politics-of-climate-change-towards-the-paris-climate-conference-2015>.

Volkan, V. *Blind Trust: Large groups and their leaders in times of crisis and terror,* Durham, NC: Pitchstone, 2004.

Chapter 11

Actionaid, 'How tax havens plunder the poor', Factsheet, 2013, accessed 11 March 2018, <http://www.gfintegrity.org/wp-content/uploads/2014/05/ActionAid-Tax-Havens-May-2013.pdf>.

Bakan, J. *The Corporation: the Pathological Pursuit of Profit and Power*, London: Constable and Robinson, 2204. For further discussion on regulatory reforms see pp. 161–167.

Cavanagh, J. & Mander, J., eds., *Alternatives to Globalization,* Oakland: Berrett-Koehle, 2004.

Cunningham, D. *The Age of Selfishness: Ayn Rand, Morality, and the Financial Crisis*, New York : Abrams, 2015. For further discussion on corporate tax and the European Parliament see pp. 204–5.

Datablog, 'FDTSE 100's use of tax havens – get the full list', *The Guardian*, 2013, accessed 11 March 2018, <https://www.theguardian.com/news/datablog/2013/may/12/ftse-100-use-tax-havens-full-list>.

Dr Dover, R., Dr Ferrett, F., Gravino, D., Prof. Jones, E. & Merler, S., 'Bringing transparency, co-ordination and convergence to corporate tax: Part 1 Assessment of the magnitude of aggressive corporate tax planning', European Parliamentary Research Service, 2015, accessed 15 May 2016, <http://www.europarl.europa.eu/RegData/etudes/STUD/2015/558773/EPRS_STU%282015%29558773_EN.pdf >.

ElBaradei, M. *The Age of Deception: Nuclear Diplomacy in Treacherous Times,* London: Bloomsbury, 2011.

Feinstein, A. *The Shadow World: Inside the Global Arms Trade,* New York: Picador, 2012.

Furnham, A. *Backstabbers and Bullies: how to cope with the dark side of people at work,* London: Bloomsbury. 2015. For further discussion on derailment leadership see pp. 18–19 & 31–38.

Goldsmith, B., 'The Foxtel-BBC deal: Implications for Australian Television and Content', *The Conversation,* April 23, accessed 23 April 2016. <https://theconversation.com/the-foxtel-bbc-deal-implications-for-australian-television-and-content-13654>.

Ireland, J., 'Gap Between Rich and Poor Growing and Will Get Worse', *The Sydney Morning Herald,* 15 September 2015, accessed 4 November 2015, <http://www.smh.com.au/federal-politics/political-news/gap-between-rich-and-poor-growing-and-will-get-worse-report-20150914-gjlxhf.html>.

Leveson Inquiry, 'Leveson Inquiry: Culture, Practice and Ethics of the Press', 2014, accessed 11 March 2018, <http://webarchive.nationalarchives.gov.uk/20140122144906/http://www.levesoninquiry.org.uk/>.

Macken, J.,'The Long Journey to Nauru', *New Matilda,* 12 January 2016, accessed 10 November 2016, <https://newmatilda.com/2016/01/12/the-long-journey-to-nauru/>.

McChesney, R. *Rich Media, Poor Democracy: Communication politics in dubious times,* Chicago: University of Illinois Press, 1999.

McDonald, H. 'Steve Killelea about the Global Peace Index', *The Saturday Paper,* September 5–11 2015, accessed 6 November 2015, <https://www.thesaturdaypaper.com.au/2015/09/05/steve-killelea-the-global-peace-index/14413752002341>.

Macintyre, Professor S. *Australia's Boldest Experiment,* Sydney: NewSouth, 2015.

McGeough, P., 'One Woman's Fight to Save Kabul's Children', *The Sun-Herald,* 6 September 2015, p. 23.

McKenna, M., 'Citizenship and its Discontent', *The Monthly,* July 2015, accessed 6 November 2015, <https://www.themonthly.com.au/issue/2015/july/1435672800/mark-mckenna/citizenship-and-its-discontents>.

Perkins, J. *Confessions of an Economic Hit Man,* San Francisco: Berrett-Koehler, 2004.

Petley, J., 'How the Murdoch Press has waged a relentless campaign against the BBC (and why it worked)', *The Conversation,*

26 August 2015, accessed 30 September
2015, <https://theconversation.com/how-the-murdoch-press-has-waged-a-relentless-campaign-against-the-bbc-and-why-its-worked-45523>.

Piketty, T. *Capital in the Twenty First Century*, London: The Belknap, Harvard University Press.

Sarah, S., 'Spanish 'radical' protest-born party challenges traditional politicians', ABC TV *Foreign Correspondent*, 25 August 2015.

Sen, A. *Inequality Re-examined*, Oxford: Clarendon Press, 1992.

Steinberg, B. *Shame and Humiliation: Presidential Decision-Making on Vietnam*, Montreal: McGill-Queen's University Press, 1996.

Stiglitz, J. *Globalization and its Discontent*, London: Norton Paperback,,2003.

Stockholm International Peace Research Institute (SIPRI), 'World military spending was $1.69 trillion in 2016', 2017, accessed 11 March 2018, <http://visuals.sipri.org>.

West, M., 'Taib Scandal could be Tip of the Iceberg.' *Sydney Morning Herald* 12 September 2015, p. 2.

Volkan, V., Itzkowitz, N. & Dod, A. *Richard Nixon: A Psychobiography*, New York: Columbia University, 1997.

Webster, V. & Brough, P., 'Assisting Organisations to deal effectively with toxic leadership in the workplace', *InPsych*, vol. 37, no. 3, 2015, pp. 24–25.

Chapter 12

Baring, A. *The Dream of the Cosmos*, England: Archive Publishing, 2013.

Dalai Lama. *Beyond Religion: Ethics for a whole world*, Noida UP: HarperCollins, 2012.

Pope Frances, *Laudato Si*, 2015, accessed 30 September 2015, <http://w2.vatican.va/content/francesco/en/encyclicals/documents/papa-francesco_20150524_enciclica-laudato-si.html>.

Jung, Carl. *The Structure and Dynamics of the Psyche*, Princeton: Princeton University Press, 1960.

Jung, C., *Man and His Symbols*, London: AldusBooks, 1964.

Manne, R., *Laudato Si:* 'A political reading: The papal encyclical is the first work that has risen to the full challenge of climate change', *The Monthly,* 2015, accessed 30 September 2015, <https://www.themonthly.com.au/blog/robert-manne/2015/01/2015/1435708320/laudato-si-political-reading>.

Conclusion

Gerhardt, S. 2004, *Why Love Matters; How affection shapes the baby's brain,* London and New York: Routledge, 2004.

Hewson, J., 'Wanted: An economy that benefits the many, not just the fortunate few', *Sydney Morning Herald,* 17 March 2017, p. 17.

www.ingramcontent.com/pod-product-compliance
Lightning Source LLC
Chambersburg PA
CBHW070805270326
41927CB00010B/2306